Web Cams For Dummies

M000237312

Common Graphics File Formats

File Extension	Basic Information
BMP	Standard bitmap graphics file format used by Microsoft Windows.
GIF	Cross-platform graphics file format commonly used in Web pages. Can be used to create simple animation.
JPG or JPEG	Cross-platform graphics file format commonly used in Web pages.
PCX	Older graphics file format still used by many Windows programs.
PICT	Standard Macintosh graphics file format.
PNG	Alternative cross-platform graphics file format designed to replace GIF.
TIFF	Bitmap graphics file format.

Common Video File Formats

File Extension	Basic Information
ASF	Newest video file format standard created by Microsoft to replace the AVI format.
AVI	Original video file format used by Microsoft Windows.
QT or MOV	QuickTime video file format that has become the standard for Macintosh computers.
MPEG	Motion Pictures Expert Group video file format.
RM	RealMedia video file format created by RealNetworks as a cross-platform video file format.

Embedding a RealVideo File

To embed a RealVideo file on a Web page, use the <EMBED> tag to define the name of a text file that ends with the .RPM file extension, as in the following example:

```
<embed src="realvideo.rpm">
```

The .RPM text file contains the name of the actual RealVideo file that you want to play, as in the following example:

```
www.mywebsite.com/realvideo.rm
```

For Dummies: Bestselling Book Series for Beginners

Web Cams For Dummies

HTML Code to Display Web Cam Images

```
<html>
<head>
<meta http-equiv="refresh" content
="XX">
</head>
<body>
```

```
<img src="filename">
</body>
</html>
```

The preceding code content = "XX" defines how many seconds to wait before refreshing the Web page, and "filename" defines an actual name of a graphic file such as dogface.gif.

Linking to an AVI, ASF, or QuickTime File

To create a Web page link to an AVI, ASF, or QuickTime file, substitute the filename in the anchor tag with something like the following example:

```
<A HREF="videofile">Plays your file.</A>
```

In the preceding code, "videofile" represents the actual filename of your video such as fire.avi, wedding.asf, or crash.mov. When the user clicks the hyperlink Plays your file, your video file downloads and plays.

Linking to a RealVideo File

To create a Web page link to a RealVideo file, create your Web page link to a text file with the .RAM file extension, as in the following example:

```
<A HREF="realvideo.ram">Plays a RealVideo file.</A>
```

Next, create a text file, ending with the .RAM file extension that contains the actual link to your RealVideo file, as in the following example:

```
www.mywebsite.com/realvideo.rm
```

Embedding an AVI, ASF, or QuickTime File

To embed an AVI, ASF, or QuickTime file on a Web page, use the following code:

```
<embed src="videofile">
```

In the preceding code, "videofile" is just the name of your video file, for example dog.avi, ballgame.asf, or parade.mov.

For Dummies: Bestselling Book Series for Beginners

Web Cams

FOR

DUMMIES®

Web Cams

FOR

DUMMIES®

By Wallace Wang

IDG Books Worldwide, Inc.
An International Data Group Company

Foster City, CA ◆ Chicago, IL ◆ Indianapolis, IN ◆ New York, NY

Web Cams For Dummies®

Published by
IDG Books Worldwide, Inc.
An International Data Group Company
919 E. Hillsdale Blvd.
Suite 300
Foster City, CA 94404
www.idgbooks.com (IDG Books Worldwide Web Site)
www.dummies.com (Dummies Press Web Site)

Library of Congress Control Number: 00-106303

ISBN: 0-7645-0743-5

Printed in the United States of America

10 9 8 7 6 5 4 3 2 1

1B/SS/RS/QQ/IN

Distributed in the United States by IDG Books Worldwide, Inc.

Distributed by CDG Books Canada Inc. for Canada; by Transworld Publishers Limited in the United Kingdom; by IDG Norge Books for Norway; by IDG Sweden Books for Sweden; by IDG Books Australia Publishing Corporation Pty. Ltd. for Australia and New Zealand; by TransQuest Publishers Pte Ltd. for Singapore, Malaysia, Thailand, Indonesia, and Hong Kong; by Gotop Information Inc. for Taiwan; by ICG Muse, Inc. for Japan; by Intersoft for South Africa; by Eyrolles for France; by International Thomson Publishing for Germany, Austria and Switzerland; by Distribuidora Cuspide for Argentina; by LR International for Brazil; by Galileo Libros for Chile; by Ediciones ZETA S.C.R. Ltda. for Peru; by WS Computer Publishing Corporation, Inc., for the Philippines; by Contemporanea de Ediciones for Venezuela; by Express Computer Distributors for the Caribbean and West Indies; by Micronesia Media Distributor, Inc. for Micronesia; by Chips Computadoras S.A. de C.V. for Mexico; by Editorial Norma de Panama S.A. for Panama; by American Bookshops for Finland.

For general information on IDG Books Worldwide's books in the U.S., please call our Consumer Customer Service department at 800-762-2974. For reseller information, including discounts and premium sales, please call our Reseller Customer Service department at 800-434-3422.

For information on where to purchase IDG Books Worldwide's books outside the U.S., please contact our International Sales department at 317-572-3993 or fax 317-572-4002.

For consumer information on foreign language translations, please contact our Customer Service department at 1-800-434-3422, fax 317-572-4002, or e-mail rights@idgbooks.com.

For information on licensing foreign or domestic rights, please phone 1-650-653-7098.

For sales inquiries and special prices for bulk quantities, please contact our Order Services department at 800-434-3422 or write to the address above.

For information on using IDG Books Worldwide's books in the classroom or for ordering examination copies, please contact our Educational Sales department at 800-434-2086 or fax 317-572-4005.

For press review copies, author interviews, or other publicity information, please contact our Public Relations department at 650-653-7000 or fax 650-653-7500.

For authorization to photocopy items for corporate, personal, or educational use, please contact Copyright Clearance Center, 222 Rosewood Drive, Danvers, MA 01923, or fax 978-750-4470.

is a registered trademark under exclusive license to IDG Books Worldwide, Inc., from International Data Group, Inc.

About the Author

Wallace Wang has written dozens of computer books that include the best-selling *Microsoft® Office For Dummies®*, *Visual Basic® For Dummies®*, and *Beginning Programming For Dummies®*. In addition to writing books, he also writes a monthly column for *Boardwatch Magazine* (www.boardwatch.com) and regularly performs stand-up comedy in Las Vegas and San Diego.

ABOUT IDG BOOKS WORLDWIDE

Welcome to the world of IDG Books Worldwide.

IDG Books Worldwide, Inc., is a subsidiary of International Data Group, the world's largest publisher of computer-related information and the leading global provider of information services on information technology. IDG was founded more than 30 years ago by Patrick J. McGovern and now employs more than 9,000 people worldwide. IDG publishes more than 290 computer publications in over 75 countries. More than 90 million people read one or more IDG publications each month.

Launched in 1990, IDG Books Worldwide is today the #1 publisher of best-selling computer books in the United States. We are proud to have received eight awards from the Computer Press Association in recognition of editorial excellence and three from Computer Currents' First Annual Readers' Choice Awards. Our best-selling *...For Dummies*® series has more than 50 million copies in print with translations in 31 languages. IDG Books Worldwide, through a joint venture with IDG's Hi-Tech Beijing, became the first U.S. publisher to publish a computer book in the People's Republic of China. In record time, IDG Books Worldwide has become the first choice for millions of readers around the world who want to learn how to better manage their businesses.

Our mission is simple: Every one of our books is designed to bring extra value and skill-building instructions to the reader. Our books are written by experts who understand and care about our readers. The knowledge base of our editorial staff comes from years of experience in publishing, education, and journalism — experience we use to produce books to carry us into the new millennium. In short, we care about books, so we attract the best people. We devote special attention to details such as audience, interior design, use of icons, and illustrations. And because we use an efficient process of authoring, editing, and desktop publishing our books electronically, we can spend more time ensuring superior content and less time on the technicalities of making books.

You can count on our commitment to deliver high-quality books at competitive prices on topics you want to read about. At IDG Books Worldwide, we continue in the IDG tradition of delivering quality for more than 30 years. You'll find no better book on a subject than one from IDG Books Worldwide.

John Kilcullen
Chairman and CEO
IDG Books Worldwide, Inc.

Eighth Annual Computer Press Awards ≥ 1992

Ninth Annual Computer Press Awards ≥ 1993

Tenth Annual Computer Press Awards ≥ 1994

Eleventh Annual Computer Press Awards ≥ 1995

Dedication

This book is dedicated to everyone who ever got frustrated trying to use a computer. Take heart. You're not stupid; it's the people who designed these infernal machines that are. We don't need to make computers easier to use. We need more people to question why computers are so hard to use in the first place.

Acknowledgments

If it weren't for the fine people at IDG Books, this book might still have been written, but not by me. So a big thanks goes to Ed Adams and Jeanne Criswell for keeping this project on track. Another big round of thanks goes to Jeff Wiedenfeld for checking to make sure this book actually makes sense within the realm of the English language.

Although they had nothing to do with the creation of this book, I like mentioning their names anyway just to thank them for their support in other areas of my life that don't involve computers: Steve Schirripa (you can catch him on the TV show *The Sopranos*) for giving me a chance as an unknown comedian to perform in Las Vegas, Patrick DeGuire for helping me start our comedy booking agency Top Bananas Entertainment (www.topbananas.com), and Leo (the man, the myth, the legend) Fontaine for helping me through the treacherous world of stand-up comedy from the beginning.

Thanks also go to Cliff Lara, D.C., for being a chiropractor extraordinaire; Denise Blake, licensed acupuncturist; and Eve Moeran and her business Milk Made at Home (milkmade@home.com) for providing valuable insight, support, and assistance in birthing and breastfeeding for my wife, Cassandra, and my son, Jordan. Additional thanks go to my cats Bo, Scraps, Tasha, and Nuit — just because they're cats.

Publisher's Acknowledgments

We're proud of this book; please register your comments through our IDG Books Worldwide Online Registration Form located at http://my2cents.dummies.com.

Some of the people who helped bring this book to market include the following:

Acquisitions, Editorial, and Media Development

Project Editors: Jeanne S. Criswell, Mica Johnson

Acquisitions Editors: Ed Adams, Carol Sheehan

Copy Editors: Tim Borek, Amy Pettinella

Proof Editors: Teresa Artman, Mary SeRine

Technical Editor: Jeff Wiedenfeld

Permissions Editor: Carmen Krikorian

Media Development Specialist: Brock Bigard

Media Development Coordinator: Marisa Pearman

Editorial Managers: Rev Mengle, Mary Corder

Media Development Manager: Laura Carpenter

Media Development Supervisor: Richard Graves

Editorial Assistant: Candace Nicholson

Production

Project Coordinator: Nicole Doram

Layout and Graphics: Amy Adrian, Joe Bucki, LeAndra Johnson, Jacque Schneider, Brian Torwelle, Julie Trippetti

Proofreaders: Andy Hollandbeck, Angel Perez, Carl Pierce, Dwight Ramsey, Marianne Santy

Indexer: York Production Services, Inc.

Special Help
Barry Childs-Helton, Christine Berman

General and Administrative

IDG Books Worldwide, Inc.: John Kilcullen, CEO; Bill Barry, President and COO; John Ball, Executive VP, Operations & Administration; John Harris, CFO

IDG Books Technology Publishing Group: Richard Swadley, Senior Vice President and Publisher; Mary Bednarek, Vice President and Publisher; Walter R. Bruce III, Vice President and Publisher; Joseph Wikert, Vice President and Publisher; Mary C. Corder, Editorial Director; Andy Cummings, Publishing Director, General User Group; Barry Pruett, Publishing Director

IDG Books Manufacturing: Ivor Parker, Vice President, Manufacturing

IDG Books Marketing: John Helmus, Assistant Vice President, Director of Marketing

IDG Books Online Management: Brenda McLaughlin, Executive Vice President, Chief Internet Officer; Gary Millrood, Executive Vice President of Business Development, Sales and Marketing

IDG Books Packaging: Marc J. Mikulich, Vice President, Brand Strategy and Research

IDG Books Production for Branded Press: Debbie Stailey, Production Director

IDG Books Sales: Roland Elgey, Senior Vice President, Sales and Marketing; Michael Violano, Vice President, International Sales and Sub Rights

◆

The publisher would like to give special thanks to Patrick J. McGovern, without whom this book would not have been possible.

◆

Contents at a Glance

Cartoons at a Glance

By Rich Tennant

"Awwrw, cool — a Web cam! You should point it at something interesting to watch. The fish bowl! The fish bowl!"

page 7

"The Web cam is finally giving me my 15 minutes worth of fame, along with several coffee machines, a few lava lamps, and a bowl of rotting fruit."

page 53

"Well that's typical. Ever since I started teleconferencing with my parents, my mother keeps looking for a toolbar function that brushes the hair off my forehead."

page 277

"The doctor wants to know if he can perform your endoscopy with a Web cam for the hospital Web site."

page 199

"Remember — if you're updating the family Web site, no more animated GIFs of your sister swinging from a tree and scratching her armpits!"

page 305

"You know, I'm pretty sure CU-SeeMe comes with an audio volume control."

page 115

Cartoon Information:
Fax: 978-546-7747
E-Mail: richtennant@the5thwave.com
World Wide Web: www.the5thwave.com

Table of Contents

....

Introduction

*I*n the early days of computing, the only things that your personal computer could display were words and numbers, usually in a sickly green or radioactive orange glow. As computers grew more powerful, they were able to display pictures, such as pie charts or bar graphs that often looked as if they had been drawn on an Etch-A-Sketch.

Gradually, the graphical displays of computers became sophisticated enough to display sharper graphics of tropical fish swimming across the monitor or fireworks exploding on the screen. As the image quality of monitors and the processing speed of computers improved, people found that they could display, edit, and print photographic images directly from their computers.

But people still wanted more from their personal computer, and so the Web cam was born. Web cams enable anyone to capture moving pictures or still images and have them appear live on their own computer monitor. Although crude compared with television and movie studio standards, Web cams have unleashed a flood of creativity all over the world. With a Web cam, you can capture moving images and view them directly on your computer. Whether you decide to save the pictures, print them, e-mail them to others, or post them on the Internet for others to view is up to you. But doing any of these things begins with a tiny camera called a Web cam, and this book can help you get the most out of any Web cam you attach to your computer.

Who Should Buy This Book

There are several reasons why you may need this book:

- ✔ You want to set up a Web site that displays live images and you want to know the type of equipment you need.
- ✔ You want to know how other people are using Web cams.
- ✔ You already own a Web cam but want ideas for different ways to use it.
- ✔ You want to know more about different Web cam resources on the Internet.

Of course you may have bought this book to spend money and keep the economy active. But whatever your reason for buying this book, rest assured it will help you better understand the wonderful world of Web cams as quickly and painlessly as possible.

Foolish Assumptions

You need either a Macintosh or a computer that runs Microsoft Windows 95, Windows 98, Windows NT, Windows 2000, or Windows Millennium Edition to use the CD-ROM included with this book.

If you don't feel comfortable using your Macintosh, you may want to buy *The iMac For Dummies* or *The iBook For Dummies,* both by David Pogue and published by IDG Books Worldwide, Inc.

If you don't feel comfortable with Windows 95/98/Millennium Edition, you may want to buy *Windows 95 For Dummies,* 2nd Edition, *Windows 98 For Dummies,* or *Windows Me For Dummies* (all by Andy Rathbone). For more information regarding Windows NT or Windows 2000, pick up a copy of *Windows NT Workstation 4 For Dummies,* 2nd Edition, or *Windows 2000 Professional For Dummies,* both by Andy Rathbone and Sharon Crawford.

How This Book Is Organized

This book contains six parts designed to guide you gently by the hand: from knowing nothing about Web cams or how they work, to being able to use one competently for sending pictures to friends or posting video images on a Web site. Each part covers a specific topic about using a Web cam. Whenever you need help, just flip through this book, find the part that covers the topic you're looking for, and then toss this book aside and get back to playing with your new toy to take pictures of yourself, your cat, or other people (with their knowledge and permission, of course).

Part 1: Meet Your Web Cam

If you have no idea what a Web cam is or what to use one for, this part of the book provides basic instructions for selecting the right Web cam and setting it up.

This part of the book also describes some unique uses for Web cams. You can see how other people are experimenting with broadcasting video and live pictures across the Internet. The whole world can see what's happening, whether viewing the Eiffel Tower or watching what another person's cat is doing at any particular time of the day.

Part II: Lights, Camera, Action!

After you have your Web cam set up, the next step is to post your pictures on the Internet for the rest of the world to see. Here you find out about the different options available, depending on whether you want to broadcast video or just an occasional snapshot of some particularly interesting object, such as a sunset over the Golden Gate Bridge or your dog taking a nap on your bed.

Part III: Videoconferencing with Your Web Cam

This part of the book explains how to use your Web cam for videoconferencing, so you can pretend you're living in a future where video phones are commonplace and computers actually don't crash every few days.

With videoconferencing, you can talk to friends, strangers, or business associates (who may be strange themselves) from the convenience of your personal computer. This part of the book also explains how to use three popular videoconferencing programs: CU-SeeMe, iVisit, and Microsoft NetMeeting.

Part IV: Having More Fun with Your Web Cam

Besides broadcasting and posting pictures from your Web cam to the Internet, you can also use your Web cam as a fun toy to customize your desktop, create your own screensaver, or send snapshots to friends via e-mail. This part of the book is meant to spark your creativity in using your Web cam to keep you and your friends entertained for hours (or at least a few minutes, anyway).

Part V: The Part of Tens

If you're still stumped on how to maximize your use of your Web cam, browse through this part of the book to get some ideas on how other people use Web cams in creative and interesting ways. Here you can find a list of popular Web cam sites, get some ideas for different ways you can use your own Web cam, and find some hints on what to do if your Web cam doesn't work properly.

Part VI: Appendixes

This part of the book provides a glossary of terms (so you can understand what the heck people are talking about when discussing Web cams), a list of popular Web cam manufacturers, a list of interesting software you may want to buy or download for use with your Web cam, and a short description of the programs available on the enclosed CD-ROM.

By using this part of the book, you can find more resources for buying and using a Web cam, whether for business or just for amusement.

How to Use This Book

This book is designed as a reference tool and a tutorial to help you understand what the heck a Web cam is and what it can do for you. The book was written to feed your mind with ideas for different ways to use your Web cam, from normal to novel uses. Don't worry about trying to read this book from cover to cover (unless you have nothing else to read). Instead, just browse through the parts that interest you and ignore the rest.

If you know nothing about Web cams, start with the first part of the book. If you already have a Web cam and feel competent in using it, feel free to skip around the book and read anything that catches your interest.

By the way, don't forget to have fun with your Web cam. The good part about Web cams is that they're inherently designed for fun, unlike a word processing or spreadsheet program, so get creative, go wild, and see what you can capture with your Web cam.

Conventions

To get the most out of the information presented in this book, you need to understand the following:

- ✔ The mouse cursor appears either as an arrow or as an I-beam pointer (depending on the program you are using). Any time you lose track of the mouse cursor, start moving the mouse around until you see something flashing across your screen. Chances are that what you're seeing is the mouse cursor.
- ✔ Clicking refers to pressing the left mouse button once and then letting go. Clicking is what you do to activate buttons on the toolbar and choose commands from pull-down menus.

✔ Double-clicking refers to pressing the left mouse button twice in rapid succession. Double-clicking typically activates a command.

✔ Dragging selects items you want to move, delete, or format. To drag, place the I-beam pointer to the left of the item that you want to select, hold down the left mouse button, and move the mouse in the desired direction. After you release the mouse button, Windows selects that item. An item is selected when it appears in white against a black background.

✔ Right-clicking means clicking the mouse's right button. (Some mice have three buttons, so ignore the middle button for now.) Right-clicking usually displays a pop-up menu on the screen.

Note: If you're left-handed and you change your mouse settings so that you use your left hand to operate the mouse, clicking means pressing the right mouse button, and right-clicking means pressing the left mouse button.

Icons Used in This Book

Icons highlight useful tips, important information to remember, or technical explanations that you can skip if you want. Keep an eye open for the following icons throughout the book:

This icon highlights important information that can be helpful for using your Web cam (provided that you remember to use the information offered in the tips, that is).

This icon marks special information or general principles that you want to keep in mind for the future.

Watch out! This icon alerts you to possible trouble if you don't follow instructions carefully.

This icon emphasizes really detailed information that's absolutely useless to know but may keep you amused for a moment or two.

Getting Started

If you haven't bought a Web cam yet, start looking for one. The first part of this book explains the different features of Web cams so that you can consider what features you want before you buy any particular brand. So turn the page, start reading, and get ready to enjoy the fun of playing with your new Web cam.

Part I
Meet Your Web Cam

"Awww, cool - a Web cam! You should point it at something interesting to watch. The fish bowl! The fish bowl!"

In this part . . .

A Web cam is nothing more than a camera that you attach to your computer, yet there are many different ways that you can use a Web cam. This part of the book shows you some of the more creative ways that people use their Web cams, including everything from trying to spot a ghost or the Loch Ness Monster to putting their own lives on display 24 hours a day.

With so many fun ways to play with a Web cam, you may want to rush out to your nearest computer store and buy one as soon as possible. Because Web cams, like any computer accessory, can vary widely in cost and features, this part of the book can help you wade through the technical details so you can find the perfect Web cam at the right price for you.

Chapter 1

The Wild World of Web Cams

*W*eb cams enable you to share still images and video with anyone around the world. If you've ever wanted to see the person you're chatting with on the Internet, send a snapshot of yourself to a friend, or broadcast live images from a specific location, a Web cam is for you. This chapter introduces you to different types of Web cams and their uses and lists many helpful Web sites that show how people are using Web cams.

What the Heck Is a Web Cam?

A Web cam is nothing more than a tiny camera that connects to your personal computer. Unlike an ordinary still or video camera, a Web cam stores and displays images directly onto your computer screen so you can edit, save, or send these images to other people.

Web cams (sometimes called "cams," which is short for cameras) get their name because the cameras are most often used to send or display images on the World Wide Web. Web cams can display two types of images:

- ✔ **Still images.** Used for taking snapshots to send via e-mail to friends, family members, or anyone else in the world who has an e-mail account.

- ✔ **Live video.** Used for videoconferencing or chatting so you can see what the other person is doing. Essentially, your Web cam acts like a miniature movie camera so whatever you see through the Web cam is what's really happening in real time. An alternative to real-time video is the use of time-lapsed still images, which displays images taken every few seconds or minutes.

The ultimate stand-alone Web cam

If you want a Web cam but don't want the hassle of connecting it to your personal computer, consider buying a special network server camera from Axis Communications (www.axis.com). Unlike ordinary Web cams, the Axis Communications camera can transmit pictures to the Internet all by itself without being connected to a PC.

Just connect an Axis Communications camera to your network, and the camera can transmit

images for posting on a Web site or to a separate computer for later viewing.

While the Axis Communications camera costs more than ordinary Web cams (approximately $499 retail price), the cost is less than buying a computer and a Web cam separately, and Axis can be especially useful for places where you don't have room to put an ordinary Web cam and a separate computer in the same place.

The Different Types of Web Cams

Depending on how much money you want to spend and the quality of the video images you want to capture, you can choose between two types of Web cams:

- ✔ Stand-alone Web cams
- ✔ Video cameras

Stand-alone Web cams

A stand-alone Web cam is a small camera that rests on or attaches to any flat surface such as the top or side of your monitor. Stand-alone Web cams are fairly inexpensive (ranging in price from $50 to $150) and create images that may appear slightly jagged or faded. Figure 1-1 shows some common stand-alone Web cams.

For maximum convenience, ease of installation, and low cost, choose a stand-alone Web cam instead of a video camera. See Chapter 2 for more information about choosing a Web cam.

The main difference between stand-alone Web cams and other types of cameras is that stand-alone Web cams need a computer to store and display their images.

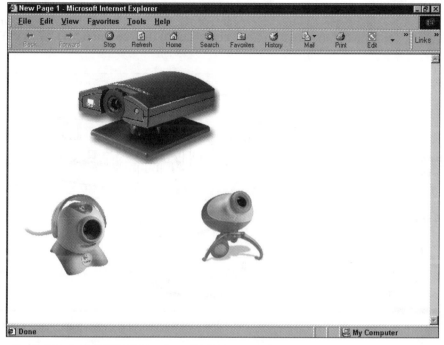

Figure 1-1:
The typical
appearance
of some
popular
stand-alone
Web cams.

Top: 3Com® HomeConnect™ PC Digital WebCam Bottom Right: ©2000 Logitech. All rights reserved. Used with permission from Logitech and may be registered. All other trademarks are the property of their respective owners. Bottom right: iREZ® Kritter™

Video cameras

Believe it or not, you can use an ordinary video camera as a Web cam. To connect a video camera to your computer, you need one of the following devices:

- ✔ Video capture card
- ✔ Video camera adapter

Get a Web cam with a laptop

Sony (www.sony.com) sells a bizarre laptop computer with a built-in Web cam for taking still or live video images. The camera is built in to the top of the display and swivels so you can take pictures of someone in front of the computer — or, by turning the camera around, you can aim it directly behind the computer.

Such a device makes a great spying tool or a portable Web cam. With the right wireless modem and Internet connection, you can have a roving Web cam anywhere you can carry it (just as long as your laptop computer's batteries don't run out).

A *video capture card* plugs into your computer's expansion slot and acts as a link between your video camcorder and your computer, enabling you to transfer images from the camcorder to the computer, as shown in Figure 1-2.

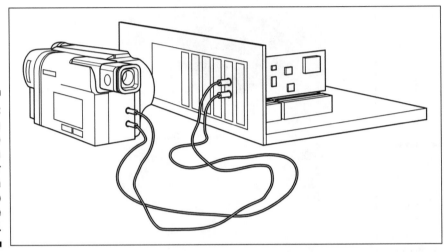

Figure 1-2: Connecting a video camera to a computer through a video capture card.

Video capture cards can be fairly expensive (ranging in price from $200 to $1,000 or more). However, video capture cards provide professional-quality editing and image quality. If you're willing to pay this premium price for quality, a video camera and a video capture card are your best options.

To find out more about the different features of video capture cards, visit the Web sites of companies that sell video capture cards, including the following:

ADS Technologies (www.adstech.com)

AITech (www.aitech.com)

Applied Technologies Manufacturing (www.wonderworks.co.uk/motionpicture)

Aspro Technologies (www.aspro.com)

Data Translation (www.datx.com/broadway)

Foresight Imaging (www.foresightimaging.com)

Pinnacle Systems (www.truevision.com)

Videonics (www.videonics.com)

Comparing video capture cards

A video capture card plugs into an expansion slot in your computer and adds a port so that you can plug in a video camcorder and transfer images from the camcorder to your computer. Some typical video capture card features include: data rate, such as 6 Mbps (the faster the better); compression ratio, such as 3:1 (the higher the compression, the lower the quality of the video); frame size and resolution, such as 640 x 480 (higher resolution gives higher quality images); and frame rate, such as 30 frames per second (the higher the frame rate, the smoother the video appears).

If you just want a fairly inexpensive video capture card, then you have to settle for adequate video speed and quality. If you're willing to pay more for a video capture card, then you can get video that is near-television quality. As a general rule, the more you spend, the sharper the video quality will be.

If you can't afford or can't justify buying a video capture card, your next option is to buy a *video camera adapter,* which is a separate box that plugs into your computer's parallel or Universal Serial Bus (USB) port. After you have plugged the video camera adapter into your computer, you can plug your video camera into the video camera adapter, as shown in Figure 1-3.

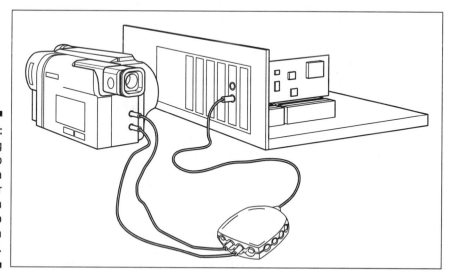

Figure 1-3:
Connecting a video camera to a computer through a video camera adapter.

For a PC video camera adapter, look at the Snappy Video Snapshot (www.play.com). For a Macintosh video camera adapter, consider the Buz multimedia producer (www.iomega.com/buz). These two products are the most well-known products for connecting a video camera to your computer.

Besides connecting a video camera to a video camera adapter, you can also plug in a VCR or TV, thereby capturing images from your favorite TV program or videotape and storing them on your computer.

A video camera combined with a video capture card or video camera adapter can capture higher-resolution images than a stand-alone Web cam, but high-resolution images take longer for people to view on a Web site.

What People Are Doing with Web Cams

To give you some ideas about what you can do with a Web cam, browse through this section to discover some of the creative ways that people are currently using their Web cams. Although some people buy Web cams exclusively for business, others get a Web cam purely for their own amusement. Think of a Web cam as a new toy and start dreaming up different ways to take advantage of having a camera attached to your personal computer.

Around the world

One of the earliest and most popular uses of a Web cam is to display views of interesting sites that people from other parts of the world may like to see. By viewing images from these Web cams, you can peek into another world from the comfort of your home.

When something as monumental as a natural or man-made disaster (such as a volcanic eruption or a riot) happens in another part of the world, someone usually connects a Web cam so others can view those events. (For your own personal rumination, think about how a Web cam could have changed the world's perception of events if everyone could have been an eyewitness to the Tiananmen Square massacre, the Bay of Pigs invasion, or the bombing of Iraq. Web cams can give you views of events free of the bias, censorship, or filtering of any agenda by the news media or government.)

American Web cams

With the majority of Internet users residing in the United States, it's no surprise that Web cams are popping up all over America like weeds after a spring rain. Browse the following Web sites to see some of your favorite American landmarks (see Figure 1-4, for example) as seen through the eye of a Web cam:

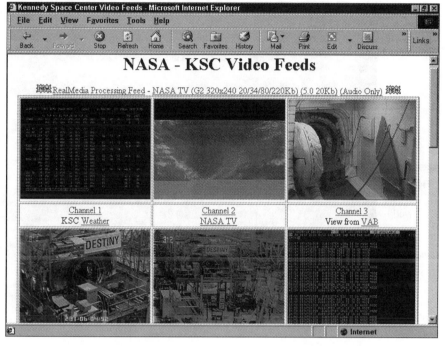

Figure 1-4:
NASA provides live video feeds of images from space and inside the Kennedy Space Center.

The Alamo Cam (www.expressnews.com/alamocam)

CapitolCam (www.townhall.com/capitalcam)

Gettysburg Battle Cam (www.gettysburgaddress.com/HTMLS/battle.html)

Golden Gate Bridge Cam (www.mapwest.com/bridgecam.html)

Polo Towers (Web cam of the Las Vegas Strip) (www.polotowers.com/Web-cam-test.htm)

Seattle Space Needle (www.spaceneedle.com/view/default.html)

The Statue of Liberty (www.sccorp.com/cam)

Yellowstone National Park Web cams (www.nps.gov/yell/tours/livecams/index.htm)

Worldwide Web cams

The next time you're planning an overseas trip, first take a peek at your favorite vacation spot via a Web cam. Or if you just want to see what it's like in another part of the world, visit that place via a Web cam, as shown in Figure 1-5.

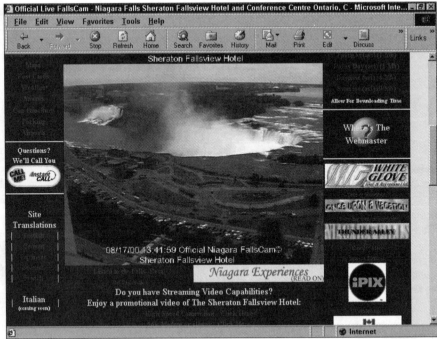

Figure 1-5:
View the
world-
famous
Niagara
Falls from
the comfort
of your
home
computer.

By looking into another country through the eyes of a Web cam, you can see how the rest of the world spends its time (perhaps looking at a Web cam that's watching you).

For a quick introduction to worldwide Web cams, visit The Fat World-Cam Web site (www.fat.co.uk/world), CyberTour (www.cybertour.com), or Szym.com (http://szym.com/cameras), which offer a variety of Web cam views from around the world. Or try some of the Web cam links listed below:

Big Ben (www.newswatch.co.uk)

European Web Cam Ring (www.fen.baynet.de/Peter.Hennig/ring.html)

Germany (www.topin.ch/de)

Hong Kong (www.dvsystems.com/hongkong.shtml)

KremlinKam (www.kremlinkam.com)

London (www.camvista.com)

MontrealCam (www.montrealcam.com)

Mount Everest (www.m.chiba-u.ac.jp/class/respir/eve_e.htm)

Niagara Falls (www.fallsview.com/English/pages/fallscam.shtml)

Panama Canal (www.pancanal.com/eng/photo/camera-java.html)

Paris (www.tf1.fr/livecam)

South Pole (http://bat.phys.unsw.edu.au/~aasto)

Tokyo Skyline (http://tokyosky.to)

The Wailing Wall (http://aish.com/wallcam or www.kotelkam.com)

Places to see

Because Web cams can go anywhere, you may want to peer inside places that you never get a chance to visit in person — such as the CNN Newsroom (www.cnn.com/EVENTS/inhouse_camera) to see if you can catch the latest headline news before the rest of the world hears about it.

For those who like to peek into the private lives of others, take a look at the Web site for the Las Vegas wedding chapel called A Little White Chapel (www.discovery.com/cams/wedding/wedding.html). A Little White Chapel has hosted weddings since 1954; numerous celebrities have said their vows there, including Judy Garland, Frank Sinatra, Michael Jordan, Mickey Rooney (twice), and Bruce Willis and Demi Moore. If you happen to visit the Web cam at the right moment, you may catch a glimpse of other Hollywood celebrities getting married in Las Vegas.

To see what may be happening on the campus of Syracuse University, visit the Live View of Syracuse University (http://emc.syr.edu/tour/webcam/hlcam.htm), which shows a view from a Web cam located on the roof of the Newhouse School of Public Communications.

In case you want an insider's view of your favorite American sporting event, visit one of the following Web cams (located in stadiums and arenas around the United States):

Chicago Cubs Wrigley Field (www.earthcam.com/usa/illinois/chicago/wrigleyville)

Denver Broncos Stadium (www.9news.com/broncosstadium)

Green Bay Packers Lambeau Field (www.packers.com/lambeau/cam)

Kansas City Chiefs Arrowhead Stadium (www.arrowheadcam.com)

University of Notre Dame Stadium (www.nd.edu/~jeremy/stadium)

Education by Web cam

While people are still debating the impact of Web cams, a few hardy souls are trying to use Web cams for educational purposes. To peer through Web cams that focus on fostering education in the general public, try one of the following Web sites to see space shuttle launches, dinosaur bones, corn fields in Iowa, or Mount St. Helens, as shown in Figure 1-6.

Discover Cam Universe (www.discovery.com/cams/cams.html)

Dinosaur Hall (www.clpgh.org/cmnh/jurassic/livecams.html)

NASA Kennedy Space Center (www.ksc.nasa.gov)

People on display

When people put their lives on display in front of a Web cam, they're often willing to show you more than you may want to see. So brace yourself when viewing certain Web cam sites, or just avoid the Web cam sites that highlight someone's real life altogether.

Figure 1-6: Through the Web cam from Discovery Online, you can see if Mount St. Helens erupts again.

Perhaps the most popular use for Web cams is to peek into the lives of other people. One of the first "Peeping Tom" Web cams occurred when a young woman named Jennifer hooked up a Web cam to enable anyone on the Internet to watch her 24 hours a day. Dubbed JenniCam (www.jennicam. org), this Web cam site provided the first look into another person's private life. Viewers can watch Jennifer in multiple situations, including flying an airplane, eating dinner with friends, and going on vacation.

The Internet world soon made her into a minor celebrity, and others quickly emulated her Web site by offering similar Web cam sites. Although the majority of these Web sites are fairly boring (does anyone do anything fascinating 24 hours a day?), you may want to visit some of the better-known Web cam sites that peer at the lives of people both famous and unknown.

Steve Wozniak (the co-creator of Apple Computers) has posted a Web cam site (http://wozcam.woz.org) so that you can see him at work. Perhaps you can catch Steve designing the latest top secret computer from Apple or finding a way to recycle his old NeXT computer.

One bizarre use for a Peeping Tom-type Web cam occurred when a man locked himself in a house for an entire year and provided Web cams for people to view his life. Calling himself the DotComGuy, (www.dotcomguy. com), this man wanted to prove that you can use the Internet for everything without ever leaving the house.

So if you can't wait for Hollywood to make your face into a celebrity, hook up your Web cam and start posting images of your own life for everyone around the world to look at. Who knows? You may become the next Internet celebrity.

Animals on display

For some odd reason, one of the more popular uses for Web cams is to look at different animals. While 90 percent of the time the animals tend to be asleep or completely absent from view, animal Web cam sites still dominate the Internet landscape.

One of the first Web cams ever was Netscape's Fish Cam (http://fishcam. netscape.com/fishcam), which enables you to watch the tropical fish swim around in a tank located somewhere inside Netscape.

To see wild animals running freely in their natural habitat, visit AfriCam (www.africam.com). AfriCam provides you with different Web cam views from some of Africa's best animal parks, as shown in Figure 1-7.

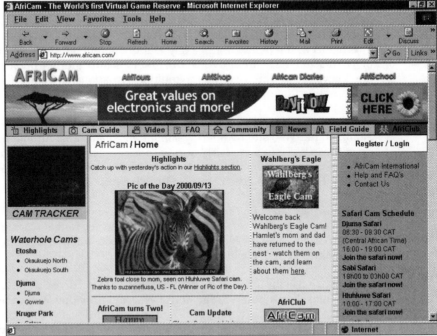

Because wild animals aren't always easy to find at any given time, you may prefer viewing animals from the Web cams located in one of the many zoos around the world. In case you want to stare at a panda bear, visit the PandaCam (`www.sandiegozoo.org/special/pandas/pandacam`) at the San Diego Zoo.

Both the National Zoo (`www.si.edu/natzoo`) in Washington, D.C., and the Toledo Zoo (`http://toledo.com/zoocams`) offer Web cams showing you everything from gorillas, tigers, lions, and elephants to Komodo Dragons and Naked Mole-Rats.

To encourage people to adopt a pet, the Humane Society set up the PuppyCam (`www.thepuppycam.com`), which shows pets around the country just waiting for a family to take them home.

Butterfly enthusiasts certainly won't want to miss the Butterfly Conservatory Web cam (`www.amnh.org/exhibitions/butterflies/cams.html`). For a part curiosity/part scientific Web cam, visit the Deformed Frog Web site (`http://freddo.pca.state.mn.us/frogcam2.html`). Operated by the Minnesota Pollution Control Agency, this Web cam shows the effects that pollution has on frogs. Some of the frogs are missing legs or organs, or they have extra limbs or organs in the wrong place.

Although aiming Web cams at animals such as gorillas or elephants may be impossible for most people, many people do point their Web cams at their pets and set up Web sites so that anyone can see their dogs, cats, parakeets, goldfish, snakes, or hamsters eating, sleeping, and playing. If you want to make your pets global superstars, put a Web cam in their face and start posting their images on the Internet.

Nature on display

In many offices lit by dim fluorescent lights, employees fight with one another for an office with a window. If you aren't lucky (or aggressive) enough to have a view of the outside world from your desk, do the next best thing and peer through a Web cam that shows you a view of a natural scene, such as a beach, mountain range, or garden.

One of the most popular beaches (especially during spring vacation) is Daytona Beach in Daytona, Florida. By visiting the Daytona Beach Cam (www.earthcam.com/usa/florida/daytona), you can see the beach bums, surfers, and sunbathers without having to get sand between your toes.

To really escape, take a peek at Mt. Fuji through the lens of the 24 Hours Mt. Fuji Live Web cam at www.sunplus.com/fuji/livee.htm. While much of the information on this Web site is written in Japanese, viewing the pictures of Mt. Fuji can be nearly as inspiring as being there in person.

To get a view of the French Alps, visit the Alpe d' Huez Web cam (www.alpedhuez.com/fr/commun/webcam.asp) and check the skiing conditions or just admire the scenery.

By browsing through different nature Web cams, you can take a virtual hike around the world without having to leave the convenience of air conditioning and indoor plumbing.

Viewing inanimate objects

To parody many of the Web cam sites, other people have aimed their Web cams at a variety of uninteresting subjects, such as paint drying on a wall, a commercial laundry washing machine in action, grass growing outside someone's window, or food decaying on a plate.

For a peek at the world's first Web cam site, visit the Trojan Room Coffee Machine (www.cl.cam.ac.uk/coffee/coffee.html), where you can view the coffeepot in the University of Cambridge's Computer Laboratory.

An unusual Web site that uses Web cam images is the HotToads! Web site (www.hottoads.com). This Web site features a man cutting a potato in half, carving a face into it, capturing images through his Web cam as the potato deteriorates, and inviting viewers to suggest which famous celebrity the rotten potato face most closely resembles, as shown in Figure 1-8.

For the easily amused or truly bored, visit the Peeling Paint Web Cam (www.mich.com/~rrreibel/paintcam.htm), where you can watch (what else?) paint peeling from a wall.

In Toronto, Canada, two enterprising young men have set up the FridgeCam (www.beerfridgecam.com), where you can see the refrigerator where they keep their beer.

A former employee of Netscape has hooked up a Linux machine to a scrolling bus sign that hangs over his desk at the Geocast Network Systems corporation. By typing in a comment at his Web site (www.weissman.org/sign), you can display a short message for him and all his co-workers to see.

As you can see, although Web cams may be great for videoconferencing, like everything else associated with personal computers, Web cams are also just plain fun to use. If you have a weird idea that you want to share with others, aim your Web cam at something weird and let other people enjoy your twisted sense of humor.

Figure 1-8: Watch a potato slowly decay into the face of your favorite celebrity at the HotToads! Web site.

Paranormal sightings

Because Web cams can transmit pictures 24 hours a day, 7 days a week, without much maintenance or supervision, they're perfect for helping people capture pictures of an elusive UFO, a ghost (as shown in Figure 1-9), the Loch Ness monster, or a host of other paranormal activities. If you've never seen a real banshee or flying saucer, visit the following links to see if someone's Web cam may have captured proof that life is not quite what we think it is.

GhostWatch (`www.irelandseye.com/ghost`)

Haunted Valley Web Cam (`www.hauntedvalley.com/webcam.htm`)

Loch Ness Live-Cam (`www.lochness.co.uk/livecam`)

Project Hessdalen (`http://hessdalen.hiof.no`)

Willard Library Ghostcam (`www.courierpress.com/ghost`)

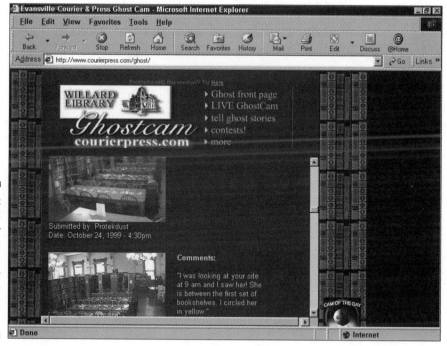

Figure 1-9: Willard Library Ghostcam captures spooky apparitions in a haunted library.

Searching for more uses for Web cams

To help you find more uses for your Web cam, browse through the following Web sites to get ideas from seeing how other people are using their Web cams. These sites offer views of things you may never have thought about looking at before.

4WebCams (`www.4webcams.com`)

AllCam (`www.allcam.com`)

Cams2000 (`www.cams2000.com`)

CollegeCams (`www.college-cams.com`)

EarthCam (`www.earthcam.com`)

EarthCam for Kids (`www.earthcamforkids.com`)

Leonard's Cam World (`www.leonardsworlds.com/camera.html`)

WebCam Central (`www.camcentral.com`)

WebCam Network (`www.webcam.net`)

WebCam Resource (`www.camcity.com/webcamresource`)

WebCam Search (`www.webcamsearch.com`)

WebCam Theater (`http://wct.images.com`)

Chapter 2

Getting the Right Web Cam

· ·

· ·

*A*fter you're convinced that you can find a productive or entertaining use for a Web cam, you may want to know how to find the best one for you. Like other computer accessories, Web cams offer a myriad of different features that may sound useful and interesting but can turn out to be useless and irrelevant for your particular needs.

So, before rushing out to buy a Web cam, take a few minutes to browse through this chapter to help you decide what type of computer equipment you need to run a Web cam and what features to look for in a Web cam.

What You Need to Run a Web Cam

Even though you may have a Macintosh or a Windows computer, you still may not be able to connect a Web cam to your computer. (Aren't computers wonderful?) That's because Web cams are fairly new accessories that need a lot of computing power to run properly.

To use most Web cams, you need four items:

✔ A Pentium (or equivalent processor) or PowerPC processor.

✔ A minimum of 16 megabytes (MB) of RAM (Random Access Memory).

✔ Either the Mac OS 8.5 (or higher) or Windows 98 (or higher) operating systems.

✔ A port for the Web cam to plug into the computer. The most common type of port needed for a Web cam is one called a *Universal Serial Bus* (USB) port. Some older Web cams, however, can connect to a serial or parallel port.

You can always find exceptions. Some Web cams can work with less memory or older processors, so compare the requirements of your particular Web cam with the capabilities of your computer.

Checking your Macintosh

All of the newer Macintosh computers, such as the iMac and the iBook, use the PowerPC processor. If you have one of these colorful Macintosh computers, rest assured that your computer has a processor powerful enough to run a Web cam.

Some of the older Macintosh computers also use the PowerPC processor. These Macintosh computers often have the words *PowerPC* or *PowerMac* plastered somewhere on the outside of the computer case.

Not all PowerPC processors are equal. Some of the earliest PowerPC processors were designated as PowerPC 640e or PowerPC 750 processors. The latest batch of PowerPC processors, found in iMacs, iBooks, PowerMacs, and the newest PowerBooks, are called PowerPC G3 or PowerPC G4 processors. Don't worry too much about the particular PowerPC processor in your Macintosh. As long as you have a PowerPC, you should have no problems running a Web cam.

What about Linux?

Most Web cams are designed to work with either a Macintosh or a Windows PC. But what if you want to use a Web cam with Linux?

Although most Web cams aren't designed to work with Linux right out of the box, Linux tends to attract computer programmers who can't resist a challenge. As a result, many Linux users have written programs that enable Linux computers to use Web cams designed for the Macintosh or for Windows.

If you own a Web cam called QuickCam, you can visit the QuickCam Third-Party Drivers Web site (www.crynwr.com/qcpc) to find the

drivers you need to run a QuickCam with Linux. For help using other Web cams with Linux, visit the Linux Help Online Web site (www.linux-help.org). You can also post your question in one of the many Linux newsgroups and ask for help from one of the many Linux supporters around the world.

Although it's not impossible to get a Web cam designed for the Macintosh or Windows to work with Linux, doing so may not be easy either. Be prepared to spend a lot of time searching for the help you need or writing your own program to get your particular Web cam to work with Linux.

If you don't have a brand-new Macintosh or a Macintosh with the words *PowerPC* written on the case, chances are good that you have an older Macintosh computer that does not use the PowerPC processor. In that case, your Macintosh may not have enough power to properly run a Web cam. Before you buy a Web cam, check to see if it can run on a Macintosh without a PowerPC processor.

In case you have a really old Macintosh, visit the Macquarium Web site (www.microserve.com/hac/interesting/macquarium) for instructions for turning your older Macintosh computer into an aquarium.

If your Macintosh has a PowerPC processor, the next step is to find out how much memory and the type of operating system your Macintosh has. Just follow these steps:

1. **Click the   icon in the upper-left corner of the screen.**

   A list of options appears.

2. **Click About This Computer.**

   The About This Computer dialog box pops up, displaying the amount of RAM and the operating system version of your Macintosh computer, as shown in Figure 2-1.

RAM   Operating system version

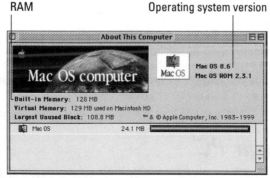

Figure 2-1: Checking the memory in a Macintosh.

At the very least, your Macintosh should have 32MB of RAM, although more RAM (such as 64MB or 128MB) ensures that you can run a Web cam along with any other programs you may want to use, such as a word processor or an Internet browser.

Most Macintosh Web cams need at least the Mac OS 8.5 or higher version of the operating system. If you have an older version of the Macintosh operating system, you may need to upgrade to a newer version.

The wonderful world of Pentiums

In the old days, Intel identified processors by numbers such as 80486. Then other companies started selling similar processors, and Intel discovered that people thought that an 80486 processor from Intel was identical to an 80486 processor from a rival company.

So when Intel released the 80586 processor, it was dubbed the *Pentium processor* because the name *Pentium* could be copyrighted, thus creating the illusion that people should only use genuine Pentium processors. (This explains why so many computers display that "Intel Inside" logo.)

When Intel released the 80686 processor, it was called the Pentium II processor (while rival companies marketed their processors as x686 technology). When Intel released the 80786 processor, it was called the Pentium III. (You can see the natural progression of Roman numerals endlessly being tacked on to the Pentium name.)

Keep in mind that a Pentium (or Pentium II or III) doesn't necessarily mean a higher-quality, faster processor. It just means that it comes from Intel. Many rival companies have created smaller, faster, and less expensive processors, but because Intel is considered the standard, the rival companies compare their processors with the Pentium processors.

As you may expect, a Pentium III is faster and more powerful than a Pentium II, which in turn is faster and more powerful than a plain old Pentium. As long as you have a Pentium processor (or a similar processor from another company), your computer can run a Web cam.

Finally, you need a USB port so that you can plug your Web cam into the computer. Once again, the iMac and iBook both have built-in USB ports. If you have an older Macintosh computer without a USB port, you may need to buy a special USB card that you can plug into your Macintosh, or buy an older Web cam that can connect to a serial or parallel port.

Checking your PC

As usual, the world of PCs is a bit more complicated than the Macintosh when it comes to determining the type of processor in your computer. At the very least, your computer should have a Pentium, Pentium II, or Pentium III processor.

If you have quick eyes, turn on your computer and watch the screen carefully for a brief display listing the type of processor and amount of RAM. However, if you want an easier way to determine your PC's processor type, operating system version, and amount of RAM, follow these steps:

1. **Right-click the My Computer icon.**

    A pop-up menu appears.

2. Choose Properties.

A dialog box appears, listing the processor type, operating system version, and amount of RAM in your computer, as shown in Figure 2-2.

Operating system version

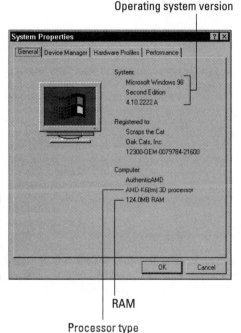

Figure 2-2:
Checking
the memory
in a PC.

RAM

Processor type

Not all computers use Pentium processors. The most popular rival processor is made by a company called Advanced Micro Devices (AMD), which sells processors that are faster and cheaper than similar Pentium processors. Another low-cost processor manufacturer is Cyrix. To compete against AMD and Cyrix processors, Intel released a lower-cost version of the Pentium II called the Celeron. If you have an AMD, Cyrix, or Celeron processor, then your computer will run a Web cam.

Table 2-1 lists the different processor types that you may find in your computer.

Table 2-1	Processor Types
Pentium Processors	*Equivalent Processors*
Pentium	AMD K5
Pentium II	AMD K6, K6-2, K6-3, Cyrix, and Celeron
Pentium III	AMD K7 (also called an Athlon or a Duron)

Most PCs can run a Web cam with a minimum of 32MB of RAM, although you should really have 64MB or 128MB to run a Web cam or other programs that will enable you to actually do something useful with your computer.

Your computer should also be running Windows 95, 98, Millennium Edition, NT, or 2000 as its operating system. If you don't have these versions of Windows, you can't run most Web cams.

Most Web cams don't work with the original version of Windows 95. To run most Web cams on Windows 95, you need the slightly updated version called Windows 95 Version 4.00.950B or 4.00.950C. Check the Web cam's requirements for specific details.

Finally, you need a USB port to plug your Web cam into the computer. The newest computers have built-in USB ports, but you can always buy a special USB card to plug into your PC. If your computer doesn't have a USB port and you don't feel like buying a USB bus expansion card, get a Web cam that connects through a parallel port.

Getting additional equipment

Some additional items you may want include a modem, sound card, speakers, and a microphone. A modem enables you to post Web cam images from your computer to a Web site or through e-mail to your friends. The slowest modem you should consider is a 56K modem, although you may want to purchase a *Digital Subscriber Line* (DSL) or cable modem for even faster Internet access.

The wearable Web cam

To show you how creative some people can get with Web cams, two students at Dearborn High School in Michigan — Russ Gibb and Michael Sassak — created a wearable Web cam. The two students read an article about wearable computers in the May 1998 issue of *Wired* magazine and decided to create the ultimate portable Web cam for a school project.

Their device consisted of Sony Glasstron display goggles connected to a computer. The computer contained 120MB of RAM and a Pentium processor packed in a case 3 inches long, 8.5 inches wide, and 5 inches deep.

Running both Windows 98 and Linux, the computer used a wireless LAN to transmit video images to a desktop PC that posted the images on a Web site.

If you visit the University of Toronto's Web site (www.wearcam.org), you can find out how engineering students are given the task of designing a wearable Web cam. Although most people may not want to create a wearable Web cam, you may be interested to see how it works. If you're a hard-core electronics/computer hobbyist, you just may find enough information to help you build your own walking video camera.

With good external speakers, your computer can play high-fidelity sounds. By adding a microphone, you can record sounds or talk to others so that you can use your Web cam for videoconferencing. Microphones usually plug directly into your computer's sound card and can be handheld or headset designs.

What to Look for in a Web Cam

If your computer has the necessary equipment to run a Web cam, congratulations! Your next step is to buy a Web cam. As you may expect, not all Web cams are created equal. Besides varying in price, they also vary drastically in picture quality and bundled software.

If you plan to hook up a video camera to your computer through a video capture card or a video adapter, you can skip this section.

Exploring basic Web cam features

When buying a Web cam, you want to carefully examine the following features:

- ✓ **System requirements.** If a Web cam requires an amount of RAM, a USB port, or a specific version of an operating system that your computer doesn't currently have, then you can't use that particular Web cam. The best Web cam is useless if it doesn't work with your computer.

- ✓ **Sensor.** The *sensor* converts focused light into electrical signals. The two types of sensors are Charge-Coupled Device (CCD) and Complimentary Metal Oxide-Silicon (CMOS). A CCD sensor offers higher resolution, lower visual distortion, and better images in low light. A CMOS sensor is less expensive to make, which translates into lower overall video quality.

- ✓ **Resolution.** *Resolution* determines the quality of the pictures that the Web cam can produce. Most Web cams offer two different resolutions — *still image* and *video*. Still image refers to individual pictures that the Web cam can take when used as a simple camera. Video refers to moving images that the Web cam can display. Common resolutions are 640 x 480 or 352 x 288. The higher the resolution, the sharper the image.

- ✓ **Graphics file format.** When a Web cam captures an image — whether a still image or a video image — it needs to store that image in a file format. The more file formats the Web cam can save your images in, the easier it will be for you to share your captured pictures with others. Common still-image file formats are JPEG, GIF, BMP, PCX, and FPX. Common digital-video file formats are AVI and IVS.

✔ **Video capture speed.** The *capture speed* refers to how many frames per second (fps) the Web cam can capture. Most Web cams can capture video images at 30 frames per second. The higher the fps rate, the smoother the video image.

✔ **Color support.** The more colors a Web cam supports, the sharper the images it can capture. Color support is often cryptically described as 16-bit (which means the Web cam can display a maximum of 64,000 colors) or 24-bit (which means the Web cam can display a maximum of 16.8 million colors).

✔ **Focus range.** This feature determines how close and far away the Web cam can capture an image. Typical focus ranges are from 2.5 centimeters to infinity (which theoretically means that your Web cam can take a picture of the edge of the universe and beyond). If you plan to use your Web cam to take close-up images, look for a Web cam with a short focus range.

Looking for the extras

Besides the basic features that every Web cam offers, look for some extra features that can make the difference between choosing one Web cam over another.

✔ **Motion detection.** Some Web cams offer a motion detection feature, so your Web cam only takes a picture of an image when something moves in front of it. These types of Web cams are especially useful for security purposes.

✔ **Video input.** A video input port enables you to plug a VCR, camcorder, DVD player, or other video source into your Web cam, so that you can display and edit images from those devices on your computer.

✔ **Included or built-in microphone.** If you plan to use your Web cam for video conferencing, you need a microphone. Some Web cams include a microphone as part of the package, while others have a built-in microphone. If a Web cam doesn't come with a microphone, plan to spend a little extra (ranging in cost from $10 to $100) to buy one. Just remember an inexpensive microphone probably won't give you the same quality as a more expensive one.

✔ **Mounting base.** The mounting base determines how you can attach your Web cam to a surface. Some Web cams can only lie on a flat surface like a dead animal. Others can clamp or stick to the side of a monitor or other piece of furniture for convenient positioning.

✔ **Cord length.** If you need to place your Web cam at a long distance from your computer, check the cord length of your Web cam. Otherwise, you may be forced to move your computer to accommodate a Web cam with a really short cord.

- ✔ **Snapshot button.** Some Web cams offer a snapshot button on the camera itself. That way, you can aim and point the Web cam at an image without having to reach across to type on the keyboard or click the mouse.

- ✔ **Privacy shutter.** Sometimes you don't want your Web cam to capture certain images, so many Web cams offer a privacy shutter, which is nothing more than a hood or shield that you can flip over the Web cam lens.

- ✔ **Games.** No one really buys a computer to balance his or her budget. More than half the time people spend in front of a computer is for leisure purposes, such as playing games. If you want a Web cam for fun, look for one that includes special game software, so you can play games with others over the Internet using your Web cam.

- ✔ **Video-editing software.** After a Web cam captures an image, you may want to touch it up or alter it slightly to reduce unwanted glare or to paste your dog's face over your boss's body. Some Web cams come with video-editing software so you don't have to buy a video-editing program separately.

- ✔ **Greeting card software.** One of the more popular uses for Web cams is to send snapshots of yourself via e-mail to friends, relatives, and co-workers. Many Web cams come with greeting card software, so you can store a captured Web cam image on a simulated greeting card that you can send to others.

Ever since Apple Computers made colors and design fashionable in the computer industry, many Web cam manufacturers have responded by creating stylish Web cams that come in different colors or look like little robots or mechanical insects that cling, stick, or rest on a tabletop, monitor, or shelf. If technical features are comparable, consider buying a Web cam for its appearance, too. After all, you're going to wind up looking at it most of the day, so you may as well get one that appeals to your sense of aesthetics as well as your technical needs.

Comparing some popular Web cams

To help you get started on your search for the perfect Web cam, take a look at some of the more popular models by visiting their respective Web sites. That way, you can compare features and find out more about Web cams through the propaganda — er, information — provided by each manufacturer. Table 2-2 points you in the right direction.

Table 2-2	Web Cam Manufacturers Online
Manufacturer	*Web Site*
3Com	www.3com.com
Creative Technologies	www.creative.com
Hawking Technologies	www.hawkingtech.com
Intel	www.intel.com
iREZ	www.irez.com
Kensington	www.kensington.com
Kodak	www.kodak.com
Logitech	www.logitech.com
Xirlink	www.xirlink.com

Chapter 3

Setting Up a Web Cam

● ●

In This Chapter

▶ Making your Web cam work

▶ Getting a Web site

▶ Finding Web cam software

▶ Uploading images using FTP

● ●

*A*lthough you can use a Web cam as an ordinary camera to take pictures of yourself seated in front of your computer, the real fun of a Web cam comes when you broadcast live images over the Internet. In this chapter, I show you how to set up your Web cam, take pictures, and then post those pictures on a Web site for everyone to admire.

As with many things that involve computers and technology, setting up a Web cam to work with the Internet is simple in theory but a bit more complicated in reality. Don't be frightened just yet. Although the entire process of connecting a Web cam to the Internet may be fraught with difficulties and problems, you'll be fine if you take the process one step at a time.

Here are the simple, theoretical steps involved in getting your Web cam to work:

1. **Install your Web cam on your computer and make sure it works correctly.**

2. **Reserve storage space on a Web hosting server.**

3. **Create a Web page to display images captured by your Web cam.**

4. **Install Web cam software to transfer your Web cam images via FTP to your Web site.**

Creating a remote-controlled Web cam

The simplest Web cam to set up is a static Web cam, which essentially aims a Web cam in a single direction, such as toward a sleeping cat or toward a volcano that may soon explode. But a more advanced setup can allow users to remotely aim, tilt, and swivel a Web cam and transmit those dynamic images over the Internet.

To create a controllable Web cam, you need two things: a remote camera mount (which contains a shelf for your Web cam to rest on) and a motor (to tilt, pan, or swivel the Web cam).

Using a special program, viewers can aim the camera in different directions. These special programs are usually written in Java or Common Gateway Interface (CGI). Both languages are often used to create Web sites that do more than just display text or pictures. In fact, many people have written games in Java or CGI so that people can play them through a Web site.

A remote camera mount is fairly expensive and creates the problem of getting the remote camera mount software to work correctly with your Web site. In addition, you really need to have a dedicated Internet connection — such as a DSL (Digital Subscriber Line) or cable modem — to provide enough bandwidth to display images and provide the necessary controls for aiming your Web cam remotely. If you're interested in creating the best possible viewing experience, consider setting up a remote-controlled Web cam.

For a remote camera mount, visit the Surveyor Corporation Web site (www.surveyor.com) or the NuSpectra Corporation Web site (www.nuspectra.com). In case you want a budget remote camera mount, visit www.doc.ic.ac.uk/~ih/doc/stepper/mount to find out how to create an inexpensive remote camera mount for any Web cam using ordinary Lego blocks, an old computer power supply, and a QBasic program.

Installing Your Web Cam

Before you can use your Web cam, you need to install it. The two most important steps to installing your Web cam are installing the software driver (program) that tells your computer how to use your Web cam and plugging in your Web cam.

The following instructions are general guidelines for installing a Web cam. Always follow the instructions that come with your Web cam.

The first, and most crucial, step to installing a Web cam is installing your Web cam software driver. Most Web cams come with the software driver on a CD-ROM. To install this Web cam software driver, just insert the CD-ROM into your computer and run the installation program, which usually has a fairly obvious name, such as INSTALL.EXE or SETUP.EXE.

After you've installed the Web cam software driver, the second step is to physically connect your Web cam to your computer, either through a USB, serial, or parallel port, depending on the type of Web cam you bought.

Finally, you may need to restart your computer so that your operating system can load the Web cam software driver. At this point (theoretically), your Web cam is ready to start taking pictures.

To help you determine if your Web cam is working properly, most Web cams come with their own software that displays images from your Web cam onto your computer screen. Just run this program and make sure you see an image from your Web cam. You may want to experiment with saving images and video from your Web cam so that you can see the quality of the images your Web cam can save.

Finding a Web Site

To set up a Web site, you need a Web hosting service. Most online services (such as America Online) and Internet service providers (ISPs, such as Prodigy or EarthLink) generously offer several megabytes of storage space for subscribers to set up their own Web site.

As an alternative to using your current ISP for hosting a Web site, you can either pay a separate Web hosting company to post your Web site or use a free Web hosting service.

Free Web hosting services make money through advertising, which means that every time someone looks at your Web site, that viewer gets bombarded by advertisements. If advertisements annoy you, then you may prefer paying for a separate Web hosting service.

Before you sign up with any Web hosting service, make sure that you can upload files to your Web site using *File Transfer Protocol* (FTP). FTP is a standard for transferring files over the Internet. If you cannot use FTP to upload files, then your Web cam is not able to send images and post them on your Web site. If you aren't sure whether a particular Web hosting service allows you to use FTP, ask.

If you want to create a recognizable domain name, such as www.dummies.com or www.idgbooks.com, you need to pay for the services of a Web hosting company. Such costs can range in price from $10 to $100 or more a month, depending on the storage space and services that you need to keep your Web site running.

The advantage of paying for a Web hosting service is that you get technical support, greater flexibility in setting up your Web site (such as offering online shopping), and a custom, easy-to-remember domain name. The disadvantage is the cost.

The advantage in using your current ISP or a free Web hosting company is that setting up and experimenting with a Web site that displays images from your Web cam doesn't cost you a thing. The disadvantage is that your domain name is often something really cryptic, like `www.members.tripod.com/Bo_the_Cat`.

If you want to experiment with a free Web site, visit one of the following Web hosting companies and set up your free account today:

AngelFire (`www.angelfire.com`)

Bizland.com (`www.bizland.com`)

FreeServers (`www.freeservers.com`)

Geocities (`www.geocities.com`)

Hypermart (`www.hypermart.net`)

LiveUniverse.com (`http://liveuniverse.com/world`)

NetColony (`www.netcolony.com`)

Stormloader (`www.stormloader.com`)

The Globe (`www.theglobe.com`)

Tripod (`www.tripod.lycos.com`)

WebProvider (`www.webprovider.com`)

Free Web sites give you the chance to experiment with designing and maintaining Web pages without any financial outlay. If you find that you like designing and maintaining Web sites, then you may want to graduate to a fee-based Web site hosting service later.

If you need help setting up a Web site, you may want to read: *Web Design & Desktop Publishing For Dummies,* by Roger C. Parker; *Setting Up an Internet Site For Dummies,* 3rd Edition, by Jason Coombs, Ted Coombs, David A. Crowder, and Rhonda Crowder; or *HTML For Dummies,* 3rd Edition, by Ed Tittel and Stephen N. James (all published by IDG Books Worldwide, Inc.).

SpotLife (`www.spotlife.com`) is a free Web hosting company specifically designed for helping people set up Web sites that display images from their Web cams.

Designing Your Web Pages

After you reserve storage space on a Web hosting server, the next step is to create the actual Web pages to display your Web cam images. You can use any Web page creation program to create your Web pages, such as Microsoft FrontPage, Adobe PageMill, or Macromedia Dreamweaver.

Programs such as FrontPage, PageMill, or Dreamweaver enable you to visually design a Web page, but you may still want to modify the actual Hypertext Markup Language (HTML) code to define exactly the way you want your Web pages to look and behave.

After you design your Web page, you need to modify the Web page to display your Web cam images. To do this, you need two HTML tags:

- ✔ The meta refresh tag
- ✔ The img src tag

The meta refresh tag appears between the `<head>` and `</head>` portion of a Web page and specifies a time interval to refresh the Web page, as in the following code:

```
<meta http-equiv="refresh" content="60">
```

The `content` value defines the number of seconds before the Web page completely reloads. In the above example, the meta tag waits 60 seconds before reloading the Web page.

After defining the time to wait before refreshing an image, the next step is to specify the image file you wish to display using the img src tag, as in the following code:

```
<img src="mycat.jpg">
```

This tag tells the Web page the particular file to display, such as a file named mycat.jpg.

You may need to specify a particular directory where the image file is stored. For example, if your Web cam image files are stored in a directory called `images`, you must specify that directory in the img src code, as you see here:

```
<img src="images/mycat.jpg">
```

So the basic skeleton of a Web page that refreshes every 60 seconds and displays an image called mycat.jpg might look like this:

```
<html>
<head>
<meta http-equiv="refresh" content ="60">
</head>
<body>
<h1>This is a picture of my cat's face.</h1>
<img src="mycat.jpg">
</body>
</html>
```

Each time the meta refresh tag reloads the Web page, the entire Web page may appear to flicker.

You can shove the meta refresh tag inside an HTML frame. That way, only the frame portion of the Web page flickers, not the entire Web page.

Displaying text with your images

Sometimes, your Web cam image may load slowly, leaving an empty space on your Web page until the Web cam image finally appears. If you want to add a little explanatory text to your image, as shown in Figure 3-1, you can use the alt attribute, which serves two purposes:

✔ To display text on a Web page while the Web cam image loads

✔ To display text as a tooltip (a tiny pop-up window) whenever the user moves the mouse over the image

To use the alt attribute, you have to include it in the img src tag, as you see here:

```
<img src="mycat.jpg" alt="Explanatory or pop-up text">
```

Rather than try to cram the entire img src tag on a single line, you can break it up so that different parts appear on separate lines, such as:

```
<img src="mycat.jpg"
alt="Explanatory or pop-up text">
```

Defining the width and height of a Web cam image

To speed up the loading of your image, specify the width and height of your Web cam image on your Web page.

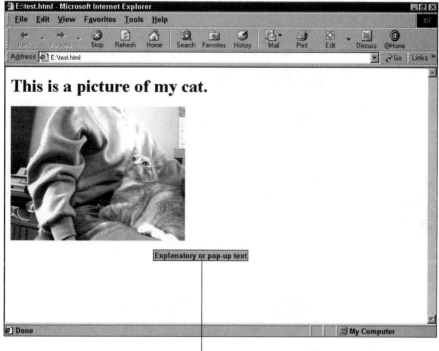

Figure 3-1:
The `alt`
attribute
displays text
in a tooltip
window
whenever
the user
moves the
mouse over
the Web
cam image.

Tooltip window

Specifying the width and height of an image enables a viewer's browser to display the Web page without waiting for the image to load first. If your Web page doesn't specify the width and height, the browser must wait for the image to appear before the browser can properly display the rest of the Web page.

If the specified width or height differs from the actual width and height of an image, the browser scales the image to fit the sizes defined in the Web page. The browser may shrink or expand the image, which can look really weird if you choose the wrong width or height for a particular image.

To specify the width and height of an image, add the `width` and `height` attributes inside the img src tag, as follows:

```
<img src="mycat.jpg" width=150 height=100>
```

or

```
<img src="mycat.jpg"
width=150
height=100>
```

The width and height are measured in *pixels,* which are the tiny little dots that make up an image on your computer screen.

Adding a border

The border attribute simply displays a border of varying thickness around your image. To define a border, just add the border attribute inside the img src tag, as follows:

```
<img src="mycat.jpg" border=3>
```

You can combine the border, width, height, and alt (text) attributes in a single img src tag, such as

```
<img src="mycat.jpg" alt="Pop-up text" width=125 height=140
        border=4>
```

Keeping text at a distance

To keep your Web pages looking pretty, you may want to specify how close text on the Web page appears next to your Web cam images. To specify how close text appears to the right and left edges of your picture, specify the horizontal spacing by using the hspace attribute. The following code tells the browser to display text around the Web cam image at a distance of 5 pixels:

```
<img src="mycat.jpg" hspace=5>
```

To specify how close text appears to the top and bottom edges of your picture, specify the vertical spacing by using the vspace attribute:

```
<img src="mycat.jpg" vspace=3>
```

Naturally, you can combine these attributes to specify both the vertical and horizontal spacing around an image, such as

```
<img src="mycat.jpg"
hspace=5
vspace=3>
```

Counting down with JavaScript

One trick to make your Web page more interesting is to display a countdown that tells viewers exactly how many seconds they have to wait before they can see an updated image from your Web cam, as shown in Figure 3-2.

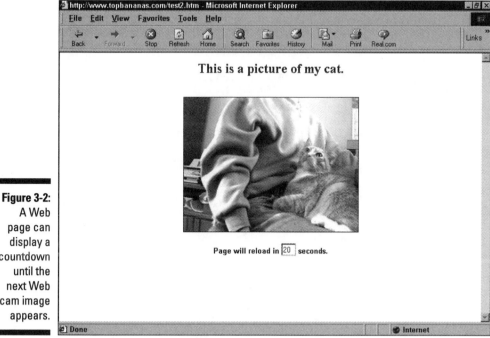

This is a picture of my cat.

Page will reload in 20 seconds.

Done   Internet

Figure 3-2:
A Web page can display a countdown until the next Web cam image appears.

To create a countdown on your Web page, you can use a programming language called JavaScript, which you can add to your Web page. First, create the meta refresh tag between your Web page's <head> and </head> tags to define how long you want your Web page to wait before reloading.

Displaying Web cam images with a Java applet

Rather than mess around with HTML code to display your Web cam images, you can mess around with Java applets instead. The AnfyTeam Web site (www.anfyteam.com) offers a shareware Java applet that you can download and copy for your own Web pages.

This Java applet can display Web cam images using special visual effects, such as overlaying another image over your Web cam image or displaying your Web cam image with a special fade-in effect.

Java applets provide more flexibility than ordinary meta refresh tags buried inside HTML code, but the price you pay for this flexibility is having to learn Java programming or, at least, how to use Java applets. Still, if you want to make your Web pages more interesting, consider Java applets as another way to display Web cam images on a Web page.

If you want to reload your Web page every 30 seconds, the meta refresh tag's `content` value is 30, like this:

```
<html>
 <head>
  <meta http-equiv=refresh content="30">
 </head>
 </html>
```

Next, sandwich the following JavaScript timer program between the `<head>` and `</head>` tags, such as:

```
<html>
 <head>
  <meta http-equiv=refresh content="30">
  <script language="JavaScript">
  <!--
  var x = 30
  var y = 1

  function StartTimer(){
   x = x-y
   if (x > -1) document.form1.clock.value = x
   timerID = setTimeout("StartTimer()", 1000)}
  // -->
  </script>
 </head>
 </html>
```

Make sure the content value specified in the meta refresh tag is equal to the value of x in the JavaScript program. In this case, the value of both is 30, which represents 30 seconds.

Next, you need to start the JavaScript timer program each time the Web page loads, by using the OnLoad command within the `<body>` tag, as follows:

```
<html>
 <head>
  <meta http-equiv=refresh content="30">
  <script language="JavaScript">
  <!--
  var x = 30
  var y = 1

  function StartTimer(){
   x = x-y
   if (x > -1) document.form1.clock.value = x
   timerID = setTimeout("StartTimer()", 1000)}
  // -->
  </script>
```

```
</head>
<body onLoad="StartTimer()">
</body>
</html>
```

Naturally, you need to display the Web cam image on the Web page by using the img src tag sandwiched inside the <body> and </body> tags, such as:

```
<html>
 <head>
  <meta http-equiv=refresh content="30">
  <script language="JavaScript">
  <!--
  var x = 30
  var y = 1

  function StartTimer(){
   x = x-y
   if (x > -1) document.form1.clock.value = x
   timerID = setTimeout("StartTimer()", 1000)}
  // -->
  </script>
 </head>
 <body onLoad="StartTimer()">
  <center>
   <h2>This is a picture of my cat.</h2>
   <img src="images/mycat.jpg"><br>
  </center>
 </body>
</html>
```

Finally, you need to display the actual countdown timer inside the <body> and </body> tags, as follows:

```
<html>
 <head>
  <meta http-equiv=refresh content="30">
  <script language="JavaScript">
  <!--
  var x = 30
  var y = 1

  function StartTimer(){
   x = x-y
   if (x > -1) document.form1.clock.value = x
   timerID = setTimeout("StartTimer()", 1000)}
  // -->
  </script>
 </head>
 <body onLoad="StartTimer()">
  <center>
   <h2>This is a picture of my cat.</h2>
```

```
<img src="images/mycat.jpg"><br>
<form name="form1"><b><font size="-1" face="Arial">Page
    will reload in </font>
<input type="text" name="clock" size="2" value> <font
    size="-1" face="Arial">seconds.</font></form>
</center>
</body>
</html>
```

For more information about JavaScript, pick up a copy of *JavaScript For Dummies Quick Reference* by Emily Vander Veer.

For more examples on displaying Web cam images on a Web page, visit one of the following Web sites, which offer free Web page samples that you can study:

GeneriCam (`www.occonnect.com/johnqpublic`)

WebCam Developers (`http://developers.Webcamworld.com`)

Finding Web Cam Software

Besides a Web cam, the most important thing you need to post live pictures on the Internet is a Web cam program. A Web cam program takes images from your Web cam and sends them over the Internet (via FTP), so they can appear on a Web page of your own creation.

Like any other category of software, Web cam programs offer a variety of features that sound good on paper but may be totally pointless for practical purposes. To help you sift through the different Web cam programs, here are some common features to look for:

- ✔ **Web cam support.** Most Web cam programs work with the most popular Web cams, but make sure that the Web cam program you're considering works with your particular Web cam.

- ✔ **FTP scheduling.** While all Web cam programs can upload your Web cam images to your Web site using FTP, some of the better programs can also schedule when to send your images, such as only between the hours of 3 p.m. and 6 p.m. every Monday through Friday.

- ✔ **Dial-up support.** Because most people are still using telephone modems to connect to the Internet, Web cam programs can dial up your Internet account, upload the images, and then disconnect as quickly as possible to avoid tying up your phone line.

- ✔ **Time-stamping.** This feature adds a time-and-date stamp to each Web cam image so that users can see when the image was last updated and, therefore, how recent (or how old) the image is.

✓ **Text and graphic stamping.** This feature adds a graphic image and/or text, such as an advertising logo and a phone number, to your uploaded Web cam images.

✓ **Prebuilt Web pages.** Because designing a Web page to display your Web cam images can be troublesome, many Web cam programs come with prebuilt Web pages that you can modify without having to write any HTML code yourself.

✓ **Streaming video.** This feature lets you display live video images from your Web cam, so people can see what your Web cam is capturing at that moment. (Because streaming videos require a fast Internet connection, most Web sites instead simply update still images periodically.)

✓ **Motion detection.** This feature automatically starts capturing images from your Web cam the moment it detects a change, such as someone turning on a light or moving in front of your Web cam. By using this feature, you can turn your Web cam into a security camera to catch intruders trying to break into a window or accessing your computer without your knowledge. To prevent someone from stealing your computer, some Web cam programs can also dial your voice or pager telephone number, send you an e-mail including pictures from your Web cam, or scare off an intruder by playing a sound file.

✓ **Audio detection.** Similar to motion detection, audio detection enables your Web cam to alert someone (by phone, pager, e-mail, and so on) or scare off an intruder by playing a sound file if the noise level around the Web cam exceeds a certain level.

✓ **Pan and tilt support.** This feature enables viewers to control your Web cam and aim or swivel it in different directions.

✓ **Password protection.** This feature prevents others from viewing a Web cam image unless they know the right password.

✓ **File format support.** This feature saves Web cam images in different file formats, such as JPEG, GIF, PCX, and BMP. Both JPEG and GIF files are great for posting on Web pages because they create small files. Other file formats, such as PCX or BMP, create large files, which you can't post on a Web site (but can edit easier because they retain more graphic details than JPEG or GIF files).

✓ **Incremental file naming.** This feature creates files with incremental file names such as MyFace1.jpg, MyFace2.jpg, and MyFace3.jpg.

Windows Web cam software

Because Windows is the most popular operating system in the world, it's no surprise that the majority of Web cam software available is designed to work under Windows. The following is a list of different Windows Web cam programs. Because most of them come in trial or demo versions, you can try these different programs until you find one that you like the best:

C3 Systems WebSnapper (www.c3sys.demon.co.uk)

CamShot (http://broadgun.com/camshot)

CompuTrust StealthWatch (www.stealthwatch.com)

Eyes&Ears (www.intech2.com)

Gotcha! (www.gotchanow.com)

HomeWatcher (www.homewatcher.com)

Honey Software (www.honeysw.com)

INetCAM (www.inetcam.com)

ISpy WebCam (www.surveyorcorp.com/ispy)

KABcam (www.kabsoftware.com)

Luminositi SoftCam (www.luminositi.com)

MSE Web Cam Control Center (www.marcweb.de)

PeleSoft NetSnap (www.netsnap.com)

SnapCap (www.snapcap.com)

Surveyor Corporation WebCam32 (www.webcam32.com)

TrueTech Webcam (www.truetech.com)

VistaX Software Web Cam Sam (www.vista-x.com)

WebCamNow (www.webcamnow.com)

Macintosh Web cam software

The Macintosh may not be as popular as Windows-based computers, but plenty of software developers have created Web cam programs for the Macintosh. Here's a list:

Evological CoolCam (www.evological.com)

NuSpectra SiteCam (www.nuspectra.com)

Oculus (www.intlweb.com/Oculus2)

PaperJet Software WebCam Too (http://webcam.paperjet.com)

StripCam (www.stripcam.org)

WebVideo (http://members.xoom.com/%5FXMCM/hsoftware/webvideo.htm)

If you really want to understand how a Web cam program works, visit the PaperJet Software Web site (http://webcam.paperjet.com) to download the complete CodeWarrior source code to the WebCam Turbo program.

Setting Up Your Dial-Up Connection

If you're one of the fortunate few who have a constant "always on" Internet connection through a cable or DSL modem, you can skip this section. For those who have to dial a telephone number to access the Internet, you need to tell your Web cam software how to use your dial-up Internet connection by defining three items:

- ✔ The phone number to call to access your Internet service provider (such as Prodigy or EarthLink)
- ✔ Your user name or ID
- ✔ Your password

Whenever you transfer Web cam images to your Web site through a dial-up connection, you're tying up a phone line in the process. While some Web cam programs can automatically send your Web cam images to your Web site and then hang up your telephone, you may want a dedicated phone line just for your computer.

When you set up your Web cam program, you may need to specify the kind of connection you have, such as a LAN connection (which also includes DSL and cable modem connections) or a dial-up connection through a phone modem. You may also want to define and store the user name and password, so the Web cam program can access your Web site automatically, without prompting you for the user name and password.

Two additional items your Web cam software may offer are the option to hang up automatically after uploading your images and the option to keep dialing your Internet access number a fixed number of times in case the line is busy. Figure 3-3 shows how to set up a Web cam program to work with a dial-up Internet connection.

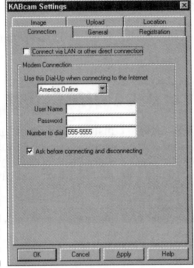

Figure 3-3:
You need to
define your
dial-up
connection
parameters
for
accessing
the Internet.

Uploading Images Using FTP

After you reserve storage space on a Web hosting server (such as America
Online or Geocities), design your Web pages to display your Web cam images,
and set up your Web cam program to dial up your Internet account, you need
to configure your Web cam program to send Web cam images via FTP. Figure
3-4 shows the typical FTP parameters needed to get your Web cam program
to upload images.

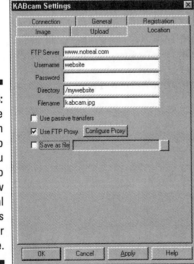

Figure 3-4:
To configure
a Web cam
program to
use FTP, you
need to
know a few
technical
details
about your
Web site.

To configure a Web cam program to connect to your Web site via FTP, you need to know four items, all of which you can get by asking your Web hosting company:

- ✔ **The name of your FTP server.** The name of your FTP server is often your domain name by itself (such as `mydomain.com`) or with `ftp` in front of it (such as `ftp.mydomain.com`).

- ✔ **Your user name (sometimes called the userid).** Your user name is often all or part of your domain name, but check with your Web hosting company to be sure.

- ✔ **Your password.** Most Web hosting services either assign you a password or let you pick one yourself. In either case, you can always change your password later.

- ✔ **The directory in which to save files.** Web hosting companies often bury users' files beneath a bizarre layer of directories within directories, such as `/home/mydomain/www`.

Check with your Web hosting company to find out your exact FTP server name, user name, password, and directory. If you have one character wrong, a period out of place, or an uppercase letter where a lowercase letter should be, your Web cam program may be unable to send your images via FTP to your Web site.

After your Web cam program uploads images to your Web site, you may want to visit your Web site using different browsers and different versions of the same browser, to make certain your Web pages properly display your Web cam images.

Part II
Lights, Camera, Action!

The 5th Wave   By Rich Tennant

"The Web cam is finally giving me my 15 minutes worth of fame, along with several coffee machines, a few lava lamps, and a bowl of rotting fruit."

In this part . . .

One of the most common uses of a Web cam is to post images to a Web site. Although doing so may sound simple in theory, it's actually slightly more complicated in practice. But don't worry. This part of the book gently guides you through the steps to place your Web cam images on a Web site, so that anyone in the world can see who you are.

This part of the book discusses how to post still images from your Web cam on a Web site and post complete video images on a Web site. It also describes the different video file formats and presents the actual HTML code for displaying different types of video file formats on your Web site.

In case you're lucky enough to be running the latest iMac or a computer with the Windows Millennium Edition operating system, your computer may also include a free copy of a video editing program called iMovie (for the iMac) or Windows Movie Maker (for Windows Millennium Edition users). To help you edit your Web cam videos, this part of the book provides brief instructions for using both iMovie and Windows Movie Maker, so you can dress up your videos with Hollywood-style special effects and create your own video masterpieces with some help from your trusty little Web cam.

Chapter 4

Capturing a Movie with Your Web Cam

*I*n this chapter, you find out about all the creative ways that you can use your Web cam to capture video images. In an ideal world, you could always display live video directly from your Web cam to your Web site, so that people all over the world could see exactly what your Web cam is capturing at that moment. Unfortunately, displaying live video through a Web cam may not be feasible, because you need a constant Internet connection so your Web cam can send a steady stream of images to your Web site.

An additional challenge with live video is the *bandwidth* requirement. Bandwidth refers to the speed and amount of data a network connection (such as the Internet) can transfer at any given time. The bandwidth of your particular Internet connection can vary depending on your location and the particular Internet service you use.

For example, connecting to the Internet on weekends and weekday evenings can often take a while because other people are trying to connect at the same time. Conversely, using a small Internet service can often speed up your connection because fewer people are competing for its resources. America Online users occasionally have trouble connecting due to the millions of America Online subscribers trying to connect simultaneously.

When setting up a Web cam, keep your Internet connection capabilities in mind. Live video takes time to send, so trying to shove live video from your Web cam through a 56K modem Internet connection can be as frustrating as trying to suck a watermelon through a straw.

Until dial-up connections through telephone modems disappear and everyone has high-speed, always-on Internet access through either cable or DSL modems, most people have to live with these technological limitations when using their Web cams. Instead of displaying live video, many people are choosing a less bandwidth-intensive method of capturing video images in a special video file. That way, they just have to send the one video file to their Web site, instead of sending a continuous stream of video images.

Understanding Movie File Formats

When you save video images to a file, you have to save them in a special video file format. The two most common video file formats are

- ✔ QuickTime
- ✔ Audio/Video Interleave (AVI)

Although QuickTime is the native video file format for Macintosh computers, you can view QuickTime files on a Windows computer if you download and install the QuickTime for Windows program from Apple Computers (www.apple.com/quicktime). QuickTime files usually end with the mov or qt file extension.

The AVI standard is the native video file format for Windows 95 and newer. Of course, Macintosh users can still view AVI files if they have the QuickTime player on their computers.

Three additional movie file formats you may run across are RealVideo (ram file extension), Advanced Streaming Format (asf file extension), and MPEG (mpg file extension). To play RealVideo movies, you need the RealPlayer plug-in, available from the Real.com Web site (www.realplayer.com). To play ASF files, you need the Windows Media Player. To play MPEG files, you can use QuickTime or the Windows Media Player.

Capturing a Video

Capturing a video with your Web cam can be as simple as pointing your Web cam at an object and running your Web cam software. (Your software may have come with your Web cam or you may have bought your software separately.) When capturing a video, you can choose several options to modify its appearance, as shown in Figure 4-1. Some options that many Web cam programs offer include the following:

✔ **File format.** Many Web cam programs save files in AVI or QuickTime formats, but you may want to experiment with different file formats to see which one you think creates the smallest files with the best image quality.

✔ **Frame rate.** Typical frame rates for Web videos range between 8 and 15 frames per second, although you can specify higher (for higher image quality at the cost of larger file size) or lower (for lower image quality in return for smaller file size) frame rates.

✔ **Resolution.** Typical Web video resolutions are 320 x 240 or 160 x 120, although you can specify higher resolutions (such as 640 x 480), which create larger files, or lower resolutions (such as 128 x 96), which create smaller files.

✔ **Color settings.** The more colors you capture, the larger the file. Black-and-white images create smaller file sizes, while 24-bit color captures sharper images at the cost of creating larger files.

Although you may be perfectly happy aiming your Web cam at an object and capturing a video, you may want to get a bit more creative and try some of the techniques originally developed by Hollywood to create interesting visual effects.

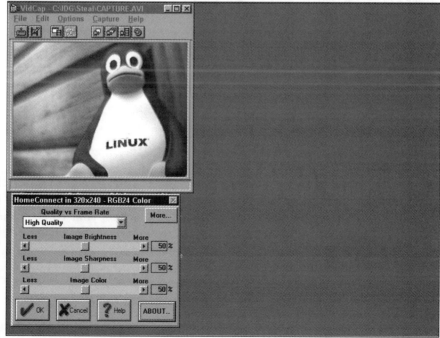

Figure 4-1:
Typical
options
available
when
capturing a
video file
through a
Web cam.

Time-lapse photography

Time-lapse video photography gives the illusion of compressing time. When viewed, a time-lapse video appears to speed up a normally slow-moving process. Examples include footage of a plant growing from a seed and blossoming into a fully grown flower, or storm clouds gathering over the sky and unleashing a tornado, making these events appear to take place in mere seconds.

To create a time-lapse video, your Web cam program needs to capture a picture at different intervals, such as every 10 minutes or every 24 hours, depending on the total length of the process you wish to capture, as shown in Figure 4-2.

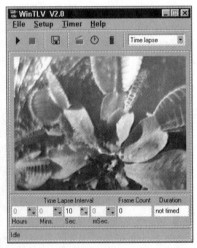

Figure 4-2:
Time-lapse
photography
condenses
a long-term
event into
a short
amount of
time.

To calculate the time intervals that your Web cam needs to capture an image, follow these steps:

1. **Determine the length of time that you want your video to show an event and multiply that by the number of frames per second you plan to capture.**

   For example, if you want a video to last 10 seconds, capturing 15 frames per second, the calculation would be

   10 seconds × 15 frames per second = 150 frames

2. **Determine the actual time of the event that you plan to capture.**

   For example, if you plan to capture an event that takes five minutes to complete, the calculation would be

   5 minutes × 60 seconds = 300 seconds

3. **Finally, divide the actual time of the event by the number of frames needed to determine the time interval for capturing images, such as the following:**

Following the same example, the calculation would be

300 seconds ÷ 150 frames = 2-second intervals

If you want to capture a 5-minute event in a 10-second video, you should set your Web cam to capture images every 2 seconds.

If your Web cam program doesn't let you define a time interval to capture a picture, grab a copy of WinTLV, which is specially designed to create time-lapse video images. A demo version of this program is available at the C3 Systems Web site (www.c3sys.demon.co.uk/tlv.htm) or on this book's CD-ROM.

Pixilation

Pixilation is an animation technique in which objects (usually people) are captured one frame at a time with intervals between each movement.

The term *pixilation* refers to using large intervals of time between frames to create magical or comical effects. For example, pixilation can show a man performing magic. The first few images show a man on stage. He snaps his fingers and magically, a cowboy hat appears on his head. He snaps his fingers again, and he's wearing a suit of armor. He snaps his fingers again, and he's wearing nothing but a loincloth.

By capturing images spaced apart in time, pixilation can create unusual effects that are more interesting than ordinary video. For example, you can have people, animals, or objects appear and disappear instantaneously.

A classic example of pixilation is Norman McLaren's 1952 Oscar-winning short anti-war film, *Neighbors,* which dramatizes the gradual escalation of a neighborly conflict from its initial misunderstanding to the climactic scene in which one neighbor destroys the homes and properties of the other neighbors.

To create pixilation, have your Web cam take images at intervals large enough for you to make any dramatic changes you wish, such as taking on and off a hat, putting on a costume, and moving to a new location. To make your video appear smooth, the people in the video need to maintain the identical pose from one frame to the next. Otherwise their image will appear to jump from frame to frame, which can have a distracting effect (unless that's what you want).

Stop-motion animation

Stop-motion is a technique used to animate objects such as clay figures. In the early days of moviemaking, Hollywood used stop-motion animation to move miniature models of King Kong, dinosaurs, and monsters that couldn't be duplicated by a stunt man in a costume.

The filmmakers shot a few frames, stopped the camera, moved the object a fraction of an inch, shot another frame or two, moved the object a little more, and so on. The overall effect is that the inanimate objects appear to move on their own. Some recent examples of stop-motion animation include the movies, *The Nightmare Before Christmas, Chicken Run,* and *James and the Giant Peach.*

Like pixilation, stop-motion animation takes time and requires a lot of patience. Move an object too far, and its movement in the video appears too jerky. Despite its limitations, stop-motion animation can help you create unique and interesting videos showing a wide variety of inanimate objects that appear to come to life.

With stop-motion animation, you can make a video of a ceramic pig walking across a kitchen table to devour a plate of cookies or a Teddy bear dancing with your daughter's favorite doll.

To create stop-motion animation, capture still images with your Web cam, then use a special video editor (described in the "Touching Up Your Video" section) that can gather multiple still images and turn them into an AVI or QuickTime video file.

Touching Up Your Video

After you create a video, you can post it on your Web site for others to download. But if you're a perfectionist, you may want to take a little time to edit your video by adding titles and sounds or touching up visual flaws (such as a red eye). You may also want to compress your video file so that it's easier for people with 56K or slower modems to download in a reasonable amount of time.

For more information about two different video-editing programs, see Chapters 6 and 7, which discuss Apple's iMovie for the Macintosh and Windows Movie Maker for (what else?) Windows.

Editing a video

Although you may not be a video professional, you may still want to do basic editing to a video file, such as adding a title to the beginning of the video, deleting certain frames to shorten the video, creating special visual transitions between frames, or adding voices or dramatic music to emphasize an image. Figure 4-3 shows QuickEditor, a shareware video-editing program for the Macintosh.

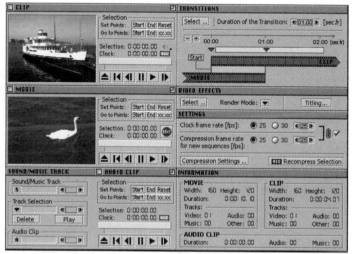

Figure 4-3:
A video-editing program gives you the control to modify individual frames of a video file.

Most video-editing programs offer the following features:

- ✔ **File format support.** Some shareware video-editing programs can only edit specific file formats, such as AVI files. Unless you know you only want to edit one or two video file formats, make sure that your video-editing program can accept a variety of different video file formats. Some video-editing programs can even convert videos from one format to another, such as from AVI to QuickTime.

- ✔ **Frame editing.** Enables you to modify colors, brightness, or overall appearance of one or more frames of your video. The capabilities may include rotating, warping, or applying other physical manipulations to a frame or applying an opaque or frosted layer over an image.

- ✔ **Video transitions.** Alters the appearance of your images using such effects as dissolve, slide, and fade-in.

- ✔ **Titling.** Enables you to create interesting Hollywood-style titles that fade in, scroll up, and swirl around the screen.

- ✔ **Audio.** Adds voice, music, or an entire soundtrack synchronized with your movie.

Video editing is a specialized field. You don't have to edit your video before posting it to a Web site, but editing it makes it look more professional.

Windows video-editing software

Here's a list of various shareware video-editing programs you can try on your PC:

Axogon Composer (www.axogon.com)

CDH Productions' Image Explorer Pro (www.cdhnow.com)

FlickerFree's VideoFramer (www.flickerfree.com)

QuickTime Pro (www.apple.com)

Zwei-Stein (www.musicref.com)

Macintosh video-editing software

Here's a list of some shareware video-editing programs you can try on your Macintosh:

iMovie (www.apple.com)

MovieWorks (www.movieworks.com)

QuickEditor (www.wild.ch/quickeditor)

QuickTime Pro (www.apple.com)

Strata Software's VideoShop (http://strata.com)

If you want to take video editing seriously, consider buying Adobe Premiere or Adobe After Effects (www.adobe.com) for either Windows or the Macintosh. Both are expensive and complicated, heavy-duty video-editing programs that professionals use.

Compressing a video

Even a simple 10-second video of your dog chasing his tail can gobble up several megabytes (MB) of disk space. Because no one wants to wait a long time to download and view a video file (no matter how interesting that video may be), video files must be kept as small as possible. You can minimize the size of your video file by reducing some or all of the following:

✔ Frame rate (the number of video frames displayed each second)

✔ Resolution

✔ Number of colors displayed

After you save your video file, you can further reduce the size of that file by compressing it using a special video file-compression program, as shown in Figure 4-4.

If you plan to post any video files on a Web site, use a video compression program. The 3-second AVI video file shown in Figure 4-4 originally took up 5.3MB of storage space. After compressing the video file with Media Cleaner, the compressed version of the same file (stored in the RealVideo file format) took up only 27KB (kilobytes) of storage space.

The average size of data is as follows:

- 1 page of ASCII text = 1 kilobyte
- 1 second of audio = 100 kilobytes
- 1 second of uncompressed video = 1000 kilobytes (1 megabyte)

To give you a rough idea of how fast (or slow) your particular Internet connection may be, look at Table 4-1.

Figure 4-4:
A typical video compression program, such as Media Cleaner, can compress a Web cam video and save it in a variety of different file formats.

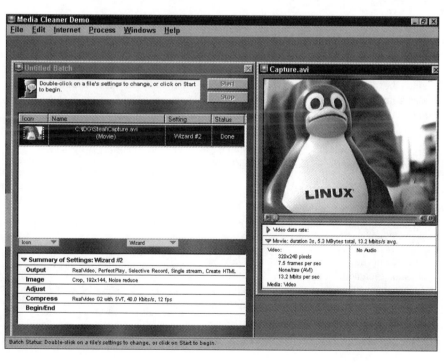

Table 4-1	Internet Download Speed
Internet Connection	*Approximate Time to Download a 1,000KB File*
28.8 Kbps	5 minutes
56.6 Kbps	3 minutes
ISDN	1 minute
Cable or DSL modem	5 seconds

Ordinary video, as seen on your TV, displays 30 frames per second. However, video files for the Web only display from 8 to 15 frames per second to keep the file size down. In a further attempt to reduce file size, video file resolution is lowered to around 160 x 120 pixels. Because of the slower frame rate and the lower resolution, video files may appear jerky and chunky when compared to TV-quality videos.

Compressing your videos

An uncompressed, large video file can gobble up a huge amount of disk space and fill up your entire hard drive. Because no one wants to waste time downloading a huge file, you need to shrink your video files by compressing them.

Some Web cam programs offer a special compression feature to help shrink your video files, but you may want to use a dedicated video file-compression program as well. Video compression works by removing redundant audio and video data, which has the drawback of reducing image quality. The trick is to reduce the file size with minimal loss of image quality.

Video compression programs use special compression techniques called *codec* (**co**mpressor/**dec**ompressor) *algorithms,* which essentially tell the computer how to reduce a video file's size. Some programs use different codecs than others, which is why two different programs can compress the same video file and create two different-size compressed video files.

To find out more about the technical details of video-compression techniques, visit the Codec Central Web site at `http://207.220.219.81/codeccentral/`.

To discover more about different video-compression programs, visit one of the following Web sites:

Cinepak (`www.cinepak.com`)

Intel Indeo (`www.intel.com`)

Media Cleaner (`www.terran.com`)

Sorenson Video (`www.sorenson.com`)

Truemotion (`www.duck.com`)

Chapter 5

Putting Your Video on a Web Site

In This Chapter

▶ Linking a video to a Web page

▶ Embedding a video on a Web page

▶ Posting videos on a Web cam hosting service

*I*n this chapter, you figure out what to do with the video you capture with your Web cam. After you capture a video file, your final step is to post the video on the Internet for everyone to look at and enjoy. Depending on your Web page editor (such as Microsoft FrontPage 2000), adding a video can be as simple as choosing a command such as Insert⇨Picture⇨Video, which automatically inserts a video file onto a Web page.

Although visually oriented Web page editors such as FrontPage may be convenient and easy to use, they hide the technical details of how a Web page actually displays video. In case you want to fine-tune the way your Web pages display video files, or if you're just curious about the specific details, keep reading this chapter.

If you don't care to know about the technical details of HTML (HyperText Markup Language), just skip to the last section, "Using a Web Cam Hosting Service," for information about posting live video on the Internet.

Writing HTML isn't hard, but if you want to get more creative in designing your Web pages, you have to know more HTML commands than this book can possibly show you. To find out more about HTML commands, pick up a copy of *HTML For Dummies,* 3rd Edition, by Ed Tittel and Steven N. James.

In case writing HTML commands is something you prefer not to do, many Web cam programs, such as CamShot (http://broadgun.com/camshot) and TrueTech WebCam (www.truetech.com), include prebuilt Web pages for displaying images from your Web cam. All you need to do is customize these prebuilt Web pages with any text or decorative graphics and then post the pages on your Web site.

Linking a Video

One of the simplest ways to post a video file on a Web page is to create a hyperlink directly on your Web page by using the anchor tag `<a href>` and `</a>`, as in this example:

```
<A HREF="videofile">Click here to view a video.</A>
```

In this example, the words, "Click here to view a video," appear as a hyperlink on the Web page. After the viewer clicks the hyperlink, <u>Click here to view a video</u>, this is what happens:

1. **The user's browser downloads the entire video file.**

   If this is a large file and the user has a slow modem, this download may take several minutes to an hour or more.

2. **The user's browser launches a video-playing program, such as the QuickTime MoviePlayer or Windows Media Player, in a separate window and plays the video.**

The drawback to linking a video to a Web page is that it forces users to download the entire video file before they can see it.

Not everyone will have the right video player to view your video, so it's a good idea to include a link on your Web page to a site where people can download the appropriate video player. For example, the QuickTime player can be found at `www.apple.com/quicktime`, the RealPlayer player can be found at `www.realplayer.com`, and the Windows Media Player can be found at `www.microsoft.com`.

Linking to an AVI, ASF, or QuickTime file

When Web cams save a video, they usually save them in one of several file formats. AVI, ASF, and QuickTime are the most widely used video formats found on the Internet. Chapter 4 describes the AVI and QuickTime formats in greater detail.

If you want to link to an AVI file, just substitute the filename in the anchor tag, as in this example:

```
<A HREF="video.avi">Plays an AVI file.</A>
```

When the user clicks the <u>Plays an AVI file</u> hyperlink, the file called `video.avi` downloads and plays as shown in Figure 5-1. (The screen looks like this in Windows 95/98, but not in Windows Me.)

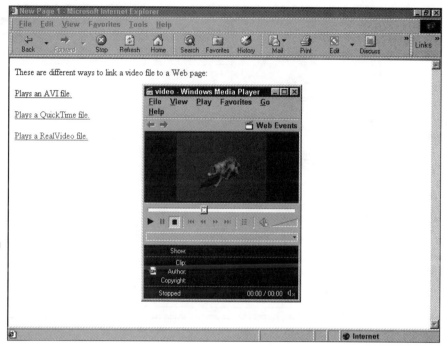

Figure 5-1:
Playing a
linked AVI
file in
Windows.

Although Microsoft originally created AVI files as the default video file for
Windows, the company recently created a new video file format called
Advanced Streaming Format (ASF). Linking an ASF file to a Web page is similar
to linking an AVI file to a Web page. All you have to do is create a Web page
link to the ASF file, as in the following example:

```
<A HREF="video.asf">Plays an ASF file.</A>
```

Instead of using an AVI or ASF file, you can substitute a QuickTime file inside
the anchor tag instead, as in this example:

```
<A HREF="quicktime.mov">Plays a QuickTime file.</A>
```

When the user clicks the Plays a QuickTime file hyperlink, the file called
quicktime.mov downloads and plays. When viewed within Windows, the
QuickTime video appears in a separate browser window. When viewed on a
Macintosh, a QuickTime video appears in a separate QuickTime window, as
shown in Figure 5-2.

Figure 5-2:
As viewed
on a
Macintosh,
the
QuickTime
window
pops up to
play a linked
QuickTime
file.

Linking to a RealVideo file

The RealVideo format from RealNetworks is another popular video file format. If you want to link to a RealVideo file, you have to go through a two-step process. First, you have to create your Web page link to a text file with the ram file extension, as in the following example:

```
<A HREF="realvideo.ram">Plays a RealVideo file.</A>
```

Next, you have to create a text file (using a simple text editor such as the Windows Notepad) that ends with the ram file extension. The contents of this text file contain the actual link to your RealVideo file, as in the following example:

```
http://www.myWebsite.com/realvideo.rm
```

When you play a linked RealVideo file, the RealPlayer program loads and displays the video, as shown in Figure 5-3.

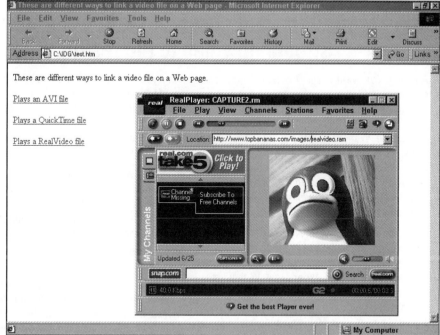

Figure 5-3:
In Windows,
the
RealPlayer
window
pops up to
play a linked
RealVideo
file.

Embedding a Video

Linking is easy to do but suffers from several drawbacks. First, after you link
a video file to a Web page, that video file runs in a separate window. Second,
linked files must be completely downloaded to the user's computer before
the user can see them.

Embedding video files is an alternative to linking them and offers the following advantages:

- ✔ Video files appear and run directly on the Web page.

- ✔ You can define the size of the video as it plays. In addition, you can also
  customize user controls that you want to appear with your video,
  thereby giving the user control over the way the video plays.

- ✔ Video files "stream" to the user, which means that users can view the
  video without first having to wait for the entire file to finish downloading.

Streaming video to the rescue

Any time you want to view a Web page, your computer (called a *client*) reaches out across the Internet and loads a Web page off another computer (called a *server*). The server simply copies the Web page off its hard drive and transfers it across the Internet to your hard drive. When your computer has a copy of all the text and graphic images that make up a Web page, you can finally look at that particular Web page on your computer.

This process of copying Web pages from the server computer to the client computer explains why slow modems make using the Internet an excruciatingly painful experience. With a slow modem, such as one running at 28.8 Kbps (kilobits per second), Web pages load as if your computer were slowly dripping molasses from the top of the screen to the bottom.

With faster 56 Kbps (56K) modems, Web pages load faster. However, people started getting bored with plain text and graphics-oriented Web pages, so the Web page creators started tossing in sound, animation, and video. Now

when you want to look at some Web pages, not only does your computer have to wait for all text and graphics to transfer from the other computer, but your computer also has to wait for all sound, animation, and video files to download as well.

Because video files can take up several megabytes (MB) of space, waiting for a video to download can take a long time, even if you have a 56K modem. If a video takes too long to download and view, most people will just jump to another Web site rather than wait.

The solution to waiting for huge video files to download is "streaming video," which displays a video almost as quickly as the video file arrives across the Internet. With streaming video, people can see a video on a Web page almost immediately, which means Web pages appear to load quickly again . . . until someone comes up with a new technique that looks cool but once more bogs down the transfer of Web pages.

The major drawback with embedding is that if a user does not have the appropriate plug-in to view your video file, your Web page can't play the video and instead displays a broken link image, as shown in Figure 5-4.

Your Web page needs to provide links so people can download the appropriate plug-in. For example, the QuickTime plug-in can be found at www.apple.com/quicktime; the RealPlayer plug-in can be found at www.realplayer.com; and the Windows Media Player can be found at www.microsoft.com/windows/windowsmedia.

Embedding an AVI, ASF, or QuickTime file

To embed an AVI, ASF, or QuickTime file, you need to use this code

```
<embed src="videofile">
```

where "videofile" is the name of your video file, such as dog.avi, ballgame.asf, or parade.mov.

Defining the size of a video window

If you want to define the size of your video as it plays, you define the height and width parameters, as in the following example:

```
<embed src="cat.mov" width="128" height="128">
```

In this case, the video appears in a window 128 pixels wide and 128 pixels high.

You can also define the width and height of your video window as a percentage of the Web page. If you want the video to appear in a window 35 percent of the width of the browser window and 55 percent of the height of the browser window, you can use the HTML code in the following example:

```
<embed src="cat.mov" width="35%" height="55%">
```

Broken link image

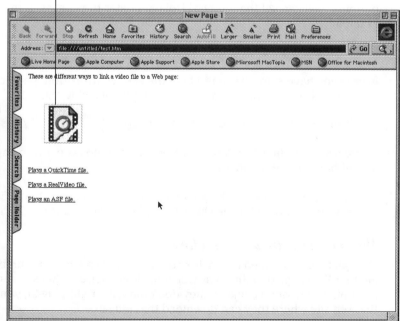

Figure 5-4: A broken link image appears when a computer does not have the appropriate plug-in to view an embedded video file.

Defining how your video plays

Normally, embedded videos play once right after the Web page appears and then stop. However, you can force the video not to play until the user clicks it and also make the video play over and over again.

To make the video wait until the user starts it, you have to set the autoplay parameter to false, as in this example:

```
<embed src="jet.asf" autoplay="false">
```

If you set the autoplay parameter to true, as shown below (or omit it altogether), the video streams in with the page and plays as soon as possible.

```
<embed src="jet.asf" autoplay="true">
```

If you want to make the video play over and over, you can set the loop parameter to true as in the following example:

```
<embed src="jet.asf" loop="true">
```

To make the video play just once, set the loop parameter to false, as in the following example:

```
<embed src="jet.asf" loop="false">
```

Adding controls to your video

If you want to display the user controls (such as the Pause, Stop, and Play buttons), you can set the controller parameter to true, as in the following example:

```
<embed src="jet.asf" controller="true">
```

In case you have some reason to hide the user controls from people, just set the controller parameter to false, as in the following example:

```
<embed src="jet.asf" controller="false">
```

Figure 5-5 shows how the Windows Media Player looks on a Web page, with and without its user controls.

You may need to adjust the height of a QuickTime video by about 15 to 25 pixels, so the controls for the QuickTime plug-in can be seen.

Making your video act like a link

You can turn your video into a link so that users can click it to jump to another Web page or a different Web site altogether. Just in case someone can't play your video because they don't have the right plug-in, you can add the Web site where they can download that plug-in.

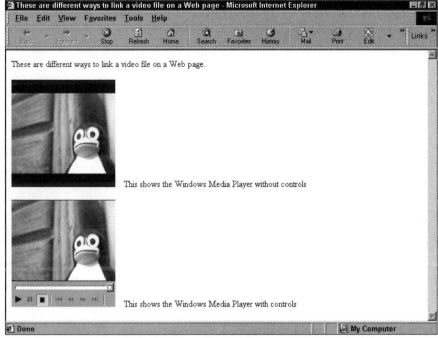

Figure 5-5:
The
Windows
Media
Player can
appear with
or without
user
controls.

If you want to turn your video into a link, just add the href code along with the exact Internet address to link to, as in the following example:

```
<embed src="glass.avi" href="http://www.dummies.com">
```

If the user clicks the glass.avi video, the link jumps to the www.dummies.com Web site.

Embedding a RealVideo file

When you embed a RealVideo file, you need to use the <embed> tag to define the following information:

✔ The name of a text file that ends with the rpm file extension, which contains the name of the actual RealVideo file that you want to play. The contents of this text file contain the actual link to your RealVideo file, as in the following example:

```
http://www.myWebsite.com/realvideo.rm
```

You can create a text file using the Windows Notepad program. Just remember to save your text file with the rpm file extension.

✔ The width and height of the window in which you want to display your RealVideo file.

✔ The type of control you want to display. To display a video, you need to set the `controls` parameter to `imagewindow`.

✔ The identity of the window to display your video, defined by the `console` parameter. If the `console` parameters are set to `_master`, any additional controls that you add, such as a Play button, affect this "master" window.

Put together, the HTML code needed to embed a RealVideo file may look something like this:

```
<embed src="images/realvideo.rpm" width="128" height="128"
       controls = imagewindow console = _master>
```

To make sure your embedded RealVideo file plays without delay, you can also set the `nojava` parameter to `true`, as in the following example:

```
<embed src="images/realvideo.rpm" width="128" height="128"
       controls = imagewindow nojava = "true" console =
       _master>
```

Setting the `nojava` parameter to `true`, keeps the browser's Java Virtual Machine from running (which can delay the playback of your video file).

Playing a RealVideo file automatically

After you embed a RealVideo file on a Web page, you still need to add more code to make the video actually play. If you want to make your RealVideo file play automatically, as soon as someone loads your Web page, you can set the `autostart` parameter to `true`, as in the following example:

```
<embed src="images/realvideo.rpm" width="128" height="128"
       controls = imagewindow nojava = "true" console =
       _master autostart = "true">
```

The above code plays the RealVideo file once and then stops. If users want to see the video again, they have to reload the Web page.

Displaying controls to play a RealVideo file

To give users more control over the playing of a RealVideo file, you can add additional buttons such as the Play, Pause, or Stop button. To define user controls, you need to create an additional `<embed>` tag and set the `controls` parameter to one of the following settings:

✓ All — displays all the user controls, as shown in Figure 5-6.

✓ ControlPanel — displays the Play, Pause, and Stop buttons, and also displays the video position slider and volume control.

✓ PlayButton — displays the Play and Pause buttons.

✓ PlayOnlyButton — displays the Play button.

✓ PauseButton — displays the Pause button.

✓ StopButton — displays the Stop button.

✓ FFCtrl — displays the Forward button.

✓ RWCtrl — displays the Rewind button.

✓ MuteCtrl — displays the Mute button.

✓ MuteVolume — displays a horizontal slider to mute the volume.

✓ VolumeSlider — displays a vertical slider to adjust the volume.

✓ PositionSlider — displays a horizontal slider to view different parts of the video.

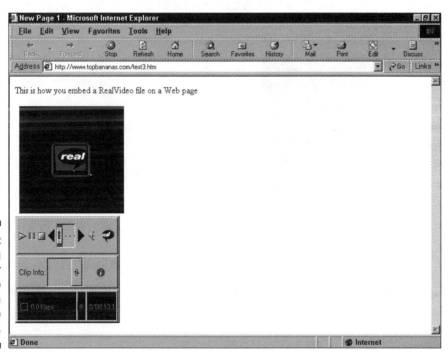

Figure 5-6:
Displaying
all the user
controls to
play a
RealVideo
file.

> ✔ `TACCtrl` — displays a button to get information about the RealVideo file.
>
> ✔ `HomeCtrl` — displays a link to the RealNetworks Web site.

So if you want to display an embedded RealVideo file, along with the control panel, you need to include the appropriate HTML code in your Web page, as in the following example:

```
<embed src="images/realvideo.rpm" width="128" height="128"
       controls = imagewindow nojava = "true" console =
       _master>

<embed src="images/realvideo.rpm" width = "128" height =
       "128" controls = ControlPanel>
```

The preceding code creates a RealVideo image window and a control panel, as shown in Figure 5-7.

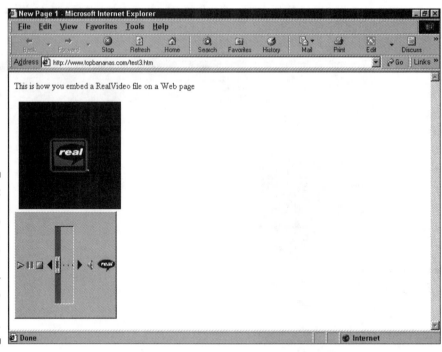

Figure 5-7:
Displaying a
RealVideo
file with
the
`control`
parameter
set to
`Control`
`Panel`.

Streaming servers: How the pros do it

Video files travel over the Internet in two ways: *HyperText Transfer Protocol* (HTTP) streaming and *Real-Time Transport Protocol/Real-Time Streaming Protocol* (RTP/RTSP) streaming.

HTTP streaming works by downloading the video file to your hard drive, which makes this type of streaming perfect for short video clips that people may want to view over and over again. This chapter explains how to use HTTP streaming for your own Web site.

Rather than storing the video file on your hard drive, RTP/RTSP streaming sends the data to your computer, displays it, and immediately discards it. This makes RTP/RTSP better for displaying things such as full-length movies, live video broadcasts of sporting events, or supermodel fashion shows.

Any Web site can display HTTP streaming. However, RTP/RTSP streaming requires a special server program, called a *streaming server*.

Apple Computers has released their Darwin Streaming Server (www.publicsource. apple.com/projects/streaming) for free as open source, which means that if you're a programmer, you can see how the program

works and modify it. The Darwin Streaming Server can be used with a Macintosh or Red Hat Linux computer to provide RTP/RTSP streaming of QuickTime video files. By providing the Darwin Streaming Server for free, Apple hopes to encourage people to make QuickTime the new video format standard.

But what if you want to use RTP/RTSP streaming with RealVideo files? Then you have to buy the RealServer software, which can cost anywhere from $695 (supporting 25 simultaneous users) to $24,000 (supporting 400 simultaneous users) or more, depending on how many people you anticipate may be downloading your RealVideo files at any given moment.

If you want to stream Microsoft AVI or ASF files, you have to use the Windows Media Services program — which is free, but requires Windows NT or Windows 2000, which you have to buy.

For Web sites that absolutely need to display long videos or live broadcasts, a streaming server is necessary. For the average person with a simple Web cam, however, ordinary HTTP streaming, by linking or embedding video files on a Web page, ought to be enough.

Using a Web Cam Hosting Service

If you want to display live video broadcasts (also called Webcasts) from your Web cam, you can either use a special streaming server (see the sidebar, "Streaming servers: How the pros do it") and wrestle with installing it correctly on a computer, or you can do it the easy way and subscribe to a special Web cam hosting service.

These services are entirely free (they make their money from advertising) and provide you with a Web site for posting still images, prerecorded Web cam videos, or live video broadcasts direct from your own Web cam and computer.

To use these services, you simply need to sign up and download their special software to connect your computer to the Web cam hosting computer. This special software takes care of the technical details of displaying your Web cam images or videos, so you can concentrate on having fun with your Web cam.

So if you want a free Web site that eliminates much of the hassle of posting video images on a Web page, take a good look at one of the following free Web cam hosting services:

Camarades (`www.camarades.com`)

EarthNoise (`www.earthnoise.com`)

Popcast (`http://ulead.popcast.com`)

Pure Broadcasting Networks (`www.purebroadcasting.com`)

SpotLife (`www.spotlife.com`)

Chapter 6

A Quick Introduction to iMovie

In This Chapter

▶ How iMovie works

▶ Editing with iMovie

▶ Adding special effects

▶ Saving your video to disk or tape

*W*hen Apple Computers introduced the iMac computer, the focus was on "the next big thing," which Apple decided must be desktop video. The idea was to make video editing as easy as desktop publishing for the average person. This dream of easy desktop video editing came true when Apple shipped certain iMac models with a free video editing program called iMovie. This chapter provides a quick introduction to using iMovie to edit and store video on your iMac computer.

The current batch of Web cams can't store video in digital video (DV) format. If you want to edit your Web cam videos, you have to use a video editing program other than iMovie.

However, iMovie does allow you to import still images captured from a Web cam. Just save your still images in GIF or JPEG format, and you can insert your still images in to iMovie, either as part of an existing video or as an altogether new video file. Then save the entire file as a QuickTime video and post it on your Web site or e-mail it to your friends.

Exploring How iMovie Works

The iMovie program is designed to edit videos in much the same way that your word processing program is meant to edit text. But unlike a word processing program, which allows you to type text directly into the program, iMovie isn't meant for you to store your video directly into the program from your video camcorder. Instead, you have to store your video on tape and then transfer that video from your camcorder to your iMac.

After you transfer a video from a camcorder into iMovie, you can use iMovie to trim your video, rearrange frames, insert still images or titles, and include transitions between frames. After you finish editing your video, you can save it on disk or transfer it back to your video camcorder and save it on tape.

If your Macintosh didn't come with iMovie, you can download a free copy from Apple's Web site at www.apple.com. Just make sure you have a Macintosh with the proper hardware, such as a fast processor, a current version of the Mac OS operating system, plenty of RAM, and a high-resolution monitor. To find out if your Macintosh can run iMovie, refer to Chapter 2 or visit Apple Computer's Web site (www.apple.com) and view the system requirements.

iMovie is only available for the Macintosh. If you're using Microsoft Windows, you have to buy a separate video editing program or just upgrade to Windows Millennium Edition, which includes a free video editing program called Movie Maker. Chapter 7 explains how Windows Movie Maker works.

To use iMovie, you need to understand its technical hierarchy. To edit a video in iMovie, you have to create a *project.* A project may represent a complete video of your family's summer vacation. You can create and save multiple projects, but iMovie only lets you load, edit, and work on one project at a time.

After you create a project, you need to load one or more *clips* into that project. Clips are the video or still image files that you put into your project. (A project without clips is like a word processing document without any words.) Each project consists of up to nine clips.

Clips can be of any length, although you may want to keep your clips to a reasonable length so you can easily edit them. For example, trying to edit a thirty-minute clip can be as unwieldy as trying to edit a thirty-page word processing document. In both cases you may find that breaking your data into smaller chunks makes it easier to view and edit.

You can store iMovie clips in two places:

- ✔ The Shelf
- ✔ The Movie Track

The Shelf is a temporary location to store, view, and edit clips, so you can pick and choose the ones you want to use before inserting them into your movie. To make your movie, you need to move clips from the Shelf to the Movie Track, as shown in Figure 6-1. When you create a movie, iMovie only uses the clips stored on the Movie Track for your newly created videofile.

The Shelf

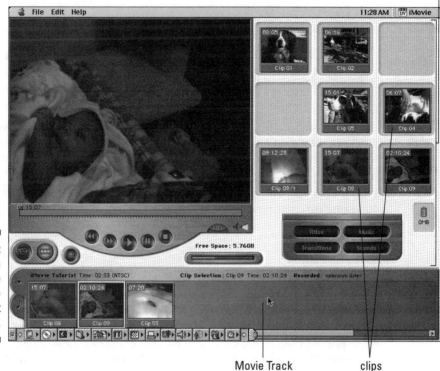

Figure 6-1:
iMovie can
load up to
nine
different
clips.

Movie Track   clips

Working with projects

To create a new project, follow these steps:

1. **Choose File⇨New Project.**

   The Create New Project dialog box appears.

2. **Type a name for your project and choose the folder where you want to store the project.**

   Storing all your projects in one place, such as inside a single folder, is a good idea. That way, you don't have to waste time trying to remember where you stored your iMovie projects.

3. **Click Create.**

   iMovie displays a blank Shelf and Movie Track.

To open an existing project, follow these steps:

1. **Choose File➪Open Project.**

   The Open Existing Project dialog box appears.

2. **Select the project you want to use and click Open. (You may have to dig through folders to find the project you want.)**

   iMovie displays any clips you have already imported to the Shelf or Movie track.

   To save the currently displayed project, just choose File➪Save Project. You may want to save your project periodically just to make sure you don't lose any work if the power goes out or your iMac crashes.

After you create or open a project, you need to add clips to it that you can edit or combine with other clips to create your entire video. You can add the following two types of clips:

- ✔ Video
- ✔ Still images

Importing a video

To import a video into iMovie, you need to capture a video using a video camcorder and then transfer that video directly into iMovie. The simplest solution is to buy one of the newer digital video camcorders that can transfer video directly to your iMac using a FireWire port (also called an IEEE 1394 port or an i.LINK port by some companies). If you have an older analog video camcorder, you need to buy a special converter to transfer your videos to your iMac.

Sony (www.sony.com) sells a special analog-to-DV (digital video) converter device called the Sony DVMC-DA2. This device converts videos stored in 8 mm, Hi8, VHS, or SVHS format to the DV format required by iMovie. Check your local video electronics retailer for more information about this device and others like it.

Before you rush out and buy a digital video camcorder, check with Apple's Web site (www.apple.com/imovie/shoot.html) first. Apple's Web site lists a handful of camcorders that have been tested to work with iMacs and iMovie. If you don't buy one of these pretested digital video camcorders, you may run into minor (or major) problems when transferring your videos to your iMac.

Video gobbles up huge chunks of hard drive space, so make sure your hard drive has at least several megabytes of available space (such as ten megabytes for a short video and several hundred megabytes for a longer video) before you try to load any video onto your iMac.

To prevent iMovie from treating an entire video as a single clip (which may be too lengthy to view and edit easily), you can tell iMovie to automatically store the video as separate clips — a different clip for each time there's a break in the video, such as whenever you stop and then restart the video camcorder. To make iMovie automatically break a large video into smaller clips, follow these steps:

1. **Choose Edit⇨Preferences.**

   The Preferences dialog box appears.

2. **Click the Import tab.**

   The Import options appear, as shown in Figure 6-2.

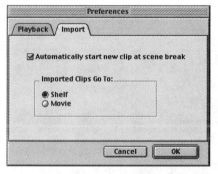

Figure 6-2:
You can customize the way iMovie stores a video.

3. **Click the Automatically Start New Clip at Scene Break check box. (Or clear the check box if you do not want iMovie to break up your video into separate clips at scene breaks.)**

4. **Click the Shelf or Movie radio button.**

   Generally you store clips on the Shelf, so you can edit and view them before moving them to the Movie Track.

5. **Click OK.**

To import a video from a digital camcorder to your iMac, follow these steps:

1. **Connect the proper cable from your iMac's FireWire port to your digital camcorder.**

The FireWire port appears on the side of the iMac. If you aren't sure where the FireWire port is, look at your iMac manual.

2. Start iMovie.

A Camera Connected message, as shown in Figure 6-3, appears to let you know that your iMac has successfully connected to your digital cam-corder. (If you do not see a Camera Connected message, check to make sure the cable is connected properly.)

3. Press the Play button on your digital video camcorder.

Your video appears in the iMovie screen.

4. Click the Import button (or press the spacebar) to start saving your video to your hard drive.

5. Click the Import button (or press the spacebar) again to stop saving your video to your hard drive.

The iMovie program saves your chosen portion of the video as a clip, displayed on the right side of the screen.

Figure 6-3:
iMovie lets you know right away if you have successfully connected your camcorder to your iMac.

Play Movie Full Screen

Edit Mode

Camera Mode

Importing a still image

Besides importing video, iMovie can also import digital camera or Web cam still images that have been stored on your hard drive as JPG, BMP, GIF, or PSD (Adobe Photoshop) files. To import a still image to iMovie, follow these steps:

1. **Choose File⇨Import File.**

   The Import File dialog box appears.

2. **Select the still image file you want to import and click Import. (You may have to dig through different folders to find the file you want.)**

   Your chosen still image appears as a clip in the iMovie program.

Editing a Clip

After you import a video into iMovie, you may want to divide it into smaller clips so each clip represents a different scene. For example, one clip could show your family at the swimming pool, a second clip could show your grandmother serving dinner, and a third clip could show your dog chewing on the steak bone from your dinner.

The two most common ways to edit a clip are cropping and splitting. *Cropping* is just a fancy word for trimming a clip, such as chopping off the first twenty seconds of a clip. *Splitting* is simply dividing one clip into two or more separate clips, so you can edit each clip individually.

Cropping a clip

Cropping a clip is "trimming" the excess scenes so that the video flows smoothly. To remove excess video footage from a clip, follow these steps:

1. **Select the clip that you want to edit.**

2. **Click directly underneath the Scrubber bar.**

   Beginning and ending crop markers appear, as shown in Figure 6-4.

3. **Drag the beginning crop marker to the left until it's at the position in your clip where you want your clip to start.**

4. **Drag the ending crop marker to the right until it's at the position where you want your clip to end.**

   For more accuracy in placing your beginning and ending crop markers, press the left or right arrow keys to move the crop markers.

5. **Choose Edit⇨Crop.**

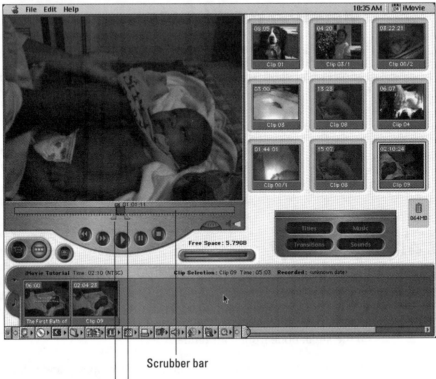

Figure 6-4:
Use the
crop
markers
to trim
the length
of a clip.

Scrubber bar

Ending crop marker

Beginning crop marker

Splitting a clip

If a clip is too long, you may want to split it into two separate clips so you can edit each clip separately. To split a clip, follow these steps:

1. **Select the clip that you want to split.**

2. **Drag the Playhead on the Scrubber bar to the location where you want to split the clip (such as in the middle).**

3. **Choose Edit➪Split Clip at Playhead.**

   iMovie displays both clips in separate parts of the Shelf with default names such as Clip02 and Clip03.

Adding Special Effects to a Clip

After you trim your clips, you can add transitions, background music, or narration to each clip.

Adding a title

A title is text that appears anywhere in your clip, but usually at the beginning or end. Titles can display the topic, such as "My Summer Vacation with Uncle Larry," or any other relevant information, such as the date the video was shot. Titles enable you to enhance a clip by adding explanatory text to the footage.

To add a title to a clip, follow these steps:

1. **Click the Titles button.**

   A preview window, title options, and text boxes for typing your title appear, as shown in Figure 6-5.

2. **Click the type of title option you want, such as Bounce In To Center or Flying Words.**

   Depending on the title option you choose, your title may appear as individual words that fly on to the screen (the Flying Words option) or that scroll to the center of the screen and bounce slightly until they settle in place (the Bounce In To Center option).

   Each time you click a different title option, such as Typewriter, iMovie shows you a preview of your title.

3. **Click in the text boxes and type the title that you want to display.**

4. **Click the Font list box and choose the font you want for your title.**

5. **(Optional) Click the Over Black check box if you want your title to appear over a black background. (If the Over Black check box is empty, your title appears directly over your initial video clip images.)**

6. **Click the Color button and choose a color for your title text.**

7. **Click the up, down, left, or right arrows to define the direction in which your title appears on your chosen clip.**

   If you click the right arrow, then your title scrolls from the left edge of the video and disappears from the right edge. Similarly if you click the down arrow, your title appears from the top of the video and scrolls down until it disappears at the bottom.

Preview window

Title options

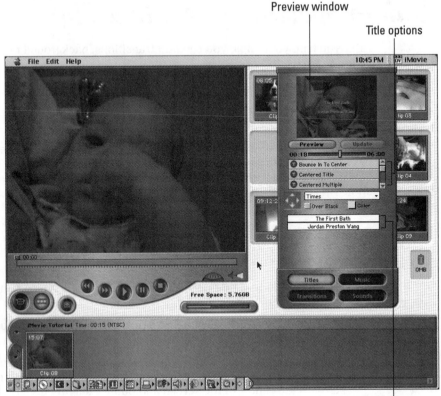

Text boxes

Figure 6-5:
Adding a
title spices
up your
video.

8. **Click the Preview button to see a preview of your clip.**

    iMovie shows you how your title appears. If you're happy with the way
    your title looks, continue to Step 9. Otherwise, go back and either start
    with a brand new title or edit your current one.

9. **Click and drag your chosen title style (such as Flying Words), to move
   the title to the Movie Track where you want the title to appear.**

    iMovie displays your title, complete with text and any visual effects
    you've chosen, on the Movie Track.

10. **Click the Titles button again to hide the different title options available.**

Adding a transition

A transition makes your clip dissolve or fade away, which creates some neat
special effects if done right or an annoying video if done wrong.

To add a transition to a clip, follow these steps:

1. **Click the Transitions button.**

   A list of transitions options appears, as shown in Figure 6-6.

2. **Select the transition option you want, such as Push Right or Cross Dissolve.**

   Each time you select a different transition option, such as Overlap, iMovie shows you a preview of your transition.

3. **Drag the slider bar to the right or left.**

   The farther left you drag the slider bar, the sooner the transition appears. The farther right you drag the slider bar, the later the transition appears.

4. **Click the Preview button to see how your transition looks.**

5. **Click and drag your chosen transition style (such as Overlap) to move the transition to where you want it to appear between the two clips on the Movie Track.**

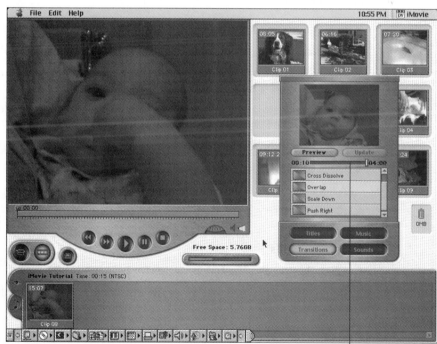

Figure 6-6: Transitions give your clip a Hollywood-style appearance.

Slider bar

6. **Click the Transitions button again to hide the transition options.**

   You can only place a transition between two clips. You cannot put a transition at the beginning or end of your video.

Adding background music

To make your video even more interesting and original, you can also add music from an audio CD or an AIFF audio file (discussed in the "Using music from an AIFF audio file" section later in this chapter) to play in the background. Music can set a mood for your video, so you can emphasize or make fun of any people or objects in your video.

Usually, nobody objects if you send a copy of a popular song as part of your video for your grandmother. However, if you plan to create videos for business, avoid using any copyrighted music.

Using music from a CD

To add music to video, follow these steps:

1. **Select the clip to which you want to add background music.**

   You can select a clip on either the Shelf or the Movie Track.

2. **Drag the Playhead to the position where you want the music to start playing in your clip.**

   For example, if you want the music to start playing in the middle of your clip, drag the Playhead to the middle.

3. **Insert an audio CD into your iMac.**

4. **Click the Music button.**

   A list of different tracks appears, as shown in Figure 6-7.

5. **Select the audio track that you want to use.**

   Your iMac starts playing your chosen audio track, so you can hear the way it sounds.

6. **Click the Record Music button to start recording.**

   iMovie displays a soundtrack at the bottom of the screen to show you how much of the audio file you have saved.

7. **Click the Stop button to stop recording.**

8. **Click the Music button to hide the music options from view.**

   iMovie displays your audio file on the Soundtrack at the bottom of the screen.

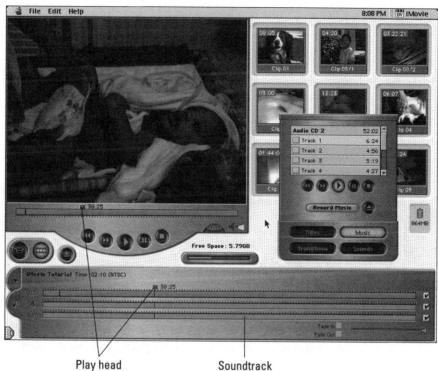

Figure 6-7:
Background
music
enhances
the mood of
your video.

Play head   Soundtrack

Using music from an AIFF audio file

Instead of using music from a CD, you can also use music (or any audio file) stored in an AIFF (Audio Interchange File Format) file, which is a special digital audio file format. You can find AIFF audio files on the Internet by visiting your favorite search engine (such as Yahoo!) and searching for "AIFF." Many Web sites offer samples of songs or sound effects stored in AIFF format.

To use an AIFF audio file, follow these steps:

1. **Select the clip you want to add the AIFF audio file to.**

   You can select a clip on the Shelf or on the Movie Track.

2. **Drag the Playhead to the position where you want the music to start playing in your clip.**

   For example, if you want to have music start playing at the beginning of your clip, drag the Playhead to the beginning.

3. **Choose File⇨Import File.**

   The Import File dialog box appears.

4. **Click the Show drop-down list box and choose AIFF Audio file.**

5. **Select the AIFF audio file you want and click Import.**

   You may have to dig through folders to find the file you want. iMovie displays your audio file on the Soundtrack at the bottom of the screen.

Adding sounds

Rather than adding music, you can add just a sound to your video, such as a dog barking, an alarm clock ringing, or your own voice narrating a portion of your video. A sound can emphasize certain points of your video, such as an alarm clock at the end to let viewers know the video's over.

You can also add multiple sounds to a clip.

Using a sound clip

iMovie comes with several prerecorded sound clips that you can use. To add a sound to a clip, follow these steps:

1. **Select the clip to which you want to add sound.**

   You can Select a clip stored on the Shelf or on the Movie Track.

2. **Click the Sounds button.**

   A list of sound options appears, as shown in Figure 6-8.

3. **Select a sound such as Dog Bark or People Laugh.**

   iMovie plays your chosen sound effect.

4. **After you find a sound you want to use, drag that sound to the Soundtrack.**

   iMovie displays your sound as a tiny box on the Soundtrack.

5. **Click the Sounds button to hide the sound options from view.**

Recording a sound clip

If you don't like any of the built-in sound clips that come with iMovie, you can record your own sounds. To record a sound, follow these steps:

1. **Select the clip to which you want to add a recorded sound.**

   You can select either a clip on the Shelf or on the Movie Track.

2. **Click the Sounds button.**

   A list of sound options appears (refer to Figure 6-8).

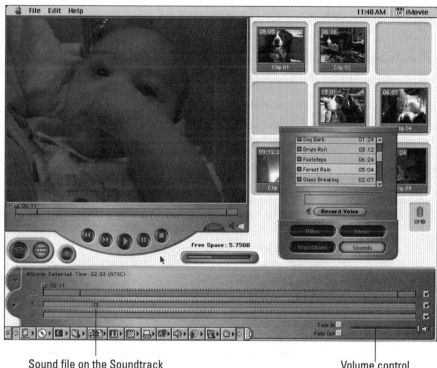

Figure 6-8:
Sound
effects
make your
video more
interesting.

Sound file on the Soundtrack   Volume control

3. **Click the Record Voice button and make a noise into your microphone.**

4. **Click the Stop button to stop recording.**

The next time you play your video, your recorded sound plays.

Editing a soundtrack

After you record or store sound or music for a clip, you may want to edit your soundtrack to move sounds to a different location, adjust the volume, or delete them completely.

Arranging sounds on the soundtrack

To arrange sounds on the soundtrack, follow these steps:

1. **Select the sound that you want to move on the soundtrack.**

2. **Hold down the mouse button and drag the sound to its new location.**

   As you drag the mouse, iMovie shows you the location where the sound will start playing.

3. **Release the mouse button.**

Adjusting the volume

Sometimes, any sounds you add to your clip may seem too loud or too soft. To adjust the volume of a sound, just follow these steps:

1. **Select the sound you want to adjust.**

2. **Drag the Volume Control slider to the left (softer) or right (louder).**

3. **(Optional) Click the Fade In check box if you want your sound to appear softly at first and then get louder.**

4. **(Optional) Click the Fade Out check box if you want your sound to gradually get softer as it ends.**

   The next time you play your video, your selected sound (in Step 1) plays at the adjusted volume you chose in Steps 2 through 4.

Deleting a sound

To delete a sound from your soundtrack, just follow these steps:

1. **Select the sound you want to delete.**

2. **Choose Edit⇨Clear.**

If you erase a sound by mistake, right away choose Edit⇨Undo to undo your deletion.

Arranging a Video

After you edit your various clips by adding sounds, transitions, or titles to them, you need to arrange them on the Movie Track, to tell iMovie the order in which you want your clips to play.

Arranging clips on the Movie Track

The Movie Track establishes the order in which your clips play. To put a clip on the Movie Track, follow these steps:

1. **Select the clip, stored on the Shelf, that you want to add to the Movie Track.**

2. **Hold down the mouse button and drag to the Movie Track.**

3. **Release the mouse button.**

   Your selected clip appears on the Movie Track.

After you have several clips on the Movie Track, you can rearrange them to change the order in which they play. To rearrange clips on the Movie Track, follow these steps:

1. **Select the clip that you want to move on the Movie Track.**

2. **Hold down the mouse button and drag the clip to a new location before or after another clip.**

3. **Release the mouse button.**

   Your clip appears in its new position on the Movie Track.

Deleting a clip

You can delete a clip by following these steps:

1. **Select the clip that you want to delete.**

2. **Choose Edit⇨Clear.**

   iMovie cheerfully deletes your chosen clip.

Rather than deleting a clip, you may want to drag the clip back to the Shelf, in case you decide to use it later.

Saving a Video

After you finish editing your video, you can save it back on tape or as a QuickTime file. Because QuickTime is a cross-platform file format, you can share your QuickTime videos with anyone who can play QuickTime files (whether Macintosh or Windows users). To download the Free QuickTime player, visit Apple Computers at www.apple.com.

Depending on what you plan to do with your video, you may want iMovie to save your QuickTime file in a compressed format. That way, you can e-mail your videos to friends and family members.

Before saving your file, you want to preview it, so you know exactly what your video looks like before you distribute it to others. Select the clip that you want to preview and press the spacebar.

Saving to tape

Saving to tape lets you keep a record of your video in your cassette library. To save your video to tape, follow these steps:

1. **Connect your video camcorder, with a blank tape installed, to your iMac.**

2. **Choose File⇨Export Movie.**

   The Export Movie dialog box appears, as shown in Figure 6-9.

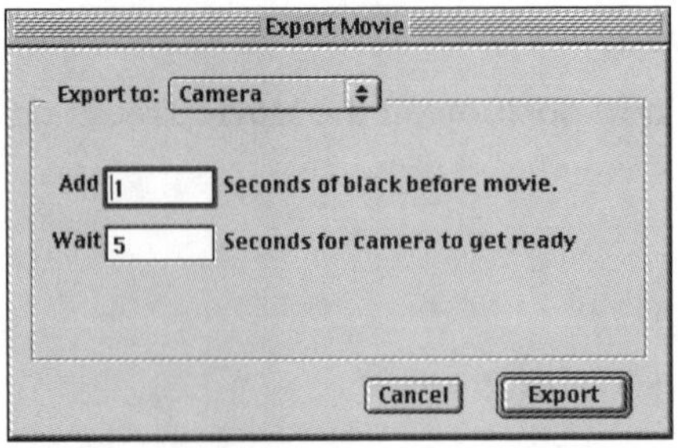

Figure 6-9:
You can
save your
edited video
back to
tape.

> Export Movie
>
> Export to: Camera
>
> Add 1 Seconds of black before movie.
> Wait 5 Seconds for camera to get ready
>
> Cancel   Export

3. **Click the Export To list box and choose Camera.**

4. **Click in the Add box and type a number to define how many seconds of black you want to appear at the start of your movie.**

5. **Click in the Wait box and type the number of seconds for your camera to get ready to record video from your iMac.**

6. **Start recording from your video camcorder.**

   Depending on your particular camcorder, this step may be as simple as pressing the Record button.

7. **Click Export.**

Generally, recording your edited video on the same tape where you recorded your original video is not a good idea. By saving your edited video on a separate cassette, you avoid possibly erasing your original video.

Saving to a QuickTime file

If you want to send your video file as e-mail or store your file on a CD, you may prefer to export your movie as a QuickTime file, because QuickTime videos can be viewed on a variety of computers including Macintosh and Windows-based computers. To export your movie as a QuickTime file, follow these steps:

1. **Choose File⇨Export Movie.**

   The Export Movie dialog box appears (refer to Figure 6-9).

2. **Click in the Export To list box and choose QuickTime.**

   The Export Movie dialog box displays a Formats list box, as shown in Figure 6-10.

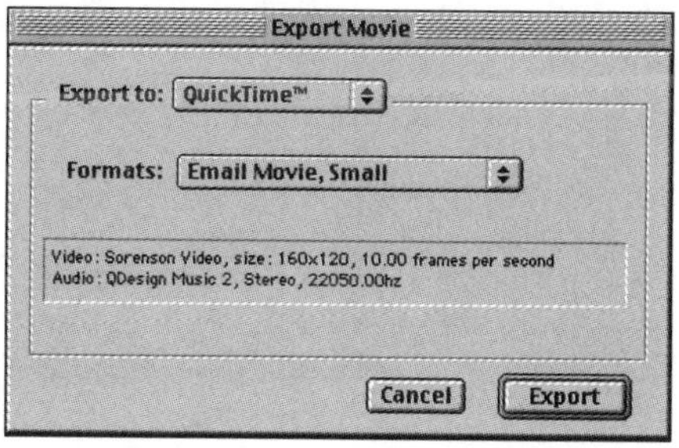

Figure 6-10:
Choosing a
format to
keep the file
size small
causes a
decrease in
video
quality.
Choosing a
format to
keep the
video quality
high causes
an increase
in file size.

Export Movie

Export to: QuickTime™

Formats: Email Movie, Small

Video: Sorenson Video, size: 160x120, 10.00 frames per second
Audio: QDesign Music 2, Stereo, 22050.00hz

Cancel   Export

3. **Click the Formats list box and choose a format, such as Email Movie, Small or CD-ROM Movie, Large.**

   The Email Movie, Small option creates the smallest file size so you can quickly transfer your video by e-mail. The CD-ROM Movie, Large option creates the largest file size but offers higher visual quality in return. The other options, Web Movie and CD-ROM Movie, Medium, provide a compromise between file size and video quality.

4. **Click Export.**

   The Export QuickTime Movie dialog box appears.

5. **Type a name for your QuickTime file and click Save. (You may want to choose a folder to store your file in as well.)**

   iMovie creates a QuickTime file that you can distribute to others.

If you like what you see in iMovie but find its features too restricting and limiting, consider buying a full-blown professional video editing package such as Adobe Premiere (www.adobe.com) or Final Cut (www.apple.com). Both programs cost several hundred dollars, but provide enough power to practice Hollywood-style video editing on your home computer. Unlike iMovie, professional video editing programs allow you to edit multiple video projects at once, save your video in a wider variety of file formats, and design your own custom special effects.

Chapter 7

Using Windows Movie Maker

In This Chapter

▶ Getting a video into Windows Movie Maker

▶ Arranging your video

▶ Viewing your video

▶ Saving your video as a file

A fter Apple introduced the iMac, which had digital video editing capabilities, Microsoft decided to add a digital video editing program with its operating system, too. So the latest version of Windows, dubbed Windows Me (short for the Millennium Edition), includes a program called Windows Movie Maker. In this chapter, you find out how to use the new Windows Movie Maker program for editing videos. Like Apple's iMovie program, Windows Movie Maker is designed to make video editing simple and painless. Just load a video onto your computer and Windows Movie Maker can help you add titles, insert transitions between scenes, and include background music or voice-over narration. Combined with your Web cam, Windows Movie Maker gives you the power to make your own movies that you can save on disk or e-mail to others.

Keep in mind that offering Windows Movie Maker for free with Windows Millennium Edition is Microsoft's subtle way of convincing everyone to upgrade from Windows 95/98. If you don't want to upgrade to Windows Me but still want a free digital video editing program, you can buy a Sony (www.sony.com) computer, which comes with Sony's own video editing program called MovieShaker. If you prefer to buy a video-editing program, look at VideoStudio (www.ulead.com) or iFilmEdit (www.cinax.com).

Putting a Video into Windows Movie Maker

To edit a video, you first have to save a video and store it on your computer using one of the following methods:

✔ Capture the video directly from your Web cam (the easy method).

✔ Import an existing video file or multiple still images. The existing video file can be one that you downloaded from the Internet or captured using a video camcorder and then transferred to your computer.

You can use any combination of the above methods, such as capturing a video from your Web cam and adding still images or existing video files.

Capturing a video or still image from your Web cam

Because you probably already have a Web cam (which is why you're reading this book), you can capture a video or still image directly from within Windows Movie Maker.

The biggest advantage of using your Web cam to capture a video is that Web cams are cheap and easy to use. The main disadvantage is that the video quality from a Web cam is grainy, fuzzy, and generally less than perfect. If you just want to have fun, use your Web cam. If you absolutely need studio-quality video images, you probably should use a video camcorder.

To capture a video from your Web cam, follow these steps:

1. **Start Windows Movie Maker by clicking the Start button and choosing Programs⇨Accessories⇨Windows Movie Maker.**

2. **Choose File⇨Record (or press Ctrl+R).**

   The Record dialog box appears, as shown in Figure 7-1.

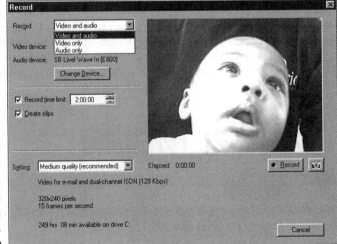

Figure 7-1: You can record a video from your Web cam and store it in Windows Movie Maker.

To reduce the size of your video file, click the Record list box and choose Video Only; then click the Setting list box and choose Low (creates small file sizes) or Medium (creates larger file sizes but with higher video quality) quality.

3. **Click the Record button.**

   Windows Movie Maker starts recording your video.

4. **Click Stop after you finish recording your video.**

   A Save Windows Media File dialog box appears.

5. **Type a name for your file in the File Name box and click Save.**

   Windows Movie Maker displays your captured video on the screen with a name such as Clip 1.

To capture a still image from your Web cam, follow these steps:

1. **Start Windows Movie Maker by clicking the Start button and choosing Programs⇨Accessories⇨Windows Movie Maker.**

2. **Choose File⇨Record (or press Ctrl+R).**

   The Record dialog box appears (refer to Figure 7-1).

3. **Click the Take Photo button that looks like a camera and appears to the right of the Record button.**

   A Save Photo dialog box appears.

4. **Type a name for your file in the File Name box and click Save.**

   You may want to choose a different folder to save your image. Windows Movie Maker stores all still images as JPEG files with the jpg file extension.

5. **Click Cancel to make the Record dialog box disappear.**

   Windows Movie Maker displays your captured still image on the screen with the name you chose in Step 4.

Importing an existing video or still image file

Instead of capturing videos from your Web cam, you can also add video files to Windows Movie Maker by using video created by other people. For example, your friend might have created a video by using her Web cam and e-mailed that video file for you to look at.

To import a video or still image file, follow these steps:

1. **Choose File⇨Import, or press Ctrl+I.**

   The Select the File to Import dialog box appears.

2. **Select the file you want to load into Windows Movie Maker and click Open.**

   Windows Movie Maker displays your chosen imported file on the screen.

   To choose more than one file, hold down the Ctrl key and select each file you want to import.

   Windows Movie Maker can import video files with the following extensions: asf, avi, wmv, and mpeg. Movie Maker can also import still image files with the following extensions: bmp, jpg, gif, and dib. If you don't have a video or still image file in any of these formats, you have to convert the file(s) you want to use to one of the acceptable file formats.

   To help you distinguish between video and still image files, Windows Movie Maker displays film sprocket holes on the top and bottom of video files, as shown in Figure 7-2.

Video file

Still image files

Figure 7-2: Windows Movie Maker imports video and still images that you can combine.

Editing a Video

After you have one or more files (video or still images) loaded into Windows Movie Maker, you can exercise your creativity by arranging and cutting video files and adding titles or background music or narration.

Arranging a video

Windows Movie Maker displays empty film frames (called the *Storyboard*) near the bottom of the window. Each frame, whether it contains a still image or a video file, is referred to as a clip. To create a video, you simply rearrange the positions of different clips (video or still images).

If you don't see empty frames at the bottom of your screen in the area that resembles a film strip, choose View⇨Storyboard. This makes the Storyboard visible at the bottom of the screen.

To arrange the clips that make up your video, follow these steps:

1. **Click the video or still image that you want to use.**

   Windows Movie Maker highlights your chosen video or still image and displays it in the larger Preview window to the right of the screen.

2. **Drag your chosen image (move the mouse) into any empty frame at the bottom of the screen.**

   The mouse pointer turns into a circle with a diagonal slash through it until you move the mouse pointer over a frame. Then the mouse pointer turns into an arrow.

3. **Release the left mouse button.**

   Windows Movie Maker displays your chosen video or still image as a frame in the Storyboard.

4. **Repeat Steps 1 through 3 for each video or still image that you want to add to your video.**

   The Storyboard displays your video and still images in the order that you want them to appear.

You can drag a video or still image to a new location on the Storyboard at a later time.

Splitting and combining clips

If you record a short video with your Web cam, Windows Movie Maker treats the whole video as a single clip. This situation may be inconvenient because it prevents you from rearranging parts of your video.

To solve this problem you can split (or combine) video clips. Splitting a clip gives you the chance to divide a normally long clip so you can rearrange the separate parts. Combining two clips makes it convenient for rearranging multiple clips as a unit, rather than rearranging them as separate clips.

You can't split or combine still images.

To split a video clip, follow these steps:

1. **Select the clip that you want to split.**

   Your clip appears in the Preview window shown in Figure 7-3.

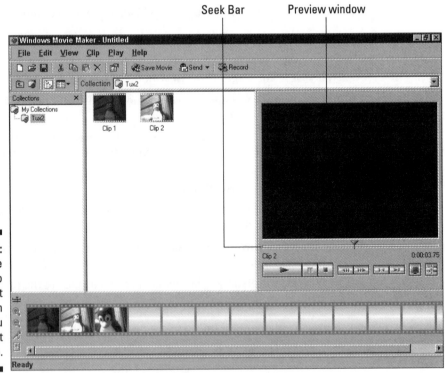

Figure 7-3:
Move the Seek Bar to the exact location where you want to split your clip.

2. **Click the Seek Bar pointer (it looks like an upside-down arrow) and drag it to the place where you want to split your clip, such as in the middle or a third of the way into your clip.**

   Your clip in the Preview window shows you the part of the clip where Windows Movie Maker will split the clip.

3. **Release the left mouse button.**

4. **Choose Clip⇨Split, or press Ctrl+Shift+S.**

   Windows Movie Maker displays your newly split clips on the Storyboard.

To combine two or more clips, follow these steps:

1. **Hold down the Ctrl key and click all the clips that you want to combine.**

   You can select more than two clips if you want.

2. **Choose Clip⇨Combine, or press Ctrl+Shift+C.**

   Windows Movie Maker combines your selected clips into a single clip.

Trimming a clip

Chances are good that sometimes your clips are too long. For example, if you have a clip of your dog walking into a room and then tripping on the carpet, you may want to cut out the early portion of the clip and just show the part where your dog trips.

Hollywood studios typically capture eight hours of film just to get three to five minutes of actual scenes that they can use in a movie. This information indicates just how much editing professionals go through to cut out extraneous scenes and irrelevant details.

You can only trim a clip that has already been placed on the Storyboard at the bottom of the screen.

To trim a clip, follow these steps:

1. **Select the clip that you want to edit.**

   Your selected clip appears in the Preview window.

2. **Drag the Seek Bar pointer to the place where you want to start your clip, such as a third of the way into the clip.**

3. **Choose Clip⇨Set Start Trim Point, or press Ctrl+Shift+Left arrow.**

   The Seek Bar pointer moves all the way to the left.

4. **Drag the Seek Bar pointer to the place where you want to end your clip.**

5. **Choose Clip⇨Set End Trim Point, or press Ctrl+Shift+Right arrow.**

   Windows Movie Maker deletes all the video footage that does not fall in between the Start Trim Point (chosen in Step 3) and the End Trim Point (chosen in Step 5). If you choose Play⇨Play/Pause (or press the spacebar), you can see how Windows Movie Maker has trimmed your clip.

To clear the trim points of a previously trimmed clip, follow these steps:

1. **Select the clip that contains the trim points you want to clear.**

   For this example, you can use the clip you trimmed in the previous set of steps.

2. **Choose Clip⇨Clear Trim Points, or press Ctrl+Shift+Del.**

   The trim points disappear, and your clip returns to its original length. If you choose Play⇨Play/Pause (or press the spacebar), you can verify that Windows Movie Maker has removed all trim points from your chosen clip.

Adding Sound to Your Video

To spice up your video, you can add narration or background music or some other sound.

Whenever you add background music, be careful about copyrights. For personal use, nobody really cares; but if you're developing a corporate presentation that you intend to broadcast to others, get permission first or just use a song in the public domain.

Windows Movie Maker can import sound files saved in the following formats: wav, snd, au, aif, aifc, aiff, and wma. If you want to import a sound file stored in another format, you have to convert the sound file to one of the formats that Windows Movie Maker can use.

Adding an existing sound file

To add an existing sound file (music, narration, or some other sound) to your video, follow these steps:

1. **Choose View⇨Timeline.**

   Windows Movie Maker displays your video clips with time markings, so you can see the approximate length of each clip.

To see time markings for shorter (or longer) durations, choose View⇨ Zoom In or Zoom Out. The Zoom In command shows your video timeline in greater detail, and the Zoom Out command shows your video timeline in less detail.

2. **Choose File⇨Import, or press Ctrl+I.**

   The Select the File to Import dialog box appears.

3. **Select the audio file you want to use and click Open. (You may have to dig through different folders to find the file you want.)**

   Windows Movie Maker displays your selected audio file as an icon on the screen.

4. **Click and drag the audio file you want to add to your video to a spot under a clip where you want the audio file to play.**

   After you release the mouse button, Windows Movie Maker displays a vertical line at the spot where you want the audio file to play, as shown in Figure 7-4. The next time you choose Play⇨Play/Pause (or press the spacebar), your chosen audio file plays at the time you specified.

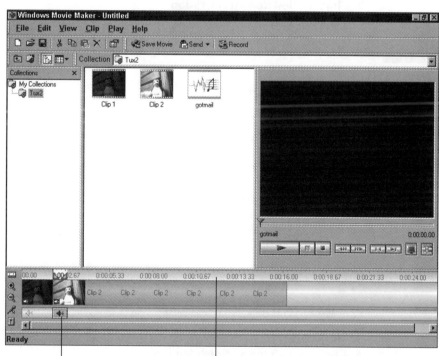

Figure 7-4:
You can add an audio file to any spot in your video.

Audio file marker   Timeline

Recording your own sound

Rather than use an existing audio file, you can record sound (such as spoken words) directly into Windows Movie Maker.

You need a microphone and a sound card to record sound. Without either of these items, you can yell and scream all you want, but Windows Movie Maker can't save any noise you make into the computer.

To record sound, just follow these steps:

1. **Choose View⇨Timeline.**

   Windows Movie Maker displays your video clips with time markings, so you can see the approximate length of each clip.

   To see time markings for shorter (or longer) durations, choose View⇨Zoom In or Zoom Out. The Zoom In command shows your video timeline in greater detail, and the Zoom Out command shows your video timeline in less detail.

2. **Choose File⇨Record Narration.**

   A Record Narration Track dialog box appears, as shown in Figure 7-5.

Figure 7-5:
The Record
Narration
Track
dialog box
indicates
the sound
level and
how much
sound you
can store
on your
hard drive.

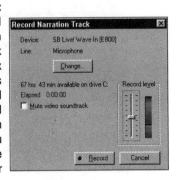

3. **Click Record and start speaking.**

   The Record button changes into a Stop button.

4. **Click Stop after you finish talking.**

   The Save Narration Track Sound File dialog box appears.

5. **Type a name for your narration in the File Name box and click Save.**

   Windows Movie Maker displays your audio file as an icon on the screen and automatically places your narration audio in the video timeline. When you choose Play⇨Play/Pause (or press the spacebar), Windows Movie Maker plays your recorded narration.

Editing your soundtrack

After you place your sound files on your video timeline, you may need to move or delete them.

To move a sound file, follow these steps:

1. **Click and drag the sound file that you want to move to a new position on the Timeline.**

2. **Release the left mouse button when you're happy with the new position of the sound file.**

To delete a sound file, follow these steps:

1. **Select the sound file that you want to delete on your video timeline.**

2. **Choose Edit⇨Delete, or press Del.**

Playing a Video

After you edit your video, take some time to view the whole thing to make sure the length is right, the transitions don't look too clunky, and any sound you recorded plays at the proper time.

Playing the entire video

To test your video, play the whole thing by following these steps:

1. **Choose Play⇨Full Screen, or press Alt+Enter.**

   Windows Movie Maker displays your video to fill up the entire screen. (You can skip this step if you don't want to see the entire video appear on your screen.)

2. **Choose Play⇨Play Entire Storyboard/Timeline.**

   Windows Movie Maker plays your video. (If you chose to display your video on the full screen in Step 1, you need to press the spacebar each time Windows Movie Maker finishes playing a single clip of your video.)

You can stop your video at any time by pressing Esc.

Playing a single clip

Instead of playing your entire video, you may want to view just a single clip. To play a clip, follow these steps:

1. **Select the clip that you want to view.**

   Windows Movie Maker highlights your selected clip.

2. **Choose Play⇨Play/Pause, or press the spacebar.**

   Windows Movie Maker starts playing your selected clip from start to finish.

If you want to jump from one clip to another, choose one of the following commands:

✔ Play⇨Back, or press Ctrl+Left arrow to view the previous clip in your video

✔ Play⇨Forward, or press Ctrl+Right arrow to view the next clip in your video

If you really want to get detail oriented, you can view the individual frames that make up a video clip by choosing one of the following commands:

✔ Play⇨Previous Frame, or press Alt+Left arrow to view the previous frame

✔ Play⇨Next Frame, or press Alt+Right arrow to view the next frame

Saving and Sending Your Video

After you arrange your clips the way you want them and add any accompanying sound files, save your video so others can watch it, too.

Saving your video as a file

To save a video, follow these steps:

1. **Choose File⇨Save Movie, or press Ctrl+M.**

   The Save Movie dialog box appears, as shown in Figure 7-6.

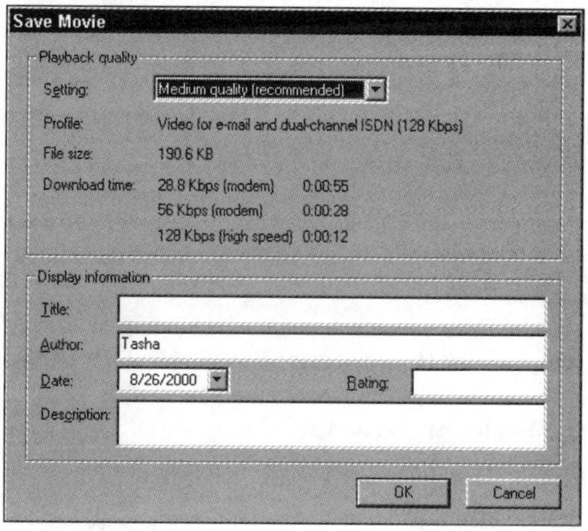

Figure 7-6:
The Save
Movie
dialog box
indicates
how big
your video
file is and
approxi-
mately how
much time
someone
will require
to download
the file
using
modems of
different
speeds.

Save Movie

Playback quality

Setting: Medium quality (recommended)

Profile: Video for e-mail and dual-channel ISDN (128 Kbps)

File size: 190.6 KB

Download time: 28.8 Kbps (modem)   0:00:55
56 Kbps (modem)   0:00:29
128 Kbps (high speed)   0:00:12

Display information

Title:

Author: Tasha

Date: 8/26/2000   Rating:

Description:

OK   Cancel

2. **(Optional) Click the Setting list box and select a different playback quality.**

   The Low quality option creates the smallest file at the sacrifice of video quality. The Medium quality option balances video quality with file size. The High quality option creates large files with the best quality. If you want to define your own options, you can choose the Other option and then click the Profile list box to select the file size optimized for particular connection speeds such as 28.8 Kbps modems.

3. **Type any information you want to store with your video, such as your name, a title, or a short description.**

4. **Click OK.**

   The Save As dialog box appears.

5. **Type a name for your video and click Save. (You may want to switch to a different folder and save your video in that folder.)**

   After Windows Movie Maker saves your file, a dialog box pops up, asking if you want to view your video right away.

6. **Click Yes or No.**

   If you click Yes, the Windows Media Player loads and plays your video. If you click No, you don't see your video play.

Windows Movie Maker saves videos in the Windows Media Video file format (*.wmv). If you want to distribute these videos to people who don't use Windows, you may need to convert the video to a different file format, such as QuickTime.

Sending your video as e-mail

Although you can save your video and send it as an e-mail attachment, Windows Movie Maker also offers the capability to send the video file directly through your e-mail program.

To send a video as e-mail, follow these steps:

1. **Choose File⇨Save Movie, or press Ctrl+M.**

   The Save Movie dialog box appears (refer to Figure 7-6).

2. **(Optional) Click the Setting list box and choose a different playback quality.**

3. **Type any information you want to store with your video, such as your name, a title, or a short description.**

4. **Click OK.**

   The Save As dialog box appears.

5. **Type a name for your video and click Save. (You may want to switch to a different folder and save your video in that folder.)**

   The E-Mail Movies dialog box appears, as shown in Figure 7-7.

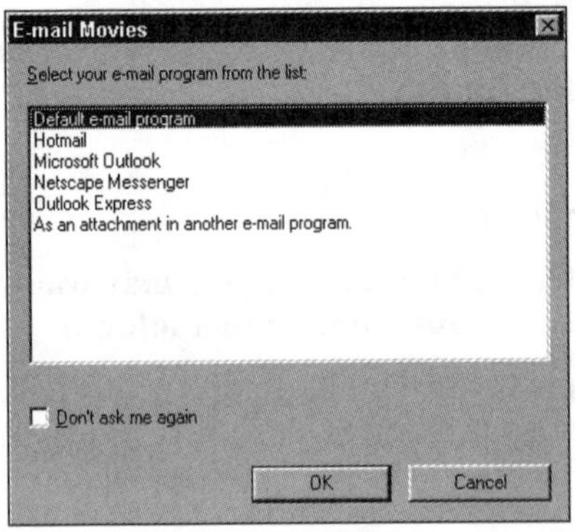

Figure 7-7:
The E-Mail Movies dialog box lets you pick which e-mail program you want to use to send out your video.

E-mail Movies

Select your e-mail program from the list:

Default e-mail program
Hotmail
Microsoft Outlook
Netscape Messenger
Outlook Express
As an attachment in another e-mail program.

☐ Don't ask me again

OK   Cancel

6. **Click the e-mail program you want to use (such as Microsoft Outlook) and click OK.**

   Your e-mail program loads with your video file already selected as a file attachment.

7. **Type an e-mail address, a subject, and any additional text you want to include with your e-mail, and then click Send.**

   Your e-mail program sends your video to your chosen e-mail destination.

By using your Web cam to send video e-mail to your friends and relatives, you can make everyone feel as if they're with you in person. If people have trouble viewing your video through e-mail, you can post your videos on your own Web site (see Chapter 5) and have your friends and relatives view your video images there instead.

Part III
Videoconferencing with Your Web Cam

The 5th Wave   By Rich Tennant

"You know, I'm pretty sure CU-SeeMe comes with an audio volume control."

In this part . . .

*V*ideoconferencing gives you a chance to see and talk to one or more people simultaneously, no matter where in the world you or the other people may be. Chat with your friends or relatives from anywhere in the world, or join a public conference to chat with and see other people.

This part of the book describes and explains how to use three of the more popular videoconferencing programs available today: CU-SeeMe (the pioneer videoconferencing program), Microsoft NetMeeting, and iVisit. With a copy of any of these programs, you're ready to jump on the Internet and start talking (and showing yourself to others with your Web cam) right away.

Chapter 8

Understanding Videoconferencing

. . . .

In This Chapter

▶ Using videoconferencing for different purposes

▶ Videoconferencing system requirements

▶ Understanding how videoconferencing works

. . . .

*I*n this chapter, I show you how to use your Web cam to communicate with others by videoconferencing. Videoconferencing enables people to hear and see each other through a communications medium, such as the telephone network. At the simplest level, videoconferencing enables two people to see and talk to each other as easily as using a telephone. On a more complicated level, videoconferencing enables groups of people to see and chat with each other from anywhere around the world.

In the past, only big corporations could afford the expensive cameras, television screens, microphones, speakers, and communications networks needed to set up a videoconference. But even with the best equipment, few companies used videoconferencing. Although videoconferencing can save money by eliminating the need to fly people to other parts of the world, most people still prefer face-to-face meetings rather than staring at someone's image on a flickering television screen. (Besides, half the fun of business trips is getting paid to sightsee in another part of the world. Videoconferencing essentially drains the pleasure out of business meetings, leaving only the drudgery and boredom.)

Today's inexpensive Web cams, however, have moved videoconferencing from corporate to individual use. Videoconferencing isn't just limited to work anymore; videoconferencing is open to people who want to use it for fun, which has the added benefit of encouraging people to experiment with videoconferencing in ways that can make it fun for use in business as well.

The next time you need to talk and see other people, but don't want to go through the hassle of making travel arrangements and accommodations, use your Web cam to conduct a videoconference so everyone can participate (just as long as they also have a Web cam).

The Picturephone: The first videoconferencing machine

Back in 1956, the engineers at Bell Systems created the first combination telephone/television set that enabled people to see the person they were calling. Eight years later, Bell Systems introduced the first experimental model, dubbed the Mod 1, at Disneyland and the New York World's Fair, so that people could talk to each other at both locations.

Unfortunately, nobody really liked the Mod 1. People complained that the Mod 1 was too bulky, the controls too hard to understand, and the picture too small to see. But Bell Systems still thought that people would like to see the person they were talking to, so they refined the system and introduced the machine as the Picturephone in 1970.

AT&T set up the first Picturephones in public buildings in New York, Washington, and Chicago, charging people $21 to make a three-minute Picturephone call. AT&T executives even predicted that by 1980, over a million Picturephones would be in use.

Not surprisingly, the Picturephone flopped because people still complained that it was too big, expensive, and uncomfortable to use. Now with inexpensive Web cams, personal computers, and Internet access, the dream of the original Picturephone has finally come true. (Now, however, people complain that *computers* are too big, expensive, and uncomfortable to use, so maybe technology hasn't made that much progress after all.)

Cool Uses for Videoconferencing

Videoconferencing originally began as a business tool for running meetings with people from around the world. But meetings aren't the most exciting part of anyone's life — has anyone on his or her deathbed ever regretted not attending enough meetings? Eventually, people soon found more interesting uses for videoconferencing that include saving lives, teaching, and even educating people about the traditions of ancient cultures.

Of course, these are just a few of the uses for videoconferencing. After you play around with your Web cam and your videoconferencing program, you may find a new use for videoconferencing that nobody else has thought about before.

Telemedicine

The right medical care can save a life. Unfortunately, too many people live far away from major hospitals and medical resources. Rather than force patients to travel long distances, the medical community has combined their equipment with videoconferencing to create a new field dubbed *telemedicine*.

Telemedicine enables doctors to examine a patient's x-rays, medical history, or the actual patient with the help of cameras, communications links, and computers. In remote places where medical treatment is either poor or nonexistent — such as Alaska, the northern region of Norway, Africa, and the isolated Pacific islands — telemedicine can provide basic health care information. Where medical treatment is adequate (major cities), telemedicine can provide specialists with the latest medical information from around the world to help local doctors diagnose and treat patients.

To find out more about what the government, military, and universities are doing with telemedicine, visit one of the following Web sites:

Alaska Telemedicine Project (www.telemedicine.alaska.edu)

American Telemedicine Association (www.atmeda.org)

Telemedicine and Advanced Technology Research Center (www.tatrc.org)

Telemedicine Information Exchange (http://tie.telemed.org)

Texas Tech University Center for Telemedicine (www.ttuhsc.edu/telemedicine)

University of California, Davis, Health System (http://telemedicine.ucdmc.ucdavis.edu)

University of Virginia Health System (www.telemed.virginia.edu)

UK National Database Telemedicine (www.dis.port.ac.uk/ndtm)

Distance learning

Going to school typically means traveling to a building and sitting in a classroom so that a teacher can give you information in the form of lectures, handouts, slides, or laboratory experiments. Unfortunately, not everyone can move near a particular school just to attend classes, so many schools use videoconferencing to offer *distance learning*.

Distance learning is any form of education where the instructor and students are physically located in separate places (as opposed to being mentally located in separate places). Correspondence courses offered the first form of distance learning by postal mail, but schools eventually provided recorded videos, live TV broadcasts, and videoconferencing to open new opportunities for students all over the world.

Distance learning enables students to attend classes from home or work, observe experiments that are conducted using specialized equipment, and learn from world-famous instructors who may be simultaneously teaching thousands of other distance-learning students.

Although people once thought that television would evolve into an educational medium, videoconferencing promises to offer true education over long distances. If the thought of sitting in a stuffy classroom located on a campus with limited parking doesn't appeal to you, then perhaps distance learning may be your best option for furthering your education.

To find out more about distance learning, visit one of the following Web sites (which in itself is a form of distance learning):

Carnegie Mellon (www.distance.cmu.edu)

Centro de Enseñanza a Distancia (www.ceac.com)

Distance Learning on the Net (www.hoyle.com/distance.htm)

Distance Learning Resource Network (www.dlrn.org)

Idaho State University (http://wapi.isu.edu)

Lacrosse University (www.lacrosseuniversity.com)

LaSalle University (www.distance.edu)

Penn State (www.outreach.psu.edu)

Rochester Institute of Technology (www.distancelearning.rit.edu)

Southern Christian University (www.southernchristian.edu)

University of Colorado (www.cuonline.edu)

University of Southern Queensland (www.usq.edu.au/dec)

U.S. Army War College (http://dde.carlisle.army.mil)

Utah Education Network (www.uen.org)

Videoconferencing Atlas (www.savie.com)

Virginia Tech Online (http://vto.vt.edu)

Washington State University (www.eus.wsu.edu/edp)

Linking remote cultures

The Cree Indians of Canada use videoconferencing to share stories and traditions of their culture with Australian aborigines. (In case you've never heard of the Cree Indians, they live in the remote reaches of northern Canada.)

Both cultures cherish their identity and use videoconferencing to spread their culture to other indigenous people around the world. Despite the odd contrast of combining ancient traditions with modern equipment, both groups say they believe tradition is enhanced by technology.

By using videoconferencing, the Cree Indians are passing on their knowledge to their children and anyone else no matter where they may be in the world. By studying other cultures through videoconferencing, you may find some new insight about life in the wisdom of the past.

To find out more about different indigenous people and their efforts to maintain their cultural identity, visit one of the following Web sites:

Center for World Indigenous Studies (www.cwis.org)

Fourth World Documentation Project (www.cwis.org/fwdp.html)

International Museum of Cultures (www.sil.org/imc)

NativeNet (http://niikaan.fdl.cc.mn.us/natnet)

NativeWeb (www.nativeWeb.org)

What You Need to Videoconference

Whether you plan to participate in telemedicine, distance learning, or cultural enrichment, or just want to goof around, you need the following equipment to run a videoconference:

- A computer (PC or Macintosh).
- A Web cam.
- An Internet connection that uses a 56K modem or better. (Higher speed connections, such as a DSL or cable modem, provide better quality video and sound, along with fewer chances of losing a connection.)
- A microphone and speakers. (Ideally, you want to use a headset to avoid feedback.)
- A sound card.
- A videoconferencing program, which sets up the video and audio connection between users.

Some important features to look for in different videoconferencing programs include

- **Text chat** — which enables users to type messages to one another.
- **Voice chat** — which enables users to speak to one another.
- **Video and audio transmission** — which enables users to see and hear one another.
- **Call screening** — which enables users to ignore certain people while accepting calls from others.

- ✓ **Whiteboard** — which provides a common screen where users can type, draw, or display text or objects on their own computer for everyone to see.

- ✓ **File sharing** — which enables users to open up a file that other users can view on their computer screens at the same time, such as a Word document or Excel spreadsheet.

- ✓ **File transferring** — which enables users to transfer documents, spreadsheets, databases, graphic images, or any other type of file to each other.

- ✓ **Remote desktop sharing** — which enables users to access another computer from a distant location.

- ✓ **Recording** — which enables users to capture an entire videoconference to a video file that they can view at a later time.

- ✓ **Cross-platform capabilities** — which enable users with different computers, such as Windows and Macintosh, to connect to each other in a conference.

- ✓ **Group conferencing** — which enables more than two users to connect with one another.

Not all videoconferencing programs work together. Some videoconferencing programs work only if everyone uses the exact same videoconferencing program. Check the specific requirements of a videoconferencing program before you purchase it.

Some videoconferencing programs, such as Microsoft NetMeeting and iVisit, are free.

Windows videoconferencing programs

Because more people use Windows than any other operating system, Windows offers a wider variety of videoconferencing programs:

ClearPhone Pro (www.clearphone.com)

CU-SeeMe (www.cuseeme.com)

ICUII (www.icuii.com)

iVisit (www.ivisit.com)

Microsoft NetMeeting (www.microsoft.com/windows/netmeeting)

Macintosh videoconferencing programs

If you're a Macintosh user, you can choose from a handful of videoconferencing programs listed below:

ClearPhone Pro (www.clearphone.com)

CU-SeeMe (www.cuseeme.com)

iVisit (www.ivisit.com)

How Videoconferencing Works

Although the exact details of videoconferencing depend on the specific videoconferencing program you use, the process of setting up a videoconference is roughly the same with all programs. For instructions on using CU-SeeMe, Microsoft NetMeeting, and iVisit, see Chapters 9, 10, and 11, respectively.

To start a videoconference with anyone, you need to know every participant's Internet Protocol (IP) address, which uniquely identifies each person (much like a telephone number). The two types of IP addresses are static and dynamic. A *static* IP address never changes. Cable modems and network connections usually have the same IP address for each computer. A *dynamic* IP address changes each time you connect to the Internet. Most dial-up accounts use dynamic IP addressing.

The reason most people get a different IP address every time they connect to the Internet is because there aren't enough IP addresses for everyone. With a limited number of IP addresses, most dial-up Internet connections assign users any available IP address the moment they connect. When they disconnect from the Internet, they no longer need an IP address, so that IP address can be assigned to someone else.

Finding your IP address

Because you need an IP address to connect to someone else to start a videoconference, everyone needs to know how to find his or her IP address. (If you're lucky enough to have a DSL or cable modem, you only need to look up your IP address once. If you have a dial-up Internet account, you have to follow the steps below to look up your IP address every time you connect to the Internet.)

To find your IP address on a Windows computer, follow these steps:

1. **Make sure that you're connected to the Internet.**

2. **Click the Start button in the Windows taskbar and choose Run.**

   A Run dialog box appears.

3. **Type** winipcfg **and click OK.**

   An IP Configuration dialog box appears, as shown in Figure 8-1.

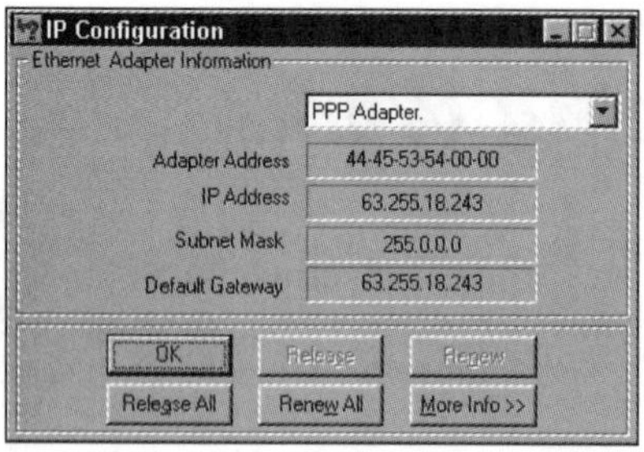

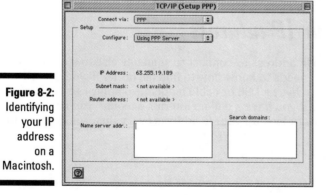

Figure 8-1:
Identifying
your IP
address in
Windows.

4. **Write down your IP address.**

5. **Click OK.**

To find your IP address on a Macintosh, follow these steps:

1. **Make sure that you're connected to the Internet.**

2. **Click the   menu in the corner of the menu bar.**

3. **Choose Control Panels⇨TCP/IP.**

   The TCP/IP dialog box appears, as shown in Figure 8-2.

Figure 8-2:
Identifying
your IP
address
on a
Macintosh.

4. Write down your IP address.

5. Click the close box in the upper-left corner of the TCP/IP dialog box.

Sharing IP addresses to start a videoconference

After everyone gets online and writes down his or her IP address, the next step is to exchange IP addresses with one another. You can share your IP address in three ways:

- ✔ Tell each other your IP address by calling on the telephone, shouting down the hall, sending an e-mail, and so forth.
- ✔ Use an instant messaging program.
- ✔ Use an Internet Locator Server (ILS).

Calling on the telephone or sending an e-mail to tell each other your IP address is an effective, but clumsy, way to coordinate a meeting. A better solution is to use an *instant messaging program,* such as ICQ, AIM, PowWow, or any of the other instant messaging programs available.

An instant messaging program notifies you the moment someone else connects to the Internet. At that time, you can swap IP addresses through the instant messaging program. After you have each other's IP address, you can connect your videoconferencing programs and start your videoconference.

Another way to get an IP address is to have each person store his (or her) name, e-mail address, and any other personal information on an *Internet Locator Service* (ILS), which is a separate computer that stores information in much the same way as a phone directory.

An ILS server can be either private or public. A private ILS server may belong to a corporation, for example, and is used solely by its employees. A public ILS server is designed for public use so people can find strangers to videoconference with at any time of the day.

If you don't know the exact IP address of someone, visit an ILS server and search for it using his or her e-mail address. If your friend is currently online, the ILS server can provide his or her current IP address. You just type that IP address into your videoconferencing program to connect with your friend and start your videoconference.

A public ILS server can also help you find total strangers to start a videoconference. Many people store their names and other information on a public ILS so that other people can randomly contact them and start a videoconference. By chatting with a total stranger, you can make a new friend (or an enemy if you're not careful).

Because most videoconferencing programs can't work with other types of videoconferencing programs, public ILS servers tend to cater to specific program users. For example, one public ILS server may list only Microsoft NetMeeting users, while another public ILS server may list only CU-SeeMe users. To find a public ILS server for your videoconference program, contact the publisher of your videoconferencing program.

Joining a group videoconference

One consideration when setting up your own videoconference is that everyone must know everyone else's IP address. For a small group of people, this can be a minor nuisance, but for a large group of people, sharing multiple IP addresses can be time consuming and overwhelming.

To solve this problem, you can join a group videoconference. Unlike a videoconference that you set up between you and a handful of your friends, a group videoconference takes place on a public conference server, which is a computer set aside specifically to coordinate communication between hundreds (or even thousands) of users simultaneously. Each person simply accesses this public conference server, and the server takes care of connecting each person to everyone else.

Whenever you attend a group videoconference, be polite and try to keep video and audio transmissions along with file transfers to a minimum. The more people who attend a public conference, the harder the public conference server computer has to work to transfer information correctly. Avoid sending large files to others or hogging precious computer resources by talking for long periods of time. If many people are connected to a public videoconference at once, and video transmission seems slow, you may want to consider turning off your Web cam to avoid clogging up the public conference server with unnecessary video transmission from your Web cam.

Group videoconferences revolve around a specific topic, such as sports, computers, or politics, but conversations between people can often deviate dramatically from the intended topic, much as conversation bounces from topic to topic during a cocktail party.

Some group videoconferences have a notable speaker who may give a lecture and answer questions afterwards, while other group videoconferences look more like a mad, free-for-all chaotic party, where nobody's in charge and everyone talks freely.

Be careful when visiting public videoconferences. People aren't always who they say they are, and many people have no qualms about having their Web cams show you certain graphic images that you may not want to see. If you don't want to risk seeing certain graphic images, you may want to avoid or restrict your use of public videoconferences altogether.

Chapter 9

Using CU-SeeMe

*I*n this chapter, you find out about using CU-SeeMe, one of the most popular videoconferencing programs for both Windows and Macintosh computers. CU-SeeMe started the videoconferencing revolution back in the early 1990s when a programmer named Tim Dorcey created the program for the Macintosh and gave it away for free from Cornell University's computers. Soon programmers developed a version of CU-SeeMe for Windows and a host of other operating systems including OS/2, Linux, and the Amiga.

As the popularity of CU-SeeMe grew, a company, dubbed White Pines Software, started marketing the program as a commercial product. Eventually the company changed its name to CUseeMe Networks (www.cuseeme.com) and abandoned the freeware version of CU-SeeMe altogether.

As the leader of the videoconferencing market, CU-SeeMe continues to grow in popularity and still maintains a healthy share of the market over new rivals, including Microsoft NetMeeting (see Chapter 10) and iVisit (see Chapter 11).

If you hunt around the Internet long enough, you may still be able to find the freeware version of CU-SeeMe floating around. Naturally, this freeware version lacks many of the more advanced features of the commercial version, so this chapter focuses exclusively on the commercial version of CU-SeeMe. But if you're on a budget, try the freeware version of CU-SeeMe, or just use NetMeeting or iVisit (which are free) instead.

Installing CU-SeeMe

To install the Windows version of CU-SeeMe, follow these steps:

1. **Insert the CU-SeeMe CD-ROM into your computer's CD-ROM drive.**

   The CU-SeeMe installation screen appears.

2. **Click the Install CU-SeeMe Pro button.**

3. **Follow the instructions on the screen to finish installing CU-SeeMe.**

If the installation screen does not appear when you insert the CU-SeeMe CD-ROM in your computer, follow these steps:

1. **Click the Start button on the Windows taskbar, choose Run, click Browse, and switch to the CD-ROM drive containing the CU-SeeMe CD-ROM.**

2. **Click the CU-SeeMePro icon.**

3. **Click Open.**

4. **Click OK.**

   The CU-SeeMe installation screen appears.

5. **Follow the instructions on the screen to finish installing CU-SeeMe.**

To install the Macintosh version of CU-SeeMe, follow these steps:

1. **Insert the CU-SeeMe CD-ROM into your Macintosh CD-ROM drive.**

   The CUSEEME window appears.

2. **Double-click the CU-SeeMe icon.**

   Depending on the version of CU-SeeMe you have, this icon may be named something cryptic such as cu313-mac.

3. **Follow the instructions on the screen to finish installing CU-SeeMe.**

Starting CU-SeeMe

For some odd reason, the Windows and Macintosh versions of CU-SeeMe look and act radically different from each other, although they can communicate with each other with no problem. Even starting CU-SeeMe is different on these platforms, depending on which version of the program you're using.

Starting the Windows version of CU-SeeMe

To start the Windows version of CU-SeeMe, follow these steps:

1. **Click the Start button, choose Programs.**

2. **Choose CU-SeeMePro⇨Conferencing Companion.**

   The CU-SeeMe Conferencing Companion window appears.

In case you want to make loading CU-SeeMe easier, follow these steps:

1. **Right-click on the Windows desktop.**

   A pop-up menu appears.

2. **Choose New⇨Shortcut.**

   A Create Shortcut dialog box appears.

3. **Click Browse.**

   A Browse dialog box appears.

4. **Click the CU-SeeMe folder and click Open.**

   You may have to dig through the folders on your hard drive until you find the CU-SeeMe Pro folder, usually stored in the C:\Program Files folder.

5. **Click the Amigo icon and click Open.**

   The Create Shortcut dialog box appears again.

6. **Click Next.**

   The Create Shortcut dialog box asks for a name for your new shortcut icon.

7. **Type a name such as CU-SeeMe and click Finish.**

   Your CU-SeeMe Pro icon appears on the desktop. The next time you want to load CU-SeeMe, just double-click this desktop icon.

Starting the Macintosh version of CU-SeeMe

To start the Macintosh version of CU-SeeMe, follow these steps:

1. **Open the CU-SeeMe folder.**

   You may have to dig through the folders on your hard drive to find the CU-SeeMe folder.

2. **Double-click the CU-SeeMe icon.**

   The CU-SeeMe program appears.

To make CU-SeeMe easier to load, follow these steps:

1. **Open the CU-SeeMe folder.**

   You may have to dig through the different folders stored on your hard drive.

2. **Click the CU-SeeMe icon.**

3. **Choose File⇨Make Alias.**

   A CU-SeeMe alias icon appears.

4. **Drag this CU-SeeMe alias icon to the Macintosh desktop.**

   Your CU-SeeMe Pro icon appears on the desktop. The next time you want to load CU-SeeMe, just double-click this desktop icon.

Calling Someone with CU-SeeMe

To chat with a friend, co-worker, or relative one-on-one, you need to know that person's IP address (see Chapter 8 for more information about identifying your IP address). After you have someone's IP address, you can call that person directly, just like dialing a telephone number.

Making a call through CU-SeeMe

To call someone, follow these steps:

1. **Connect to the Internet.**

   If you have a DSL or cable modem, your computer is always connected to the Internet. If you have a dial-up account, you have to dial up your Internet service provider (ISP) first.

2. **Start CU-SeeMe.**

   The Conferencing Companion window or the Macintosh version appears, as shown in Figures 9-1 and 9-2.

3. **Get the IP address of the person you're calling.**

   DSL and cable modem users have a static IP address that never changes. But if you're trying to reach someone who uses a dial-up account, you may have to ask for that person's IP address by typing a message through an instant messaging program such as ICQ or AIM.

4. **Choose Tools⇨Manual Dial (or Call⇨Manual Dial for the Macintosh).**

   A Manual Dial dialog box appears, as shown in Figure 9-3.

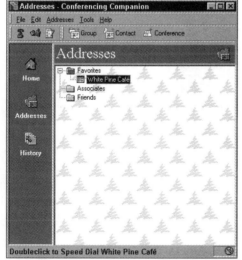

Figure 9-1:
The
Conferencing
Companion
window
appears
after you
load the
Windows
version of
CU-SeeMe.

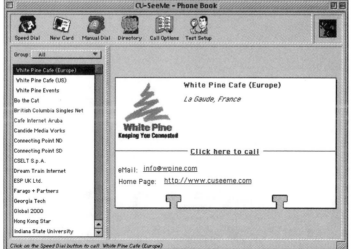

Figure 9-2:
The
Macintosh
version of
CU-SeeMe.

5. Type the person's IP address in the Address box.

If you want to send video from your Web cam, make sure a check mark appears in the Send Video check box.

6. Click Manual Dial.

An Incoming Call Notification dialog box appears on the receiver's screen, as shown in Figure 9-4. As soon as the person clicks the Accept button, the CU-SeeMe window appears, as shown in Figure 9-5, so you can start communicating with one another.

Figure 9-3:
The Windows version of the Manual Dial dialog box for typing an IP address.

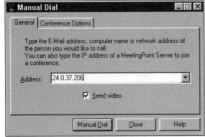

Figure 9-4:
The Incoming Call Notification dialog box lets you know when someone is trying to call you.

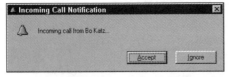

Figure 9-5:
The CU-SeeMe program shows two video windows — one for the caller and one for the receiver.

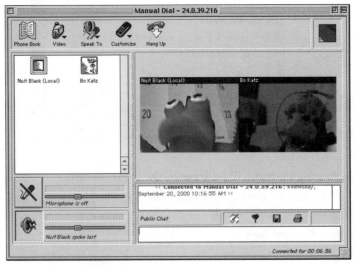

After you finish a particular call, just choose Conference⇨Hang Up. CU-SeeMe disconnects you from your call.

Storing an IP address

If some of your friends have static IP addresses (such as a DSL modem, cable modem, or local-area network connection), you can store their names and IP addresses so you don't have to type them each time you want to call.

If some of your friends use dial-up accounts, they have *dynamic* IP addresses, which change every time they connect to the Internet. Therefore, saving a dynamic IP address is a waste of time.

Using Windows

To save an IP address using the Windows version of CU-SeeMe, follow these steps:

1. **Open the Conferencing Companion window (refer to Figure 9-1).**

   Refer to the "Starting the Windows version of CU-SeeMe" section for instructions on opening the Conferencing Companion window.

2. **Click in the folder where you want to store your saved IP address, such as in the Friends or Favorites folder.**

3. **Choose Addresses⇨New Contact.**

   A New Contact dialog box appears, as shown in Figure 9-6.

Figure 9-6:
The New
Contact
dialog box
lets you
store an IP
address.

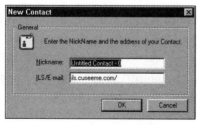

4. **Type a name in the Nickname box.**

5. **Type the IP address in the ILS/E-mail box.**

6. **Click OK.**

The next time you want to call your contact, look in the Conferencing Companion window and double-click the name of the person you want to call.

You can always drag the contact to a different folder later.

Using a Macintosh

To save an IP address using the Macintosh version of CU-SeeMe, follow these steps:

1. **Choose File⇨New Contact Card Assistant.**

   A New Contact Card Assistant dialog box appears.

2. **Click Next.**

   The New Contact Card Assistant asks for a name, IP address, and other information that you want to save, as shown in Figure 9-7.

	New Contact Card Assistant

Step 1. Enter calling information

Enter any information about the person or place you wish to contact. It's OK if you don't enter all the information, but you must type at least the e-mail or the IP address.

Name :
Company :
E-mail :
IP Address :   [Advanced...]

[Cancel]   [Finish]   [< Back] [Next >]

Figure 9-7: The New Contact Card Assistant guides you through the process of storing a name in CU-SeeMe.

3. **Type a name in the Name box and then type the IP address in the IP Address box.**

4. **Click Next.**

   The New Contact Card Assistant informs you that you've completed Step 1.

5. **Click Next.**

   The New Contact Card Assistant dialog box asks if you want to classify your contact as personal or professional information.

6. **Click the Personal or Professional Information radio button and then click Next.**

   The New Contact Card Assistant asks for more information about your contact, such as a telephone number and postal address.

7. **Type in the information you want to save about your contact and click Next.**

Another New Contact Card Assistant dialog box appears, informing you that you've completed Step 2.

8. **Click Next.**

The New Contact Card Assistant dialog box asks if you want to add a picture to your contact card.

9. **(Optional) Click the Browse button and choose a picture.**

You can skip this step if you want.

10. **Click Next.**

The New Contact Card Assistant dialog box displays a preview of your contact card, as shown in Figure 9-8.

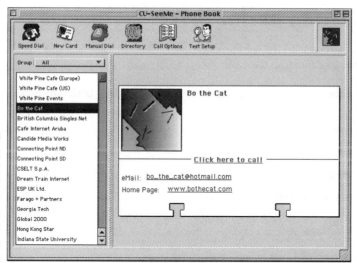

Figure 9-8: Displaying the final version of a contact card in CU-SeeMe.

11. **Click Finish.**

The next time you want to call your contact, click the name of the person you want to call and then click the Click here to call link that appears in the middle of the contact card.

Joining a CU-SeeMe Conference

In case none of your friends are available to chat online, you can also visit a public conference to meet and chat with new people. Or you can also use a conference to coordinate a meeting with your friends. That way, you don't have to know their exact IP addresses.

To join a conference, you need to get a directory server address, which typically begins with ILS (which stands for *Internet locator service*). CU-SeeMe lists several popular ILS servers, such as ils.2cuseeme.com, but if you want to find a different Internet Locator Service, visit one of the following Web sites:

CU-SeeMe World (http://cuseemeworld.com)

Visitalk.com (www.visitalk.com)

Choosing an ILS server (Windows)

After you pick an ILS to use, you need to tell CU-SeeMe to use that particular server by following these steps:

1. **Open the Conferencing Companion window (refer to Figure 9-1).**

   Refer to the "Starting the Windows version of CU-SeeMe" section for instructions on opening the Conferencing Companion window.

2. **Choose Tools⇨Preferences.**

   A Preferences dialog box appears.

3. **Click Directory Services.**

   The Directory Services options appear, as shown in Figure 9-9.

Figure 9-9:
The Preferences dialog box is where you can change all your CU-SeeMe settings.

4. Click the Edit button.

A Directory Edit dialog box appears, as shown in Figure 9-10.

Figure 9-10:
You can add
or delete an
ILS server
name from
the Direc-
tory Edit
dialog box.

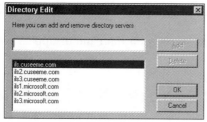

5. Type the ILS server name you want to add and click OK.

6. Click in the list box in the Directory group and select the ILS server name you want to use.

If you want others to be able to contact you through the server, make sure that a check box appears in the Advertise on the Directory At check box.

7. Click the Personal, Business, or Adults-Only radio button in the Category group.

8. Click Personal Information.

The Personal Information options appear, as shown in Figure 9-11.

Figure 9-11:
You can
store
personal
information
that you
want to
share with
others in a
conference.

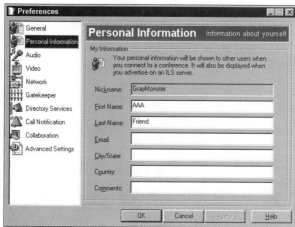

If you advertise yourself on an ILS server, anyone can read your personal information. You may want to delete your e-mail address or use a Web-based e-mail account such as HotMail to protect your privacy.

9. **Type any information you want to share, such as your name and e-mail address.**

10. **Click OK.**

The Preferences dialog box stores your data and disappears.

Connecting to an ILS server (Windows)

After you've chosen an ILS server, the next step is to connect to that server so you can chat with people all over the world.

To connect to an ILS server, follow these steps:

1. **Open the Conferencing Companion window (refer to Figure 9-1).**

Refer to the "Starting the Windows version of CU-SeeMe" section for instructions on opening the Conferencing Companion window.

2. **Choose Tools⇨Directory.**

A Directory window appears, as shown in Figure 9-12.

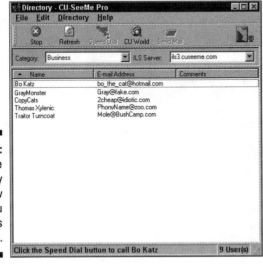

Figure 9-12:
The Directory window shows you who's online.

3. **Click the ILS Server drop-down list and choose the ILS server you want to use.**

   Choosing an ILS server is like choosing a TV channel. Different ILS servers appeal to different types of people, so you may want to explore different ILS servers until you find a few that you like.

4. **Click the Category drop-down list and choose a category such as Business or Personal.**

5. **Double-click the name you want to contact.**

   If the person you're contacting accepts your call, the CU-SeeMe window appears and you can start chatting.

To stop talking with someone, just choose Conference⇨Hang Up.

Choosing an ILS server (Macintosh)

Before you can chat with people in public conferences, you need to choose an ILS server for your copy of CU-SeeMe to use.

To choose an ILS server to use with the Macintosh version of CU-SeeMe, follow these steps:

1. **Start CU-SeeMe.**

2. **Choose Call⇨Directory.**

   A Directory dialog box appears.

3. **Choose Edit⇨Preferences.**

   A Preferences dialog box appears, as shown in Figure 9-13.

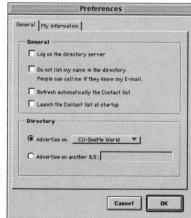

Figure 9-13:
The
Preferences
dialog box
in the
Macintosh
version of
CU-SeeMe.

4. **Click the General tab and select the Advertise on Another ILS radio button.**

5. **In the adjacent text box, type the ILS server name you want to use.**

6. **Click the My Information tab and type any information you want to share with others, such as your e-mail address or name.**

If you advertise yourself on an ILS server, anyone can read your personal information. You may want to delete your e-mail address or use a Web-based e-mail account, such as HotMail, to protect your privacy.

7. **Click OK.**

The Preferences dialog box stores your data and disappears.

Connecting to an ILS server (Macintosh)

After you choose a particular ILS server, you need to connect to that ILS server to chat with other people.

To connect to an ILS server, follow these steps:

1. **Choose Call⇨Directory.**

The Directory window appears.

2. **Click the ILS Address drop-down list and choose the ILS server you want to use.**

Because some ILS servers may be more crowded than others, you may want to experiment with different ILS servers.

3. **Click the Category drop-down list and choose a category such as Personal or Business.**

4. **Double-click the name you want to contact.**

If the person you're contacting accepts your call, the CU-SeeMe window appears (refer to Figure 9-5), and you can start chatting.

To stop talking with someone, just choose Conference⇨Hang Up.

Chatting with Others

You can chat using either audio or text. Audio lets you hear exactly what the other person says in real-time, although the sound quality may be muffled or garbled, especially if one of the users has a slow modem.

Because of the limitations of audio, many people just chat by typing text instead. Typing text may be slower than speaking, but doing so provides a written record of your chat, while avoiding misunderstandings due to sound quality.

Chatting with audio

If you want to talk to another person on CU-SeeMe as easily as you talk to someone on a telephone, both you and the other person need a microphone and speakers. To talk to someone, make sure you're connected with that person (the person's name must appear in the CU-SeeMe window) and then follow these steps:

1. **Click the Turn On/Off Microphone button.**

   The Microphone is turned off if the button appears faded or with a slash through it. Make sure you turn on the microphone.

2. **Talk into your microphone.**

Audio sounds best when everyone has a high-bandwidth Internet connection, such as a DSL or cable modem. If you only have a 56K or slower modem, sound may come out garbled.

You can adjust both the microphone and speaker levels by clicking the Turn On/Off Microphone button and the Turn On/Off Speaker button and clicking the Microphone and Speaker sliders, as shown in Figure 9-14 and Figure 9-15.

Chatting in text mode

As long as you don't mind typing, chatting in text mode can be much simpler and more reliable. The Chat window displays two windows (see Figures 9-14 and 9-15). The top window contains everything that you or other chat room members have typed. The bottom window is where you type your message so that other people can read it.

Typing a message

To type a message in the Chat window, follow these steps:

1. **Click in the bottom window of the Chat window.**

2. **Type your message.**

You can always edit, delete, or modify your message at this time. After you press the Enter key to send your message, you cannot make further modifications, so be sure that you don't say anything that you may regret later.

3. Press Enter after you're sure you want to send your message.

When your message appears in the top half of the Chat window, other chat room members can read the message.

Turn On/Off Microphone

Turn On/Off Speaker

Figure 9-14:
Modifying the microphone and speaker volumes in the Windows version of CU-SeeMe.

In case you want a little privacy, you can send a private text message to someone by choosing Conference➪Chat To and then clicking the name of the person you want to receive your text messages.

Saving a chat room conversation

You can save a chat room conversation in two ways: by saving it to a file or by printing it out. To save a chat room conversation as a file, follow these steps:

1. **Choose File⇨Save Chat.**

   A Save As dialog box appears.

2. **Type a name for your file.**

   You may want to switch to a different folder to save your text mode conversations.

3. **Click Save.**

   CU-SeeMe saves your chat room conversation as a text file that you can open and edit using any word processing program.

Turn On/Off Microphone

Figure 9-15:
Modifying
the
microphone
and speaker
volumes
in the
Macintosh
version of
CU-SeeMe.

Turn On/Off Speaker   Clear Chat Window

Rather than saving the entire chat room conversation as a text file, you can highlight the text you want to save, choose Edit⇨Copy, and then paste the text into a separate word processing document.

To print out your chat room conversation, follow these steps:

1. **Choose File⇨Print.**

   A Print dialog box appears.

2. **Choose the print options (such as picking the printer to use and how many pages you want to print out) and then click OK.**

   Your chat room conversation prints out (as long as your printer is working properly, that is).

Clearing the Chat window

With extended chats, your Chat window can get cluttered. To clear the top part of the Chat window in Windows, follow these steps:

1. **Click anywhere inside the top part of the Chat window.**

2. **Choose Edit⇨Delete.**

   All the text in the top part of the Chat window disappears.

To clear the chat window in the Macintosh version of CU-SeeMe, click the Clear Chat Window button.

Make sure there isn't anything you want to save in your chat room before clearing the Chat room window. If you clear the chat room window, you can't print or save the text to a file later on.

Chapter 10

Using Microsoft NetMeeting

*T*he success of videoconferencing programs like CU-SeeMe prompted Microsoft to release its own videoconferencing program dubbed Microsoft NetMeeting. Like the creators of the original version of CU-SeeMe, Microsoft decided to give away NetMeeting so they could develop a large user base as quickly as possible.

Not only does Microsoft NetMeeting provide the usual video, audio, and chat features, but the program also comes loaded with business-oriented features such as file transfers, application sharing, and a whiteboard for displaying text and graphics for all videoconferencing participants to see.

In this chapter, you discover how to use the different features of Microsoft NetMeeting so you can chat with friends, hold conferences online with co-workers, and share ideas with others without leaving the comfort of your computer screen.

Installing NetMeeting

Because NetMeeting is free, you can download the latest version from the NetMeeting home page at `www.microsoft.com/windows/netmeeting`. After you download NetMeeting, you see the following instructions:

1. **Click the Download Now button above.**

2. **In the File Download dialog box, select Run This Program From Its Current Location.**

3. **Click OK to continue.**

Following these instructions, NetMeeting installs itself and lets you use it right away. After you install NetMeeting, you still have to start the program.

NetMeeting automatically places an icon on the Windows desktop. To start NetMeeting quickly, just double-click this icon.

You can also start NetMeeting by following these steps:

1. **Click the Start button on the Windows taskbar.**

   A pop-up menu appears.

2. **Choose Programs⇨NetMeeting.**

   The NetMeeting window appears.

NetMeeting only works with Windows 95 and later versions of Windows. If you want to videoconference with a Macintosh, you have to use CU-SeeMe (see Chapter 9), iVisit (see Chapter 11), or run NetMeeting from within a Windows emulator on your Macintosh.

Calling Someone with NetMeeting

To chat with a friend, co-worker, or relative one-on-one, you need to know the other person's IP address (see Chapter 8 for more information on identifying your IP address). After you have someone's IP address, you can call that person directly, just as easily as you can dial a telephone number. To call someone, follow these steps:

1. **Connect to the Internet.**

   If you have a DSL or cable modem, your computer is always connected to the Internet. If you have a dial-up account, you first have to dial up your Internet service provider.

2. **Start NetMeeting.**

   The NetMeeting window appears.

3. **Get the IP address of the person you're calling.**

   DSL and cable modem users have a static IP address that never changes. But if you're trying to reach someone who uses a dial-up account, you may have to get that person's IP address through an instant messaging program such as ICQ or MSN Messenger.

Instant messaging programs, like ICQ or MSN Messenger, are separate programs that can notify you the moment a friend connects to the Internet.

4. Choose Call⇨New Call or press Ctrl+N.

The Place A Call dialog box appears, as shown in Figure 10-1.

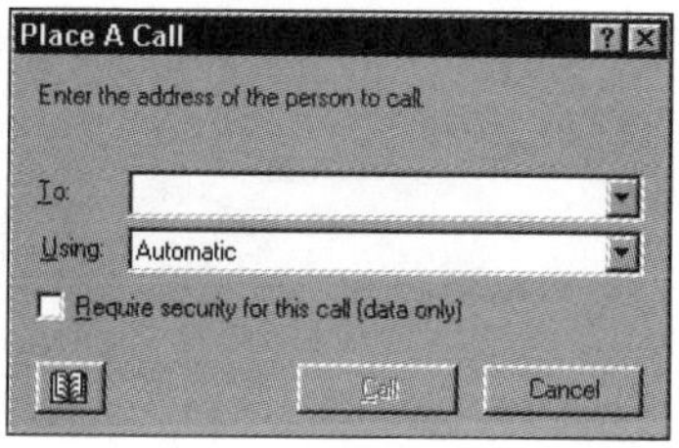

Figure 10-1:
The Place A
Call dialog
box is
where you
type the IP
address of
the person
you want to
contact.

> **Place A Call** ? ✕
>
> Enter the address of the person to call.
>
> To: [   ] ▾
> Using: [Automatic   ] ▾
> ☐ Require security for this call (data only)
>
> [▦]   [Call]   [Cancel]

5. Type the person's IP address in the To box and click Call.

After the other person accepts the call, that person's name appears in the bottom of the NetMeeting window. At this point, you're connected with that person.

Displaying video during a call

In case you want to see how you look to another person through your Web cam, you can display your own video on the screen. NetMeeting gives you two options for displaying your own video:

- ✔ **My video (New Window).** The other person's video fills the entire NetMeeting screen, and your own video appears in a separate window.

- ✔ **Picture-in-Picture.** The other person's video fills the entire NetMeeting screen, and your own video appears in a corner of the NetMeeting screen, as shown in Figure 10-2.

To choose how to display your video, choose View⇨Picture-in-Picture or My Video (New Window).

You can click the Start Video button in the NetMeeting window to start sending video. Or you can determine whether to send or receive video by choosing Tools⇨Video. When a pop-up menu appears, click Send or Receive to select or deselect each option.

Start Video/Stop Video

Figure 10-2:
You can
tuck your
own video
inside the
corner of
the screen.

Because video can take a long time to transfer from one computer to another (especially over a 56Kbps modem), NetMeeting gives you the option of modifying the way video appears, to improve the video quality, or to turn the video display off (or on) altogether.

To modify the way NetMeeting displays video, follow these steps:

1. **Choose Tools⇨Options.**

   The Options dialog box appears.

2. **Click the Video tab, as shown in Figure 10-3.**

3. **Select the options you want, such as Automatically Send Video at the Start of Each Call, or move the slider closer to Faster Video or to Better Quality in the Video Quality group.**

4. **Click OK after you make your changes.**

Storing an IP address

If you regularly need to call someone who has a static IP address (such as someone using a DSL, cable modem, or the same network as you), you can save the person's name and IP address so you don't have to type these each time you want to call.

If someone uses a dial-up account, that person has a dynamic IP address that changes each time he or she connects to the Internet. So you need not bother trying to save that person's IP address.

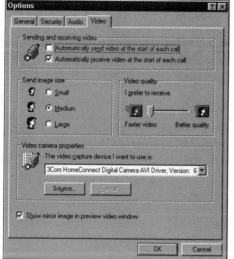

Figure 10-3:
Using the Video tab, you can adjust the way NetMeeting displays and receives video.

To save an IP address, follow these steps:

1. Choose Call⇨Create Speed Dial.

A Create SpeedDial dialog box appears, as shown in Figure 10-4.

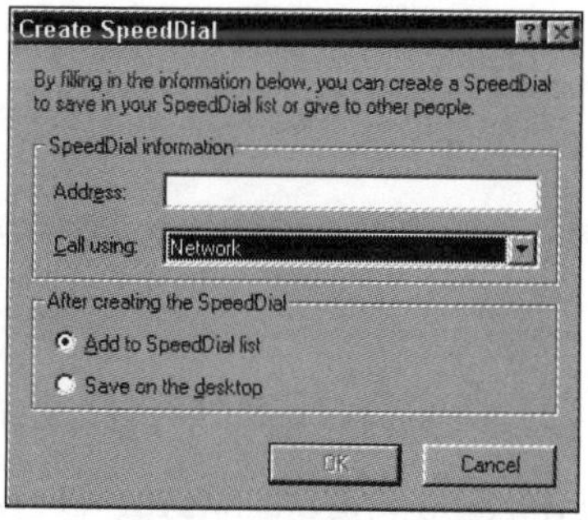

Figure 10-4:
You can save a frequently called IP address.

2. Type the IP address in the Address box.

3. Click the Call Using list box and choose Directory or Network.

Choosing Directory lets you store an IP address in a list of users on a particular ILS server. Choosing Network stores the IP address so you can directly connect to that person without first connecting to an ILS server.

4. Select the Add to SpeedDial List or Save on the Desktop radio button.

5. Click OK.

NetMeeting stores the IP address and displays the NetMeeting window.

Calling a previously stored IP address

After you save a frequently called IP address, you can retrieve it any time you want to call that particular person. If you save the IP address as an icon on the desktop, you can just double-click that icon to load NetMeeting and make a call.

If you previously stored the IP address, you can retrieve that IP address by following these steps:

1. Choose Call⇨New Call (or press Ctrl+N).

The Place A Call dialog box appears, as shown in Figure 10-5.

Figure 10-5:
Retrieving a
previously
stored IP
address.

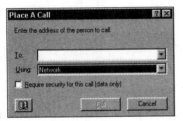

2. Click the Using list box and choose Network or Directory.

3. Click the To list box.

A list of all your saved IP addresses appears.

4. Click the IP address you want to call.

NetMeeting attempts to connect you with your chosen IP address.

Receiving a call with NetMeeting

At any time, you can choose one of the following options for receiving incoming calls:

✔ **Do Not Disturb** prevents anyone from contacting you.

✔ **Automatically Accept Calls** enables anyone to contact you.

✔ **Choose to Accept Calls** enables you to decide at the time of the call whether to answer.

To ignore any calls, follow these steps:

1. **Choose Call⇨Do Not Disturb.**

   A dialog box appears, informing you that you will not be able to receive calls until you turn off the Do Not Disturb option.

2. **Click OK.**

   If you click the Call menu, you will see a check mark in front of the Do Not Disturb option.

To turn off the Do Not Disturb option, repeat the same steps you used to turn it on, only remove the check mark from the Do Not Disturb option in the Call menu.

To automatically accept any calls, choose Call⇨Automatically Accept Calls. When this option is turned on, a check mark appears in front of the Automatically Accept Calls option in the Call menu.

To turn off the Automatically Accept Calls option, repeat the same steps you used to turn it on, only remove the check mark from the Automatically Accept Calls option in the Call menu.

If you have not chosen either the Do Not Disturb or the Automatically Accept Calls option, NetMeeting displays an Incoming Call dialog box whenever someone tries to call you. Just follow these steps:

1. **Connect to the Internet.**

2. **Start NetMeeting.**

   When someone calls you, the Incoming Call dialog box pops up, as shown in Figure 10-6.

Figure 10-6:
You can choose to accept or ignore a call.

3. **Click the Accept or Ignore button.**

After you finish with a particular call, just choose Call⇨Hang Up.

Joining a NetMeeting Conference

Although you can just call people you know, you may be interested in chatting with new people once in awhile, just to have fun and socialize with someone different for a change.

Conferences are also great ways to meet your friends without having to go through the nuisance of typing their exact IP addresses.

To find a conference, you need to get a directory server address, which typically begins with ILS (which stands for *Internet locator service*). To find an Internet locator service, visit one of the following Web sites:

> The NetMeeting Zone (`www.netmeet.net`)
>
> Visitalk.com (`www.visitalk.com`)

Defining and logging on to an ILS server

After you find an ILS to use, you need to tell NetMeeting to use that server by following these steps:

1. **Choose Tools⇨Options.**

   The Options dialog box appears.

2. **Click the General tab.**

   The General tab appears, as shown in Figure 10-7.

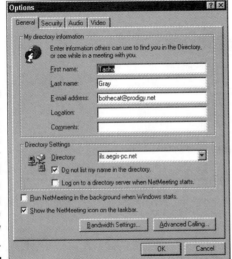

Figure 10-7:
The General tab displays your personal information along with the directory settings.

3. **Click in the Directory box and type the ILS address of the server you want to use.**

   In the example, the address is `ils.aegis-pc.net`.

   If you previously typed the ILS server addresses here, just select the specific address you want to use.

   To protect your privacy and yourself, you may not want others to know your real e-mail address. Therefore, either don't type in an e-mail address, or set up a free e-mail account with HotMail or Yahoo! and use that e-mail address instead. For additional privacy, you can also select the Do Not List My Name in the Directory check box.

   If you select the Log On to a Directory Server When NetMeeting Starts check box, you can skip Step 5.

4. **Click OK.**

   The NetMeeting window appears again.

5. **Choose Call➪Directory.**

   The Find Someone window appears, as shown in Figure 10-8, listing all the people currently logged on to the chosen ILS server.

6. **Double-click the person you want to chat with.**

   If the person accepts your call, his or her video and name appear in your NetMeeting window (refer to Figure 10-2).

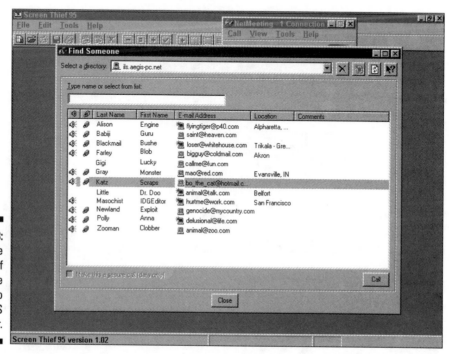

Figure 10-8: Viewing the names of people logged on to an ILS server.

Logging off from an ILS server

After you connect to someone through an ILS server, you don't need to stay logged on to that ILS server anymore. To log off from an ILS server, choose Call⇨Log Off. This disconnects you from the ILS server. You may also want to close the Find Someone window that displays the listing of people currently on the ILS server.

REMEMBER

After you connect with another person through the ILS server, you remain connected to that person until you hang up on that person.

Hosting a Meeting

NetMeeting also enables you to host a meeting in which you and several other people get together to collaborate online. The main advantage of hosting a meeting is that you can define the controls and privileges of other people.

To host a meeting, follow these steps:

1. Choose Call⇨Host Meeting.

A Host a Meeting dialog box appears, as shown in Figure 10-9.

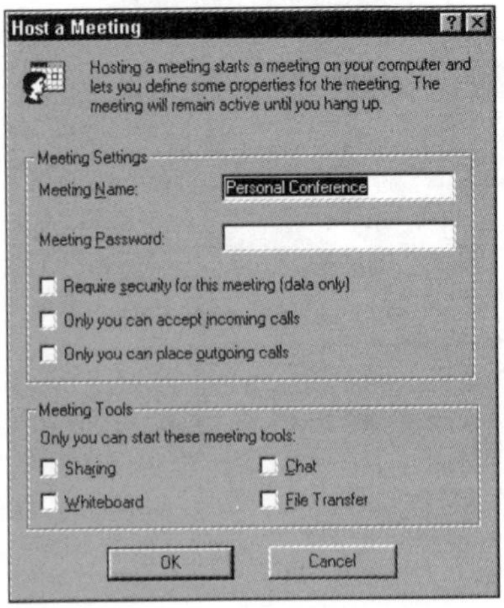

Figure 10-9:
When you
host a
meeting,
you can
define your
own rules
for the
meeting.

> **Host a Meeting**
>
> Hosting a meeting starts a meeting on your computer and lets you define some properties for the meeting. The meeting will remain active until you hang up.
>
> **Meeting Settings**
> Meeting Name: `Personal Conference`
> Meeting Password: `                    `
>
> ☐ Require security for this meeting (data only)
> ☐ Only you can accept incoming calls
> ☐ Only you can place outgoing calls
>
> **Meeting Tools**
> Only you can start these meeting tools:
> ☐ Sharing   ☐ Chat
> ☐ Whiteboard   ☐ File Transfer
>
> [OK]   [Cancel]

2. Click in the Meeting Name box and type a name.

This name is purely for your own benefit and has no effect on the way NetMeeting runs.

3. **Click in the Meeting Password box and type a password.**

   If people try to join your meeting, they have to type the password first. Otherwise, they're locked out of the meeting.

4. **Select the check boxes to define any additional options you want, such as enabling only you to accept incoming calls or only you to start a whiteboard or shared application.**

5. **Click OK after you finish.**

6. **Wait for others to call you, or call others to invite them to your meeting.**

Chatting with Others

With NetMeeting, you can chat by audio or text. Audio lets you hear exactly what the other person says in real time, although the sound quality may be muffled or garbled, especially if one of the users is connected by a slow modem. Because of the limitations of audio, many people choose to chat using text instead. Typing text may be slower than speaking, but doing so provides a written record of your chat and helps avoid misunderstandings that may result from iffy sound quality.

Chatting with audio

Talking with someone on the other side of the world, country, or street can be fun, although the audio quality may vary, depending on your computer's speakers. To talk and listen to other people, both parties need a microphone and speakers.

Audio sounds best when everyone has a high-bandwidth Internet connection, such as a DSL or cable modem. If you only have a 56 Kbps or slower modem, the sound may come out garbled.

To talk to someone, make sure you're connected with that person (the person's name appears at the bottom of the NetMeeting window) and then start talking.

You can adjust both the speaker and microphone volume levels by clicking the Adjust Audio Volume button and moving the microphone or speaker volume sliders shown in Figure 10-10.

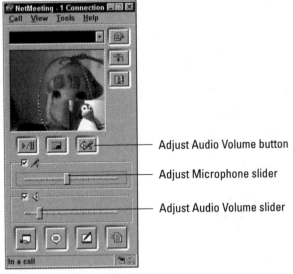

Figure 10-10:
To adjust
the sound
levels, you
can move
the
microphone
and speaker
volume
sliders.

Adjust Audio Volume button

Adjust Microphone slider

Adjust Audio Volume slider

Chatting in text mode

The problem with chatting by audio is that the sound may be muffled or distorted. So many people just prefer to type messages to each other. That way, you can clearly see what the other person is writing rather than trying to guess what the other person is saying. So rather than talk, you can chat in text mode.

The Chat window displays two text boxes, as shown in Figure 10-11. The top text box contains everything that you or other chat room members have typed. The bottom text box, called the Message box, is where you can type your message so other people can read it.

Send Message button

Figure 10-11:
The Chat
window
displays
the entire
conversation
and a
separate box
in which
you type
your own
messages.

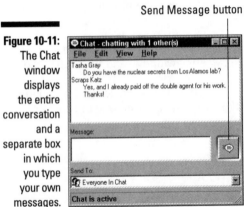

Typing a message

The bottom-left corner of the Chat window may display two messages: `Chat is not active` or `Chat is active`. The `Chat is active` message means that anything you type can be seen by other chat room members. To type a message in the Chat window, follow these steps:

1. **Use one of the following methods to open the Chat window (refer to Figure 10-11):**

   - Press Ctrl+T.

   - Click the Chat button.

   - Choose Tools⇨Chat.

2. **Click in the Message box of the Chat window.**

3. **Type your message.**

   You can edit, delete, or modify your message at this time. After you press the Enter key to send your message, however, you cannot modify it, so make sure that you don't say anything that you may regret later.

4. **Press Enter or click the Send Message button after you're sure you want to send your message.**

   After your message appears in the top half of the Chat window, other chat room members can read it and you can no longer edit it.

Saving a chat room conversation

You can record a chat room conversation in two ways: by saving it to a file or by printing it out. To save a chat room conversation as a file, follow these steps:

1. **Choose File⇨Save As in the Chat window.**

   The Save As dialog box appears.

2. **Type a name for your file.**

   You may want to switch to a different folder in which to save your text mode conversations.

3. **Click Save.**

   NetMeeting saves your chat room conversation as an HTML file, as shown in Figure 10-12.

Rather than save the entire chat room conversation as a text file, you can highlight the text you want to save, choose Edit⇨Copy, and paste the text into a separate word-processing document.

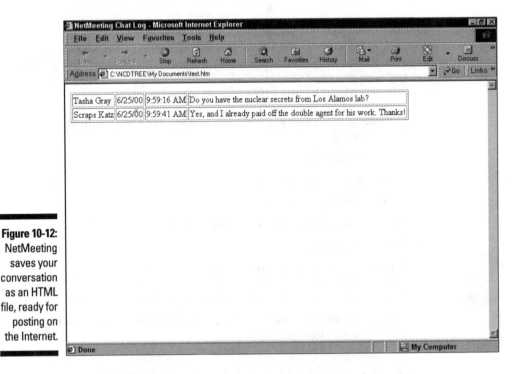

Figure 10-12:
NetMeeting
saves your
conversation
as an HTML
file, ready for
posting on
the Internet.

If you prefer to just print out your chat room conversation, follow these
steps:

1. **Choose File⇨Print.**

   The Print dialog box appears.

2. **Set the print options (such as the printer you want to use and the
   number of pages you want to print out) and click OK.**

Clearing the Chat window

Sometimes, a chat room conversation can contain so many messages from
different people that your Chat window gets cluttered. If you want to clear
the top text box of the Chat window, choose Edit⇨Clear All.

Make sure there isn't anything you want to save in your chat room before
clearing the Chat window. If you clear the Chat window, you can't print or
save the text to a file later on.

Defining your chat room settings

Just to give you a feeling of control, NetMeeting lets you modify the way your
Chat window works by choosing the font, type size, and the way in which the
Chat window highlights conversations.

To define your chat room settings, follow these steps:

1. **Choose View⇨Options in the Chat window.**

   The Options dialog box appears, as shown in Figure 10-13.

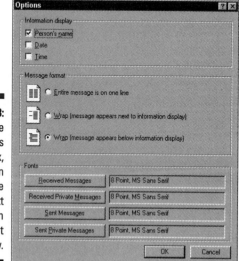

Figure 10-13: In the Options dialog box, you can modify the way text appears in your Chat window.

2. **Click the option you want to change, such as the Sent Messages button to choose a different font.**

3. **Click OK after you finish making the changes you want.**

   The Chat window displays your chosen options the next time someone types you a message.

Using the Whiteboard

Because drawing can often get a point across faster than text or spoken language, NetMeeting provides a special feature called a *whiteboard,* which provides a screen where anyone can draw, type, or copy text or pictures for everyone else to see simultaneously. To open the whiteboard screen, choose Tools⇨Whiteboard, or press Ctrl+W. The Whiteboard window appears, as shown in Figure 10-14, and you can start typing, drawing, or modifying text or graphics.

Whatever you draw or type on the whiteboard may take a few seconds or minutes to appear on other people's screens, depending on the speed of the connection between you and everyone else. A network connection quickly transfers your text or picture. If someone's using a 56 Kbps modem, on the other hand, the transfer is slower.

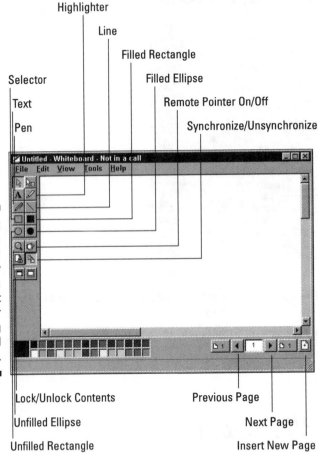

Highlighter

Line

Filled Rectangle

Filled Ellipse

Selector

Remote Pointer On/Off

Text

Pen

Synchronize/Unsynchronize

Figure 10-14:
The
Whiteboard
window
acts as a
simple paint
program for
displaying
text and
graphics.

Lock/Unlock Contents

Previous Page

Unfilled Ellipse

Next Page

Unfilled Rectangle

Insert New Page

Typing text on a whiteboard

Text can appear on the whiteboard in different fonts and colors. To type text on the whiteboard, just follow these steps:

1. **Click the Text tool.**

   The mouse pointer turns into an I-beam icon.

2. **Move the mouse pointer to wherever on the whiteboard you want to type and then click the left mouse button.**

   A box with a blinking cursor inside appears.

3. **Type your text.**

   If you want to modify the color, size, or font of your text, continue to the next step. Otherwise skip to Step 7.

4. **Highlight any text you want to modify and click the color you want to use, such as yellow or red.**

5. **Click the Font Options button.**

   The Font dialog box appears.

6. **Select your font options and type size, and then click OK.**

7. **Click the Pointer tool after you finish.**

   Clicking the Pointer tool shows you how your text looks to other people viewing the whiteboard.

If you want to edit text again, click the Text tool and then click the text that you want to edit.

You can emphasize text by choosing the Highlighter tool, clicking a color at the bottom of the Whiteboard window, and dragging over the text you want to highlight in bright colors such as yellow or blue.

Drawing shapes on a whiteboard

You can draw simple rectangles or ellipses on the whiteboard by following these steps:

1. **Click the Unfilled or Filled Rectangle or Ellipse tool.**

   The mouse pointer turns into a crosshair icon.

2. **Click a line width in the left side of the Whiteboard window.**

   The line widths appear directly under the various Whiteboard tools (refer to Figure 10-14).

3. **Click the color that you want for your object.**

4. **Move the mouse where you want to draw your object, hold down the left mouse button, and drag the mouse to draw the object.**

5. **Release the left mouse button after you finish drawing.**

   Your object appears on the whiteboard for everyone to see.

Drawing lines on a whiteboard

In case you want to draw something freehand, you can choose between the Pen and the Line tool. To use the Pen tool, follow these steps:

1. **Click the Pen tool.**

   The mouse pointer turns into a pen icon.

2. **Click a line width in the bottom-left corner of the Whiteboard window.**

   The line widths appear directly under the various Whiteboard tools (refer to Figure 10-14).

3. **Click a color for your pen.**

4. **Click the spot where you want to start drawing and drag the mouse to draw your line.**

5. **Release the left mouse button after you finish.**

To use the Line tool, follow these steps:

1. **Click the Line tool.**

   The mouse pointer turns into a crosshair icon.

2. **Click the spot where you want to start drawing the line and drag to the position where you want the line to end.**

3. **Release the left mouse button.**

   Your line appears on the whiteboard for everyone to see.

Deleting objects on a whiteboard

In case you want to delete text, objects, or lines from the whiteboard, follow these steps:

1. **Click the Pointer tool.**

2. **Click the object you want to delete.**

   NetMeeting highlights your chosen object.

3. **Press the Delete key.**

Your chosen object disappears.

If you accidentally delete an object, press Ctrl+Z right away to bring the object back again.

Adding and deleting pages from the whiteboard

You can always add or delete pages from the whiteboard. To add a page, choose one of the following:

✔ Choose Edit⇨Insert Page.

✔ Press Ctrl++ (Hold down the Ctrl key and press the + key).

✔ Click the Insert New Page button (the button in the lower-right corner with the page icon and + sign).

To delete a page from the whiteboard, follow these steps:

1. **Click the Previous Page or Next Page button until the page you want to delete appears.**

2. **Choose Edit⇨Delete Page, or press Ctrl+− (Hold down the Ctrl key and press the − key).**

A Whiteboard dialog box appears, asking if you're sure you want to delete the page.

3. **Click Yes.**

NetMeeting deletes your chosen page.

Saving and loading a whiteboard

You can save a whiteboard in a special file so you can load it again in NetMeeting to view it or continue editing it. To save a whiteboard, follow these steps:

1. **Choose File⇨Save, or press Ctrl+S.**

The Save As dialog box appears.

2. **Type a name for your whiteboard file.**

You may want to choose a different folder or drive in which to store your whiteboard.

3. Click Save.

NetMeeting saves the whiteboard as a file on your computer.

You can print out your whiteboard by choosing File⇨Print.

To reload your whiteboard in NetMeeting, follow these steps:

1. Choose File⇨Open, or press Ctrl+O.

An Open dialog box appears.

2. Select the whiteboard file you want to load.

3. Click Open.

NetMeeting displays your previously saved whiteboard file.

Transferring Files

Sometimes you may need to transfer files to one or more people attending the online meeting. Rather than send the files as e-mail attachments, you can transfer them through NetMeeting. To transfer a file, follow these steps:

1. Choose Tools⇨File Transfer, or press Ctrl+F.

The File Transfer window appears.

2. Click the Add Files button.

The Select Files to Send dialog box appears.

3. Click the file you want to send.

If you want to send multiple files, hold down the Ctrl key and click each file that you want to transfer.

To highlight a range of files, hold down the Shift key, click the first file you want to transfer, and then click the last file you want to transfer. NetMeeting highlights all the files in between the first and last files you clicked.

4. Click Add.

The File Transfer window displays the files, as shown in Figure 10-15.

If you want to send files to only one person in the conference, click the list box in the upper-right corner of the File Transfer window and select the name of the person you want to send your files to. (By default, this list box is set to Everyone, which means everyone in the conference receives any files you send.)

Add Files

Remove Files

Send All

Stop Sending

View Received Files

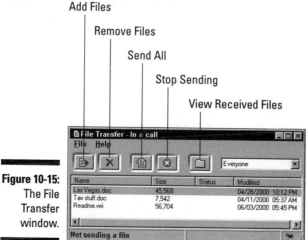

Figure 10-15:
The File
Transfer
window.

If you change your mind about sending a particular file, you can click
that file and then click the Remove Files button.

5. Click the Send All button.

Sharing Applications

Using the whiteboard feature gives everyone a chance to share ideas by
drawing or typing, but what if you want to share data from a major application such as Microsoft Word or Excel?

That's the idea behind the capability for sharing applications. For example, if
you want to collaborate on a Microsoft Word document, you can share that
document through NetMeeting. Only one person (the one doing the sharing)
needs to have a copy of Microsoft Word, but anyone else can see, edit, and
control Microsoft Word from his or her computer.

Shared applications can run extremely slow if you're communicating over a
56 Kbps or slower modem. If you're going to share applications, make sure all
the computers have plenty of memory, along with a high-speed Internet connection if possible.

Sharing applications enables you to collaborate using the commands and
files of your favorite application. To share an application, follow these steps:

**1. Load the application that you want to share, such as Microsoft Word
(or even a game if you prefer).**

2. **Make sure that you're connected to at least one other person through NetMeeting.**

3. **Choose Tools⇨Sharing, or press Ctrl+S.**

   The Sharing dialog box appears, as shown in Figure 10-16.

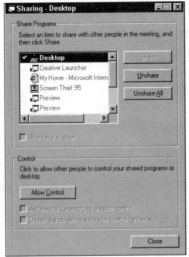

Figure 10-16:
The Sharing
dialog box
lets you pick
which
currently
running
application
to share
with others
through
NetMeeting.

4. **Click the file you want to share.**

5. **Click the Share button.**

   A check mark appears next to the chosen application. A window showing the application and the currently loaded file opens on the other person's computer screen.

Granting control over a shared application

When you share an application, you can either control it completely or enable others to edit and modify files located on your hard drive through the shared application. To grant control over a shared application, follow these steps:

1. **Choose Tools⇨Sharing, or press Ctrl+S.**

   The Sharing dialog box appears (refer to Figure 10-16).

2. **Click the Allow Control button.**

3. **Select the Automatically Accept Requests for Control check box.**

   Your chosen shared application appears on other users' computer screens. You may want to click the Close button on the Sharing dialog box to make it go away.

After you enable control of a shared application, other users can request control of the shared application by choosing Control⇨Request Control. That way they can control the shared application as if they were running it on their own computers, which means they can type or open windows.

Stop sharing an application

Any time you want to stop sharing an application, just follow these steps:

1. **Choose Tools⇨Sharing, or press Ctrl+S.**

   The Sharing dialog box appears (refer to Figure 10-16).

2. **Click any application you want to stop sharing.**

3. **Click the Unshare or the Unshare All button.**

   If you want to stop sharing all shared applications, click the Unshare All button. If you just want to selectively stop sharing applications, click the Unshare button.

4. **Click Close.**

   Any applications that you chose to unshare in Step 2 now disappear from other users' computer screens.

Sharing applications can be a great way to collaborate in real time using your computer. That way you can actually get some useful work done without wasting time gathering people together in one place and lugging laptop computers around. With a little creativity and experimentation, you may find even more uses for NetMeeting, its Whiteboard features, and its capability for sharing applications.

Chapter 11

Using iVisit

In This Chapter

▶ Installing iVisit

▶ Calling someone using iVisit

▶ Receiving a call

▶ Attending an iVisit conference

▶ Chatting with iVisit

▶ Dealing with rude people

*I*n this chapter, you learn how to use one of the newest videoconferencing programs: iVisit. Like Microsoft NetMeeting, iVisit is free to use, copy, and pass around to your friends. By giving away the program, the company hopes more people will use it, thereby increasing the company's share of the video-conferencing market.

The History of iVisit

After creating the CU-SeeMe program in 1992 and starting the videoconferencing revolution for personal computers, its creator, Tim Dorcey, redesigned the program and it became known as iVisit.

The first version of iVisit was released in 1997, and the program is continually being upgraded. With support for both Windows and the Macintosh, iVisit has quickly garnered loyal support from many users. Best of all, like the original version of CU-SeeMe, the program is free!

Perhaps the most crucial difference between CU-SeeMe and iVisit is that when connecting large numbers of people in a videoconference, CU-SeeMe requires the use of a reflector (a server), which is a separate computer that coordinates communication between all users. iVisit does not require a separate server but instead links users directly to one another, which improves responsiveness for all participants. In addition, iVisit is faster and more efficient than CU-SeeMe.

Installing iVisit

You can download the latest version of iVisit for both Windows and the Macintosh from the iVisit Web site at `www.ivisit.com`.

Installing the Windows version of iVisit

To install the Windows version of iVisit, follow these steps:

1. **Connect to the iVisit Web site and click the link to download the iVisit program.**

   The File Download dialog box appears.

2. **Click the Run This Program from the Current Location radio button and click OK.**

   The iVisit installation program downloads to your computer and starts installing the program.

3. **Follow the instructions on the iVisit installation program screens to finish installing iVisit.**

   When the iVisit installation program is done, you can start the iVisit program.

Installing the Macintosh version of iVisit

To install the Macintosh version of iVisit, follow these steps:

1. **Connect to the iVisit Web site and click the link to download the iVisit program.**

   The Download Manager dialog box appears and starts the download process to your Macintosh.

2. **Close the Download Manager window after the download is complete.**

   You may also want to close any other programs, such as your Web browser, to prevent interference with the installation of iVisit.

3. **Double-click the iVisit installer icon on your Macintosh desktop.**

   The iVisit installation program appears.

4. **Follow the instructions on the iVisit installation program screens to finish installing iVisit.**

   When the iVisit installation program is done, you can start the iVisit program.

To make sure people use only the latest version of iVisit, the iVisit program expires after a certain number of months. When it expires, all you need to do is download the latest free version from the iVisit Web site and reinstall the program.

Starting the Windows version of iVisit

To start the Windows version of iVisit, follow these steps:

1. **Click the Start button on the Windows taskbar.**

   A pop-up menu appears.

2. **Choose Programs⇨iVisit⇨iVisit.**

   The iVisit program appears.

Starting the Macintosh version of iVisit

To start the Macintosh version of iVisit, follow these steps:

1. **Open the iVisit folder.**

   You may have to dig through several folders to find the iVisit folder.

2. **Double-click the iVisit icon.**

   The iVisit program appears.

Calling Another Person with iVisit

If you know someone's IP address (see Chapter 8 for more information about identifying your IP address), you can call that person directly, much the same way you dial the person's telephone number. To call someone, just follow these steps:

1. **Connect to the Internet.**

   If you have a DSL or cable modem, your computer is always connected to the Internet. If you have a dial-up account, you first have to dial your Internet Service Provider.

2. **Start iVisit.**

After you start iVisit, the program displays three windows, as shown in Figure 11-1:

- A Video window (so you can see yourself through your Web cam)

- A Chat window (in which you can type and read messages)

- A Directory window (in which you can connect to others through the iVisit network)

3. Get the IP address of the person you're calling.

DSL and cable modem users have a static IP address that never changes. But if you're trying to reach someone who uses a dial-up account, you may have to get that person's IP address through an instant messaging program such as ICQ or MSN Messenger.

Instant messaging programs, such as ICQ or MSN Messenger, are programs that notify you the moment a friend connects to the Internet.

You can find your own IP address from within iVisit by choosing Windows⇨Network Stats. The Network Statistics dialog box that appears, as shown in Figure 11-2, lists your IP address.

Figure 11-1:
The three
iVisit
windows.

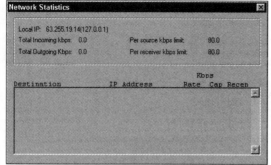

Figure 11-2:
The
Network
Statistics
dialog box
helps you
identify your
own IP
address.

4. **Choose File⇨Connect IP.**

The Edit Bookmark dialog box appears, as shown in Figure 11-3.

Figure 11-3:
The Edit
Bookmark
dialog box is
where you
type the IP
address of
the person
you want to
contact.

5. **Click the Connect button.**

Another Video window appears, confirming that you have successfully
connected with the person you just called.

Video quality may look chunky and poor, especially if one or both of the
people involved are using an ordinary 56 Kbps or slower modem.

Saving someone's IP address

If you plan to regularly call someone who has a static IP address (such as
with a DSL or cable modem), you can save the person's name and IP address
so you don't have to type that information in each time you want to call.

If someone uses a dial-up account, that person has a dynamic IP address that changes each time he or she connects to the Internet. Saving a dynamic IP address is pointless.

To save an IP address in iVisit, follow these steps:

1. **Choose File➪Connect IP.**

   An Edit Bookmark dialog box appears (refer to Figure 11-3).

2. **Type the name of the person in the Name box.**

3. **Type that person's IP address in the IP Address box.**

4. **Click the Save button.**

Retrieving someone's IP address

After you save someone's IP address, you can retrieve it any time you want to call that person. To retrieve a previously saved IP address in iVisit, follow these steps:

1. **Click the Mode drop-down list in the Directory window and choose Bookmarks.**

   If the Directory window isn't visible, choose Windows➪Directory. After choosing Bookmarks in the Mode drop-down list, several folders appear, including the Saved folder, as shown in Figure 11-4.

Figure 11-4:
The Saved folder contains your bookmarked list of IP addresses.

2. **Double-click the Saved folder.**

   A list of your previously saved names and IP addresses appears, as shown in Figure 11-5.

Figure 11-5:
The
Directory
window
stores your
saved
names
and IP
addresses
in the Saved
folders
in the
Bookmarks
mode.

Connect to User button

3. **Double-click a name, or click the name and then click the Connect
   to User button.**

   The iVisit program attempts to connect to the person you want to
   contact.

Receiving a Call with iVisit

To receive a call, follow these steps:

1. **Connect to the Internet.**

   If you have a DSL or cable modem, your computer is always connected
   to the Internet. If you have a dial-up account, you first have to dial your
   Internet Service Provider.

   (If necessary, you may need to give out your IP address to the person
   trying to call you, for example, through an instant messaging program,
   which is a special program that can notify you the moment a friend connects to the Internet.)

2. **Start iVisit.**

   As soon as the other person tries to call you, the Connection Request
   dialog box appears, as shown in Figure 11-6, with the name and IP
   address of the caller.

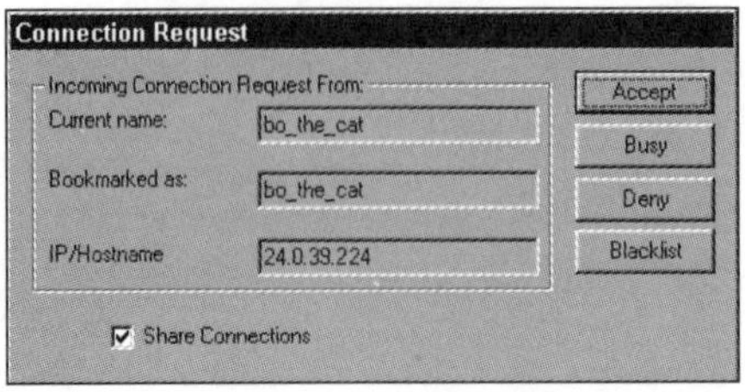

Figure 11-6:
The
Connection
Request
dialog box
gives you
the option to
accept a
request to
connect.

Connection Request

Incoming Connection Request From:
Current name: bo_the_cat
Bookmarked as: bo_the_cat
IP/Hostname   24.0.39.224

Accept
Busy
Deny
Blacklist

☑ Share Connections

3. **Select one of the following options:**

• **Accept** connects you to the caller.

• **Busy** displays a Busy message to the caller.

• **Deny** displays a Connection Refused message to the caller.

• **Blacklist** displays a Blacklisted message to the caller.

If you choose the Accept option, iVisit displays a video window of your caller.

Use the Blacklist option to permanently keep someone from calling you. This feature can be useful to screen out stalkers, obnoxious people, or just people you don't like.

If you don't select one of the options in Step 3, the iVisit program displays a No Answer message to the caller.

Joining an iVisit Conference

In addition to calling other people you know, you can also join a videoconference of total strangers — to meet new people, discuss a particular topic, or socialize from the convenience of your Web cam and personal computer.

Conferences are organized according to topics, such as Business, Arts & Leisure, Romance, or Games. Within each conference topic are additional subtopics. You can join two types of conferences:

✔ Chat rooms
✔ Listings

Chat rooms enable two or more people to chat with one another. Think of a chat room as an open room where anyone can see and hear anyone else.

Listings are more like phone directories; you can add your name to a list, but someone has to call you first to talk to you.

The most popular conferences are the adult-oriented and romance conferences. If you don't want to participate in anything that may embarrass you or make you uncomfortable, stick to conferences focusing on safer topics such as sports, business, or entertainment.

Protecting your privacy in a conference

Anyone, including celebrities, ordinary people, and online stalkers, can join a public conference. So for privacy, you may not want others to know your real e-mail address. To protect yourself, don't type an e-mail address; set up a free e-mail account with HotMail or Yahoo! and use that e-mail address instead.

To change your e-mail address in iVisit, follow these steps:

1. **Choose Settings⇨Preferences.**

   The Preferences dialog box appears, as shown in Figure 11-7.

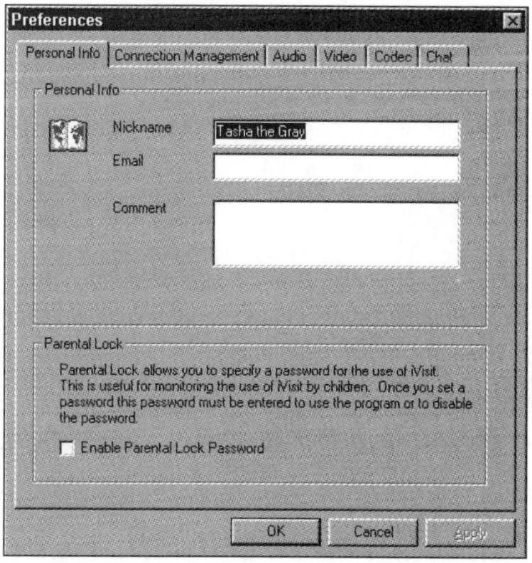

Figure 11-7:
You can define your nickname and e-mail address on the Personal Info tab.

> Preferences
>
> Personal Info | Connection Management | Audio | Video | Codec | Chat
>
> Personal Info
>
> Nickname: Tasha the Gray
>
> Email:
>
> Comment:
>
> Parental Lock
>
> Parental Lock allows you to specify a password for the use of iVisit. This is useful for monitoring the use of iVisit by children. Once you set a password this password must be entered to use the program or to disable the password.
>
> ☐ Enable Parental Lock Password
>
> OK | Cancel | Apply

2. **Click the Personal Info tab and type a nickname, your e-mail address, and any comment you want others to know about you.**

3. **Click OK.**

   iVisit saves your personal information.

Joining a chat room or listing

To join a chat room or listing, follow these steps:

1. **Make sure the Directory window appears.**

   If it does not, choose Windows⊅Directory.

2. **Click the Mode drop-down list and choose Server.**

   The Directory window displays a list of different conference folders, such as Arts & Leisure or Education.

3. **Double-click a conference folder.**

   A list of different chat rooms and listings appears, as shown in Figure 11-8.

Figure 11-8:
The
Directory
window
lists all the
available
conference
folders and
chat rooms
that you
can visit.

4. **Double-click the chat room or listing you want to visit.**

   A list of current chat room members appears, as shown in Figure 11-9.

   By browsing through the list of current chat room members' names, you can get a rough idea of the type of people in that chat room. If you find too many chat room members' names with sexual references, you may want to avoid that chat room.

Figure 11-9:
The
Directory
window lists
all current
members in
a chat room.

Join Selected Room button

5. Click the Join Selected Room or Join Selected Listing button.

The Join Selected Room and Join Selected Listing buttons appear in the same location, depending on whether you're currently highlighting a room or listing.

If you join a chat room, the Guest List window appears, as shown in Figure 11-10, and you see tiny video windows of all the current chat room members. You can start chatting with these people immediately (see the "Chatting" section later in this chapter).

If you join a listing, you have to double-click another person's name to start chatting with that person.

Figure 11-10:
The Guest
List window
displays the
video
window of
all current
members in
the chat
room.

After you click the Join Selected Room or Join Selected Listing button, it turns into the Leave Selected Room or Leave Selected Listing button. To leave click either the Leave Selected Room or Leave Selected Listing button.

Changing your server

The friendly folks that make the iVisit program also provide a special computer that other iVisit users can use to join or start a conference. The iVisit server address is `http://directory.ivisit.com`, but you can always choose another server to use if you want.

For example, your company or an organization may start a private server so employees or members can use iVisit to create and join conferences without the hassle of the general public interfering.

To switch to a different server, follow these steps:

1. **Choose Settings⇨Preferences.**

   The Preferences dialog box appears.

2. **Click the Connection Management tab.**

   The Connection Management tab appears, as shown in Figure 11-11.

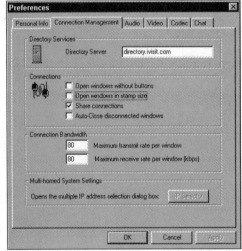

Figure 11-11: The Connection Management tab displays your current Directory Server.

3. **Click in the Directory Server box and type the address of the server you want to use.**

   If you want to switch to a different server, you have to get the exact Directory Server name from the person running the server you want to use.

4. **Click OK.**

   iVisit saves your new server listing.

Chatting

iVisit offers two modes in which to chat: audio or text. Audio lets you hear exactly what the other person is saying in real-time, although the sound may seem muffled or garbled, especially if one of the users has a slow modem. Audio, however, gives you the illusion of talking on a futuristic telephone, which is what makes videoconferencing fun.

Because of audio's limitations, many people choose instead to chat in text mode. Text mode may be slower than speaking, but it provides a written record of your chat and avoids any misunderstandings due to sound quality.

Chatting with audio

Perhaps the most exciting part of videoconferencing is that you can chat with another person just by talking, as if you were using a telephone. While the audio quality may vary, depending on your computer's speakers, talking to someone is usually much faster than typing a message.

Audio sounds best when everyone has a high-bandwidth Internet connection, such as a DSL or cable modem. If you only have a 56 Kbps or slower modem, sound may come out garbled.

Talking to someone

To talk and listen to others, both parties need a microphone and speakers. The quality of both the microphone and the speakers can affect the audio quality, but if you don't mind a less-than-crystal-clear sound, you can have fun chatting in real time.

If you want to talk privately, click the Send Private Audio/Chat button in the video window of the person you want to talk to.

To talk to someone, follow these steps:

1. **Hold down the Ctrl key or move the mouse pointer over the Talk button and hold down the left mouse button. (Macintosh users can hold down the Control key or move the mouse pointer over the Talk button and hold down the mouse button.)**

   You must hold down the Ctrl (or Control) key or hold down the mouse button over the Talk button the whole time you talk or else iVisit assumes you're done talking and won't transmit any more sounds from your microphone.

2. **Talk into your microphone.**

   As you speak, a green bar appears beside the microphone icon, to show you the microphone's sensitivity.

3. **Release the Ctrl (Control) key or the mouse button after you finish talking.**

   With the Windows version of iVisit, you can adjust both the speaker and microphone levels by clicking the minus (–) or plus (+) sign next to the speaker and microphone icons.

Recording and playing a video while chatting

In case you need to preserve a video of someone doing something particularly interesting or unusual, you can record that video in a separate file.

To record a video, follow these steps:

1. **Click the Start Recording button in the video window of the person you want to record, as shown in Figure 11-12.**

   iVisit starts recording your video and tracking the elapsed time, approximate file size, and approximate download time for a 28.8 Kbps modem.

Figure 11-12: You can record a video of anyone for future reference.

Pause button

Start Recording button

You can click the Pause button to temporarily stop recording and then click it again to continue recording.

2. **Click the Stop button to stop recording.**

   The Save As dialog box appears.

3. **Type a name for the video file and then click Save.**

You may want to change folders before saving your video.

After you save a video, you can only view the video again from within the iVisit program.

To play a saved video recording, follow these steps:

1. **Choose File⇨Play File.**

   The Open dialog box appears.

2. **Select the video file you want to view and then click Open.**

   A video window appears, displaying the video file.

3. **Click the close box in the upper right corner of the video window to make it go away.**

Defining your audio and video settings

Although the quality of your video and audio relies mostly on your Internet connection, you may still want to tweak some of the video and audio settings to optimize iVisit.

To define your audio and video settings, follow these steps:

1. **Choose Settings⇨Preferences.**

   The Preferences dialog box appears.

2. **Click the Audio tab.**

   The Audio tab appears, as shown in Figure 11-13.

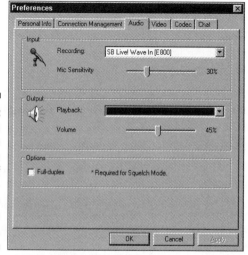

Figure 11-13: You can adjust the audio quality of your video-conference through the Audio tab.

3. **Choose any options you want to change, such as increasing the microphone sensitivity or increasing the volume by dragging the slider.**

   The options available in the Audio tab include the following:

   - **Mic Sensitivity** adjusts the microphone to be more or less sensitive to sounds. The maximum sensitivity is 100% and the minimum sensitivity is 3%.

   - **Volume** adjusts the volume from your speakers, in case another person is talking too loudly or softly.

   - **Full Duplex** turns on full-duplex mode (which lets you talk and listen to others at the same time). If the check box is clear, then iVisit is using half-duplex mode (which lets you either talk or listen but not both simultaneously).

4. **Click the Video tab.**

   The Video tab appears, as shown in Figure 11-14.

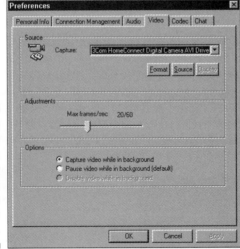

Figure 11-14: You can sharpen video quality by modifying the options on the Video tab.

5. **Select the option(s) you want to change, such as increasing the number of frames per second.**

   The options available in the Video tab include the following:

   - **Source** enables you to change the resolution, size, and image quality of your video.

   - **Adjustments** adjusts the number of frames to display per second.

   - **Options** enables you to capture video all the time or to pause when the video window is in the background. Pausing can prevent your video transmission from slowing down the iVisit program.

6. Click OK after you make any changes.

The higher the quality of your video and audio settings, the slower iVisit works. In general, don't set the audio and video settings to their maximum unless you have a high-bandwidth Internet connection, such as a cable modem or T3 line.

Chatting in text mode

Talking over the computer can be fun, but sometimes you may prefer to type your messages, such as when you want to make sure the other person doesn't misunderstand your words. So rather than talking, you can chat in text mode.

Text mode appears in the Chat window, which displays two windows. The top window contains everything that you or the other chat room members type. The bottom window is where you type your messages so other people can read them.

Typing a message

The bottom-left corner of the Chat window may display one of two messages: Ready or Not Connected. The Ready message tells you that you're connected to a chat room and anything you type and send will be seen by other chat room members. If the Not Connected message appears, nothing you type will be seen by anyone else until you connect with another person by contacting them directly (see the "Calling Another Person with iVisit" section) or through a conference (see the "Joining an iVisit Conference" section).

If you want to send a private message to another person, click the Send Private Audio Chat button in the video window of the person you want to chat with in private, as shown in Figure 11-15.

Figure 11-15: You can hold a private conversation through iVisit.

Send Private Audio Chat button

To type a message in the Chat window, follow these steps:

1. **Click in the bottom window of the Chat window.**

2. **Type your message.**

   You can edit, delete, or modify your message at this time. After you press the Enter key to send your message, you cannot modify it, so make sure you don't say anything really stupid or insulting that you may later regret.

3. **Press Enter after you're sure that you want to send your message.**

   When your message appears in the top half of the Chat window, other chat room members can read it.

Saving a chat room conversation

Sometimes you may join a chat room and find the conversation so interesting that you want to save it for future reference (or as evidence against someone breaking the law).

The iVisit program saves chat room conversations in an ordinary text file, which can be opened and modified by any word processing program. To save a chat room conversation, follow these steps:

1. **Choose File⇨Save in the Chat window.**

   The Save As dialog box appears.

   If you want to save your chat room conversation under a different name, choose File⇨Save As. Doing so can be handy if, after you have already saved the existing conversation in a file, someone adds new text that you want to save as well. Rather than erase the old file, just save the conversation in a new file.

2. **Type a name for your file.**

   You may want to switch to a different folder to save your text mode conversations.

3. **Click Save.**

   iVisit saves the current chat room as a file.

Rather than save the entire chat room conversation as a text file, you can highlight the text you want to save by choosing Edit⇨Copy and then pasting the text into a separate word processing document.

Clearing the Chat window

Sometimes a chat room conversation can contain so many messages from different people that your Chat window starts to look cluttered. If you want to clear the top window of the Chat window, choose Edit⇨Clear.

If you clear the chat room window, you can't save the text in a file. So if there's something you want to save in the Chat window, save it before clearing the window.

Defining your chat room settings

To give you a feeling of control, iVisit lets you modify the way your Chat window works by enabling you to choose the font, type size, and the way the Chat window highlights conversations.

To define your chat room settings, follow these steps:

1. **Choose Settings⇨Preferences in the Chat window.**

   The Preferences dialog box appears, as shown in Figure 11-16.

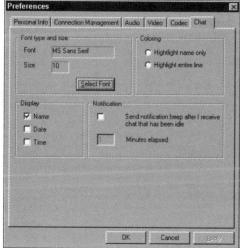

Figure 11-16:
The Preferences dialog box lets you modify the way text appears in the Chat window.

2. **Click the Chat tab.**

3. **Click any options you want to change.**

   For example, clicking the Select Font button allows you to choose a different font, type size, and color for your text. Some of the other options on the Chat tab lets you display the name, date, and time with each person in a chat room (instead of just a name), which could be useful if you plan to save the text of a chat room for later reference.

4. **Click OK after you make all your changes.**

   iVisit saves your changes.

Making your own chat room

Visiting public chat rooms can be an enjoyable way to meet other people, but sometimes you may want to create a private chat room for just you and your friends, where strangers aren't wandering in and getting in the way. To make your own chat room, follow these steps:

1. **If the Directory window isn't visible, choose Windows⇨Directory.**

   The Directory window appears (see Figure 11-17).

2. **Click the Mode drop-down list and choose Server.**

3. **Double-click the conference folder in which you want to create your chat room. For example, if you want to create a chat room inside the Business folder, double-click that folder.**

4. **Click the Create Server Heading button, as shown in Figure 11-17.**

   The Create New Room/Listing dialog box appears.

Figure 11-17:
Making your
own chat
room is
easy.

Create Server Heading button

5. **Click the Room radio button.**

6. **Type a name for your private chat room in the Name box.**

7. **Type any additional information you want others to know about your private chat room in the Comment box.**

8. **Type a password in the Password box.**

   If you don't care who joins, leave the Password box empty. Otherwise, people will need the password to join, which you can give them through an instant messaging program like ICQ, which can notify you immediately as your friends connect to the Internet.

9. **Type the maximum number of people you want the chat room to hold in the Size Limit box.**

10. **Click OK.**

Your private chat room is ready for others to enter.

After you finish using your chat room, click the Delete Owned Heading button, as shown in Figure 11-18, to remove the chat room.

Figure 11-18:
You can delete a chat room of your own creation after you're done using it.

Delete Owned Heading button

Dealing with Strangers (Or Strange People)

No matter how careful you may be, you're likely to run into some obnoxious or deranged person who wants to say something obscene or show you body parts or other disgusting objects that you'd prefer not to see. To deal with these less-than-desirable people, click one of the following four toggle buttons, shown in Figure 11-19, to stop the connection:

- ✔ Stop Receiving Video
- ✔ Stop Incoming Chat
- ✔ Stop Incoming Audio
- ✔ Stop Private Audio Chat

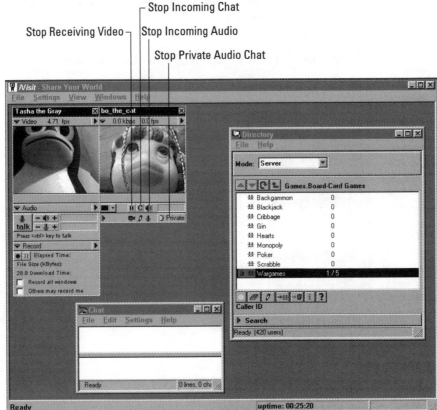

Stop Incoming Chat

Stop Receiving Video ⌐ Stop Incoming Audio

Stop Private Audio Chat

Figure 11-19:
Keep these
buttons
handy for
cutting off
someone
in a hurry.

By clicking any of these buttons in the video window of the person you want to ignore, you can avoid hearing or seeing anything that person may have to say or show.

For greater privacy, you can send a private message to another person by clicking the Send Private Audio Chat button in the video window of the person you want to chat with in private. (See the "Chatting with audio" section.) Or you can create your own chat room and password protect it so that no one except you and your friends can get together to chat. (See the "Making your own chat room" section.)

Chapter 12

Playing Games with Your Web Cam

In This Chapter

▶ Understanding how Web cam games work

▶ Playing Web cam games

▶ Making your own games

*B*esides using a computer for work or business, many people use their computers for playing games, chatting with friends, or goofing off (so they don't have to do any work). Furthermore, most people don't use their Web cams just for videoconferencing. Besides taking goofy pictures of themselves or their pets, people use their Web cams to play interactive games, courtesy of a new company called Reality Fusion.

Reality Fusion gives away several of its games with some Web cams, such as certain models sold by Intel and Logitech. Reality Fusion also provides several games for free that you can download from its Web site at www. realityfusion.com. This chapter introduces you to some of the free Web cam games developed by Reality Fusion.

Keep in mind that the Reality Fusion games work only with Windows. If you have a Macintosh, you have to use a Windows emulation program such as Virtual PC by Connectix (www.connectix.com) or SoftWindows by FWB Software (www.fwb.com).

How Reality Fusion Games Work

Instead of making games that require virtual reality helmets, goggles, and handheld controls, Reality Fusion makes games that work by using your Web cam to display your image directly into a game.

After your image appears inside the game, you control the game by moving, waving your hand, jumping up and down, or kicking. The game uses motion-detection technology to determine when your arm (or other body part) makes contact with an object, such as a ball. When the game detects that contact has been made, the object bounces away as if you had physically hit it yourself. Playing a Reality Fusion game may give you more exercise than going to the gym!

Installing a Reality Fusion game

Although this book includes some of the many Web cam games available from Reality Fusion, you may also have some Reality Fusion games that came with a CD-ROM bundled with your Web cam, or you may have downloaded some additional games from the Reality Fusion Web site.

To install a Reality Fusion game using the CD-ROM that came bundled with your Web cam, follow these steps:

1. **Insert the Reality Fusion CD-ROM.**

   When you insert the Reality Fusion CD-ROM into your computer, an installation screen appears. If an installation screen does not appear, click the Start button on the Windows taskbar, choose Run, click Browse, and search the CD-ROM drive (usually identified as drive D or E) to find a file with a name such as SETUP.EXE or INSTALL.EXE. Click Open and then click OK.

2. **Follow the instructions on the installation screen.**

   The installation program may ask you to define the directory where you want to store your game.

3. **Choose the options you want (such as defining a new directory) to install your games.**

   The installation program installs your games to your hard drive.

To install a Reality Fusion game that you have downloaded from the Reality Fusion Web site, follow these steps:

1. **Download the Reality Fusion game that you want.**

   The game will be stored in a file with a name such as SETUP.EXE or INSTALL.EXE.

2. **Click the Start button on the Windows taskbar and choose Run.**

   A Run dialog box appears.

3. **Click Browse.**

   The Browse dialog box appears.

4. **Click the Reality Fusion file you just downloaded (you may have to search through different drives or folders) and click Open.**

   The Run dialog box appears again.

5. **Click OK.**

   The Reality Fusion installation program starts running.

6. **Follow the instructions on the installation screen.**

   The installation program may ask you to define the directory where you want to store your game.

7. **Choose the options you want (such as defining a new directory) to install your games.**

   The installation program installs your games to your hard drive.

To install a Reality Fusion game from the enclosed CD-ROM, follow these steps:

1. **Insert the CD-ROM from this book into your computer's CD-ROM drive.**

   The installation screen appears.

2. **Choose the Reality Fusion games and click OK.**

   The installation program installs the Reality Fusion games on your hard drive.

Configuring your Web cam

After the Reality Fusion installation is complete, a dialog box appears to help you configure your Web cam to work with the games. Of course, you can always configure your Web cam at a later time by following these steps:

1. **Click the Start button on the Windows taskbar and choose Programs⇨Reality Fusion.**

   A pop-up menu appears. Instead of displaying the exact name "Reality Fusion," the menu may display a name such as "Reality Fusion Game Cam" or some other slight variation.

2. **Choose the Reality Fusion Camera Connection Wizard.**

   The Reality Fusion Camera Connection Wizard dialog box appears, showing you how your Web cam images will look in a Reality Fusion game, as shown in Figure 12-1.

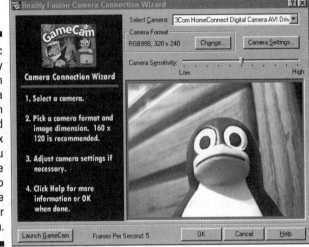

Figure 12-1:
The Reality
Fusion
Camera
Connection
Wizard
dialog box
lets you
adjust the
video
appearance
from your
Web cam.

3. **Choose the options you want to adjust on your Web cam's video image.**

    For example, you may need to adjust the image size or sensitivity of your Web cam.

4. **Click OK after you finish adjusting your Web cam.**

    You're ready to start playing a Reality Fusion game.

Although most Reality Fusion Web cam games work with all brands and models of different Web cams, the games may not work with your particular Web cam. If this happens, you either have to buy a different Web cam or contact Reality Fusion to see if a patch or update is available for your particular Web cam.

Playing a Reality Fusion Game

After configuring your Web cam to work with Reality Fusion games, you're ready to start playing a Web cam game. After you load the Reality Fusion game (depending on the version and type of Reality Fusion games you have), you may see an interface like the one shown in Figure 12-2.

Figure 12-2:
The Reality
Fusion
GameCam
provides an
easy-to-use
interface for
choosing
the games
you want to
play.

This interface displays buttons that represent the various Web cam games available and the current image displayed from your Web cam. (If this image looks bad, you may need to reconfigure your Web cam, as explained in the previous section, "Configuring your Web cam.")

Three of the more common types of games Reality Fusion offers include the following:

✔ **Ball games.** In these games, you try to shoot a ball into a basketball hoop, as shown in Figure 12-3, or over a volleyball net.

✔ **Fighting games.** In these games, you kick or punch at a cartoon target that is trying to kick and punch you right back, as shown in Figure 12-4.

✔ **Silly diversions.** These aren't so much games as they are amusing ways to use your Web cam. One playful use is to paste a Web cam image over the face of an existing photograph, as shown in Figure 12-5.

Figure 12-3:
You can
bounce a
basketball
off your
head, hand,
or leg (or
other body
part).

Figure 12-4:
Practice
your martial
arts skills by
fighting an
animated
figure.

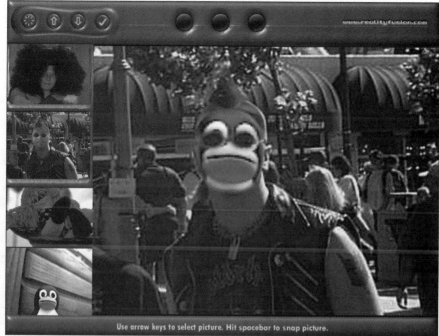

Use arrow keys to select picture. Hit spacebar to snap picture.

Figure 12-5:
Have fun
with your
Web cam by
creating
silly images.

Customizing a Reality Fusion game

You may want to customize some of the Reality Fusion games to modify the
difficulty level, change the animated opponents on the screen, or include an
image from your Web cam in the game. Figure 12-6 shows an option that
enables you to capture someone's face and paste that image onto your
opponent's body.

Playing a Reality Fusion game

The Reality Fusion games work by capturing an image from your Web cam and
displaying that image in a box within the Reality Fusion game. To get maximum enjoyment from these games, you may want to follow these guidelines:

✔ Focus and configure your Web cam to work with the Reality Fusion
   games. (See the "Configuring your Web cam" section earlier in this chapter.) If the image from your Web cam is blurry, the game won't properly
   detect any movement you make in front of your Web cam.

✔ Wait until the game ball (or other object) appears inside the box that
   contains the video image from your Web cam before you try to hit it.

✔ Move slowly and precisely. Waving your hands rapidly in front of your Web cam displays a blur, which the game may interpret as empty space and allow a game ball or other object to pass right through.

✔ Avoid wearing baggy clothing, dangling bracelets, or other objects that may move at the same time you move your arm or hand. The Web cam games work by detecting movement, and they can't determine the difference between a moving hand or a moving bracelet. (If your bracelet moves, it could hit the ball.)

Figure 12-6:
Some Reality Fusion games let you paste an image from your Web cam to appear on an opponent or in the background.

Developing Your Own Games

If you're really motivated by the technology you see in the Reality Fusion games, you can make up your own games or applications that use motion-detection technology. Create the next killer game where players hunt down monsters in a maze, or make a presentation kiosk (a free-standing video screen and computer) that doesn't require a touch screen (which results in messy fingerprint smudges) for people to look up information at museums, airports, or any other public location. For you hardy souls who are willing to dig into programming, Reality Fusion sells a Software Development Kit (SDK) that enables you to write your own programs for detecting motion through a Web cam. Currently the SDK only supports C or C++ programming, but future versions of the SDK will support more popular languages, such as Visual Basic or Java.

Part IV
Having More Fun with Your Web Cam

The 5th Wave   By Rich Tennant

"The doctor wants to know if he can perform your endoscopy with a Web cam for the hospital Web site."

In this part . . .

To help you get the most out of your Web cam, this part of the book describes some of the more offbeat ways to use your Web cam. One intriguing use for Web cams is to play special Web cam games. Instead of forcing you to wear bulky and expensive virtual reality gear, these latest Web cam games let you point a Web cam at yourself to see your image projected on the screen. Whenever you move, your image moves within the game, giving you a chance to hit moving objects around the screen.

If you don't like playing games, don't worry. This part of the book also shows you how to use Web cam images to create your own desktop images and screen savers. For more fun, use your Web cam to send still and video images to others via e-mail. Your Web cam can do much more than you think. Just read this part of the book and start experimenting today.

Chapter 13

Customizing Your Desktop

• •

In This Chapter

▶ Customizing the Windows desktop

▶ Customizing the Macintosh desktop

▶ Customizing your startup screen

▶ Customizing your icons

▶ Designing and editing your own icons

• •

*T*his chapter explains how to change the way your Windows or Macintosh computer displays its desktop. The *desktop* is the background image that appears as soon as you start your computer, before you start running programs such as games, word-processing programs, or Web browsers. Generally, the desktop shows a plain color along with some icons that represent the various programs.

Although functional, a plain desktop is not very interesting to look at. So, to spice up your computer, both Windows and Macintosh computers offer the option of changing the appearance of your desktop to display different colors and pictures, including images captured from your Web cam.

Changing the Windows Desktop

You can add any BMP, GIF, or JPEG graphic file to your Windows desktop in three different ways:

✔ **Center.** This method displays a single image in the middle of the screen and is best for large images that are easy to see.

✔ **Stretch.** This method enlarges a single image to fill the entire screen, as shown in Figure 13-1.

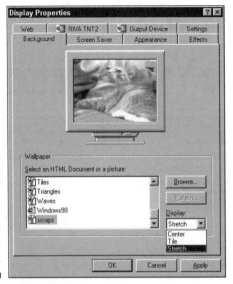

Figure 13-1:
The
Windows
desktop
can display
a bitmap
image
to fill up
the entire
screen.

✔ **Tile.** This method fills the entire screen with multiple copies of a single image and is best for displaying repetitive patterns, as shown in Figure 13-2.

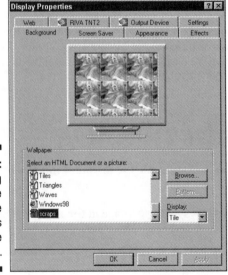

Figure 13-2:
Tiling
places the
same image
in rows
across the
screen.

Windows 95 can use only BMP files.

To customize your Windows desktop, follow these steps:

1. **Store or convert your designed image into a bitmap (BMP) file format.**

2. **Click the Start button on the Windows taskbar and choose Settings⇨Control Panel.**

   The Control Panel window appears.

3. **Double-click the Display icon.**

   The Display Properties dialog box appears.

4. **Click the Background tab.**

   The Background tab shows your current desktop.

5. **Click the Browse button.**

   A dialog box appears, offering a range of files you can open.

   This dialog box has an ongoing identity crisis; what you see on-screen depends on the version of Windows you're running. Windows 95 calls the box *Browsing for wallpaper;* in Windows 98, an Open dialog box appears. In Windows Me, it's a Browse dialog box.

6. **Click the bitmap image you want.**

   If you click the File Name pull-down list box, you can select a graphic image that you have chosen before.

   Click the icons in the middle of the dialog box. If you want to select a previously chosen bitmap image, click in the pull-down or scroll-down list of filenames. You may have to change drives or folders to find the file you want.

7. **Click Open (OK in Windows 95).**

8. **Select the Center, Tile, or Stretch option from the Display drop-down list box.**

   In Windows Me, this box calls itself the Picture Display list box; in Windows 98, it's just a Display list box. The struggle for box identity rages on, accompanied (as ever) by temporary confusion.

   The Display Properties dialog box shows how your chosen image looks, as shown in Figure 13-3.

9. **Click OK.**

   Your chosen image appears on your Windows desktop.

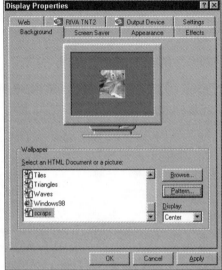

Figure 13-3:
The Display
Properties
dialog box
shows a
preview
of your
desktop
with the
selected
image.

Choose your desktop image carefully. Some images make your icons extremely difficult to see. If an image looks horrible as a tiled image, it may look better as a stretched or centered image, or vice versa.

Changing the Macintosh Desktop

The Macintosh gives you the choice of placing PICT, TIFF, GIF, or JPEG files on your desktop in five different ways:

- ✔ **Tile on Screen.** This method displays multiple copies of a single image across your desktop.

- ✔ **Center on Screen.** This method displays a single image in the center of the screen.

- ✔ **Scale to Screen.** This method proportionally enlarges a single image to fill up the screen. Unlike the Fill Screen option below, this option won't stretch or unnaturally distort an image to fill up the screen.

- ✔ **Fill Screen.** This method enlarges a single image to fill the entire screen. For some images, this option may stretch the image and distort its appearance.

- ✔ **Position Automatically.** This method places your image on the desktop as Scale to Screen or Center on Screen, depending on the size of the image.

To change the appearance of your desktop, follow these steps:

1. In the Apple menu choose⇨Control Panels⇨Appearance.

The Appearance dialog box appears.

2. Click the Desktop tab, as shown in Figure 13-4.

Figure 13-4:
The Appear-
ance dialog
box shows
a preview
of your
desktop
with your
chosen
image.

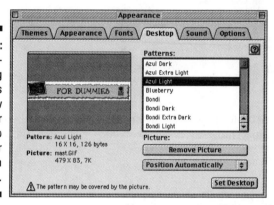

If you drag a picture to the sample screen shown in the Appearance
dialog box, you can skip Steps 3 through 5.

3. Click the Place Picture button.

The Choose a File dialog box appears.

4. Select the PICT, TIFF, GIF, or JPEG file that you want to use.

You may need to change folders to find the file you want.

5. Click Choose.

The Appearance dialog box shows you what your chosen graphic file
looks like.

**6. Click the list box directly under the Remove Picture button and
choose an option for displaying your chosen image, such as Tile on
Screen or Fill Screen.**

Figure 13-5 shows the result of choosing Tile on screen.

7. Click the Set Desktop button.

Your chosen image appears on your desktop.

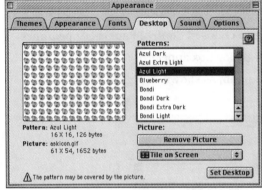

Figure 13-5:
Tiling
displays
multiple
copies of
the same
image on
the desktop.

If you want to remove a picture from your desktop, follow the preceding Steps 1 and 2, click the Remove Picture button, and then click the Set Desktop button.

Changing Your Startup Screen

After your computer starts up, a startup screen appears, usually the Windows 98 or Mac OS logo. Because this image isn't exactly exciting, you may want to create your own startup screen, using an image that you created or captured from your Web cam.

To create a startup screen for Windows, start with an image that's 640 x 480 pixels in size. If you plan to use an existing image, you may need to resize that image using a graphic editing program, as shown in Figure 13-6.

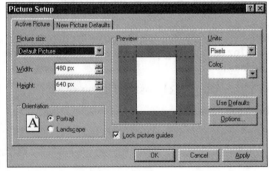

Figure 13-6:
Microsoft
PhotoDraw
can resize
an existing
graphic
image.

If you plan to use an image captured through your Web cam, make sure you save your Web cam image using the 640 x 480-pixel dimensions, as shown in Figure 13-7.

Figure 13-7:
Web cam
programs
give you an
option for
capturing
images at a
certain size.

Changing the Windows startup screen

Windows 95 stores the startup screen in a bitmap file called LOGO.SYS, located in the C:\WINDOWS directory. To change a Windows 95 startup screen, you need to replace this LOGO.SYS file with another bitmap file of your choice and name your new file LOGO.SYS.

Make a copy of your original Windows 95 LOGO.SYS file and name it LOGO.OLD or something similar, just in case you ever decide to use the original Windows startup screen again.

Unlike Windows 95, Windows 98 stores its startup screen image in a file called IO.SYS. To replace your Windows 98 startup screen image, you just need to copy any bitmap image to your C:\ directory and save the file under the name LOGO.SYS. The next time Windows 98 starts up, it will use the image stored in the LOGO.SYS file instead of the normal startup screen stored in the IO.SYS file.

To create a startup screen image for Windows, follow these steps:

1. **Click the Start button and choose Programs⇨Accessories⇨Paint.**

   The MS Paint program loads.

2. **Choose File⇨Open.**

   The Open dialog box appears.

3. **Select the image you want to use for your startup screen and click Open.**

4. **Choose Image⇨Attributes.**

   The Attributes dialog box appears, as shown in Figure 13-8.

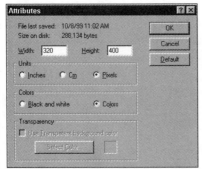

Figure 13-8:
Resize your
image in the
Attributes
dialog box.

5. **Select the Pixels radio button in the Units group.**

6. **Change the width of the image to 320 and the height to 400.**

7. **Click OK.**

The Paint program stores the height and width dimensions you chose in
Step 6.

8. **Choose File⇨Save As.**

The Save As dialog box appears.

9. **Select the C:\ directory in the Save In drop-down list box.**

10. **In the File Name text box, type "logo.sys" including the quotation marks.**

If you neglect to type the quotation marks, Windows won't save your file
with the proper .sys file extension.

11. **In the Save As Type list box, select 256 Color Bitmap (*.bmp; *.dib).**

12. **Click Save.**

The next time you start up your computer, Windows uses your new LOGO.SYS
image as your startup screen.

You can also change your Windows shutdown screens (which are stored in
two files in the C:\WINDOWS directory called LOGOS.SYS and LOGOW.SYS).
The LOGOS.SYS file contains the Windows logo along with the words Windows
is shutting down. The LOGOS.SYS file displays the words It's now safe
to turn off your computer. Just create your own bitmap graphic images
and save them in the C:\WINDOWS directory as LOGOS.SYS or LOGOW.SYS.

Changing the Macintosh startup screen

Normally, after you turn on a Macintosh, you see an image of the Mac OS
happy face with the Welcome To Macintosh salutation underneath.

However, you can change your Macintosh startup screen to display any image stored in the PICT file format.

Many graphics programs (such as LightningPaint) can save any picture as a Macintosh startup screen file type. To find a shareware graphics program that can do this, visit www.macdownload.com.

Not all graphics programs can save an image as a startup screen; so if your graphics program does not offer this feature, you may need to try another graphics program.

To save a picture as your startup screen by using a painting program, load the image you want to use or create a new image by using your graphics program. Then save the picture as a StartupScreen file type and give it the name StartupScreen, as shown in Figure 13-9.

Copy the StartupScreen image file into your System folder. The next time you start up your Macintosh, your image appears as the new startup screen.

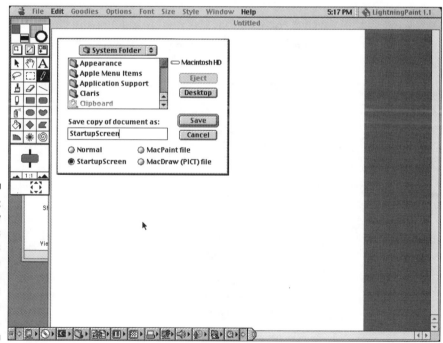

Figure 13-9:
Many graphics programs can save an image directly as a startup screen file.

Changing Your Icons

Both the Windows and Macintosh desktops display icons that represent some of the many programs stored on your hard drive. In case you don't like the look of your program icons, you can always edit them or create brand new ones of your own using an icon-editing program. (The end of this chapter lists some popular Windows and Macintosh icon-editing programs.)

You can turn any image into an icon, including any image that you previously captured from your Web cam. For best results, make sure the main object or person in your image appears as close to the center of the picture as possible. That way if you need to edit your icon, you can cut off the edges without losing any part of the main image.

Changing an icon in Windows

To change an icon in Windows, follow these steps:

1. **Right-click the icon that you want to change and choose Properties.**

   The Properties dialog box appears, as shown in Figure 13-10.

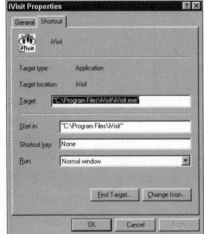

Figure 13-10: The Properties dialog box enables you to change icons.

2. **Click the Change Icon button.**

   The Change Icon window appears, as shown in Figure 13-11.

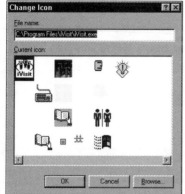

Figure 13-11:
The
Change
Icon
window
displays
alternate
icons you
can pick.

3. **Click Browse to choose the icon that you want to use.**

   (This icon can be an image that you captured with your Web cam and edited, or an image that you created from scratch using an icon-editing program.)

   A Change Icon dialog box appears.

4. **Select the icon file you want to use.**

   You may have to switch folders or drives to find the file you want.

   If you click a program file in Step 4, you can see and choose any alternate icons already created for that particular program.

5. **Click Open.**

   The Change Icon window shows your chosen icon. (Or if you clicked a program file, you see several alternate icons created for that particular program.)

6. **Click the icon that you want to use and then click OK.**

   The Properties dialog box appears again, showing your chosen icon.

7. **Click OK.**

Changing an icon on the Macintosh

To change an icon on a Macintosh, follow these steps:

1. **Copy (by selecting the image and choosing Edit⇨Copy) the new graphic image that you want to use for your icon.**

   You may need to load a graphics program first to display the image you want to use for your new icon.

2. **Select the icon on your desktop that you want to change.**

3. **Choose File⇨Get Info⇨General Information (or press ⌘+I).**

   The Navigator Info window appears, as shown in Figure 13-12.

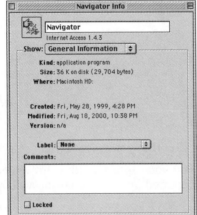

Figure 13-12:
Change
icons
in the
Navigator
Info
window.

4. **Click the icon that appears in the upper-left corner of the Navigator Info window.**

   A black line appears around the icon.

5. **Choose Edit⇨Paste.**

   The image you copied in Step 1 now appears in place of the icon in the Navigator Info window.

6. **Click the close box of the Navigator Info window.**

   The Navigator Info window disappears. Your icon now appears on the desktop.

Making your own icons

If you're really ambitious, you can draw your own icons from scratch, or use your Web cam to capture an image that you can edit and save for use as an icon. To make your own icons, you just need a little creativity and a special icon-editing program. Some features that most icon-editing programs offer include the following:

✔ **File format compatibility.** This feature enables you to convert a BMP, GIF, or JPEG graphic into an icon file.

✔ **Pixel editing.** This feature enables you to modify individual pixels, as shown in Figure 13-13, so you can create or edit a picture as part of your icon.

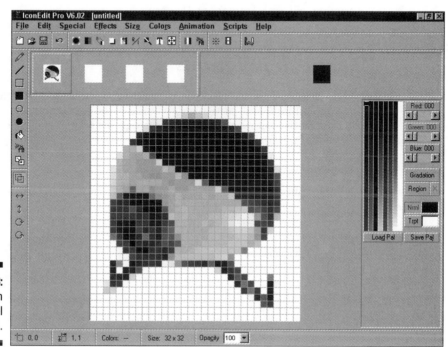

Figure 13-13:
Editing an
icon pixel
by pixel.

Creating your own icons can be stimulating and rewarding or tedious and boring, depending on how fancy and detailed you get with your icons.

Many freeware and shareware developers create entire libraries of icons that contain images from movies and TV shows, such as *Star Wars, James Bond,* or *The Simpsons.* You can find these icon libraries at Web sites such as www. download.com or www.macdownload.com.

Windows programs

If you want to customize your Windows desktop, try one of the following programs to help you create custom icons for all your programs and files:

AX-Icons (www.axialis.com)

IconBook (www.geocities.com/SiliconValley/Lab/2355)

IconForge (www.cursorarts.com)

Microangelo (www.impactsoft.com)

Macintosh programs

Because Macintosh people tend to believe they're more creative than the average person (and endearingly more modest, too!), you may want to get your hands on the following icon-editing programs so you can create and modify your Macintosh icons:

IconDropper (www.iconfactory.com)

Iconographer (www.mscape.com/products/iconographer.html)

Icon Machine (www.iconmachine.com)

Chapter 14

Making a Screen Saver

In This Chapter

▶ Creating your own screen saver

▶ Finding a screen-saver-creation program

▶ Writing your own screen-saver program

*A*fter discovering some of the more common ways to use your Web cam for posting images on a Web site or sending video e-mail to friends and relatives, you may be wondering what else you can do with your Web cam.

Because you've probably already used your Web cam to take pictures of everything within reach of your Web cam's attached cable, you may want to put some of those Web cam images to good use by using them in a screen saver.

A screen saver blanks out your monitor after a period of inactivity (for some people, that period of inactivity could be the entire time they're at work) and displays a constantly changing image on the monitor.

In the old days, screen savers protected against a problem known as "phosphor burn-in," which occurs when the same image appears on a monitor for long periods of time. Eventually that image physically etches itself on the screen, essentially ruining the monitor.

Fortunately, today's monitors are often smart enough to turn themselves off automatically after a period of inactivity to prevent phosphor burn-in. People still use screen savers nowadays, for fun (to display sports stars or celebrities) or for business (to advertise their business). In this chapter, you find out how to turn images from your Web cam into a screen saver for any Macintosh or Windows computer.

Making Your Own Screen Saver

Although you can use the screen savers that came with your computer, you may want to create your own. Many people create screen savers for fun that display pictures of their dog or parakeet. Some people use screen savers as a marketing tool, making a really cool screen saver with images that others will want to put on their own computers (and thus display their company logo in the process).

To make a screen saver, you need two items: video or still images (such as any image captured through your Web cam) and a screen-saver-creation program. To create a screen saver, you need to follow these steps:

1. **Capture one or more video or still images with your Web cam.**

   Depending on your screen-saver-creation program, you may need to save your Web cam images in a specific file format such as AVI, BMP, or GIF. You can also use still images from other sources, such as scanned images or artwork created using a graphics program such as Adobe Photoshop.

2. **Start your screen-saver-creation program.**

3. **Load the video files or still images that you want to appear in your screen saver.**

   If you import multiple still images, such as GIF or JPEG files, into your screen-saver-creation program, as shown in Figure 14-1, you can create a slideshow-type screen saver that displays one image for several seconds before displaying the next one.

After Dark: The granddaddy of screen savers

One of the most popular screen savers of all time was called After Dark, marketed by Berkeley Systems www.berksys.com. After Dark single-handedly created the screen saver market with a popular screen saver program that displayed flying toasters and slices of bread that would float from one side of the screen to the other.

Sales of After Dark initially soared, but sales have been slowly shrinking now that most computer monitors have special energy-saving features that automatically shut off the screen after a specified amount of time. In addition, the latest versions of Windows have built-in screen savers. Even worse is that the current version of After Dark no longer runs on the latest version of Macintosh and Windows computers.

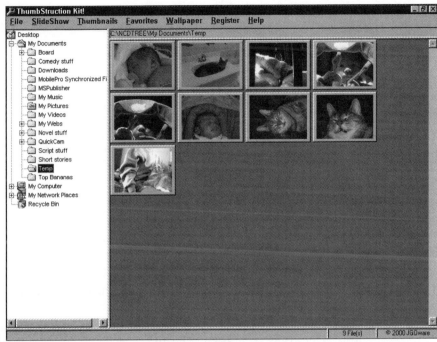

Figure 14-1:
Multiple graphic files create a slideshow effect for your screen saver.

To help keep in touch with loved ones, create a screen saver showing you and your family in different poses. Then give your screen-saver file to your friends and relatives, so they can see your family pictures whenever their screen saver starts up.

As an alternative to creating a slideshow-type screen saver, many screen-saver-creation programs also let you import video files such as AVI or QuickTime videos, so you can play your video when your screen saver runs. (For example, you can have a video of yourself waving at your Web cam.)

4. **Edit your images.**

   After you import a graphic image into your screen saver, you may want to rearrange its position, flip or rotate it, or resize the image to fit the entire screen. Many screen-saver-creation programs provide simple editing capabilities so you can change the way the images appear on the screen. Your screen saver can use Hollywood-style movie effects such as sliding images from left to right; bursting on the screen like a firecracker; or showing images fade, dissolve, or wipe away from the screen, as shown in Figure 14-2.

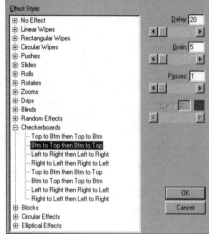

Figure 14-2:
Transitions
give your
individual
screen
saver
images a
Hollywood-
style effect.

5. **Add any audio recordings (such as music or recordings of your voice captured from a microphone) to your screen saver.**

   Audio files can be as simple as brief sound effects, such as a bell ringing or a clock ticking, or as complicated as an entire song or speech. You can make your screen saver a little more interesting by playing your favorite song, your own voice stating affirmations (such as "I am losing weight every day" or "I will find a better job and get out of this company"), or goofy insults that you install on your boss's computer for extra laughs . . . just kidding, of course.

   Because you're going to listen to the same sound every time the screen saver starts up, you may want to pick an unobtrusive sound such as a babbling brook, waves crashing on a shore, or a thunderstorm. Sounds such as these are pleasant and won't distract others.

   Use sound sparingly. Although the novelty of having your screen saver play heavy metal music whenever your computer is idle may be tempting, ask yourself if you really want to hear the same song every time your screen saver runs. If you work in a crowded office, your colleagues probably don't want to hear your screen saver making noises whenever you leave your computer, either. When in doubt, leave the sound out.

6. **Save your screen saver as a separate file.**

   Windows screen-saver-creation programs often give you the choice of saving your file in the Windows screen saver format (with an scr file extension) or as a self-installing exe file that you can distribute to others.

7. **Install your screen saver on your computer.**

   If your screen-saver-creation program allows you to create an installation program that will install your screen saver automatically, you can just run that installation program. But some screen-saver-creation programs create a screen-saver file that you must install manually. If that's the case, see the next sections.

To see how you can give away screen savers to help promote your business, visit the Resources for Success Web site (www.newdreams.com) or the Options Success Coaching Web site (www.successoptions.com), where you can download a free screen saver that provides motivational, inspirational, and humorous quotes on your screen.

Installing a screen saver in Windows

Windows comes with a built-in program to display screen-saver images. When you use a separate screen-saver-creation program to create a screen saver, you're actually creating the images you want to appear when the Windows screen saver program runs.

To install a screen saver to run within Windows, you need to save your screen saver in the C:\Windows\System folder as shown in Figure 14-3.

Figure 14-3:
A screen-saver-creation program automates the process of saving your screen saver in the proper file format and folder on your hard drive.

Windows screen-saver files always end with the scr file extension.

After you store your screen saver in the C:\Windows\System folder, you still need to select that screen saver to run when your computer is idle. To choose a screen saver, follow these steps:

1. **Click the Start button on the Windows taskbar.**

   A pop-up menu appears.

2. **Choose Settings⇨Control Panel.**

   A Control Panel window appears.

3. **Double-click the Display icon.**

   The Display Properties dialog box appears.

4. **Click the Screen Saver tab.**

   The Display Properties dialog box displays a Screen Saver list box for choosing the screen saver you want to use, as shown in Figure 14-4.

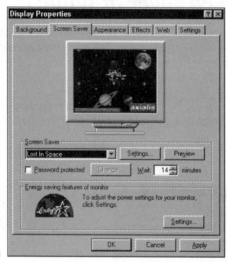

Figure 14-4:
From the Display Properties dialog box you can preview the different screen savers available on your computer.

5. **Click in the Screen Saver list box and choose the name of the screen saver you want to use, such as Flying Windows or 3D Maze.**

   The Display Properties dialog box displays a preview of your chosen screen saver.

6. **Click in the Wait text box and type the number of minutes you want Windows to wait before running your screen saver.**

7. **(Optional) Click in the Password protected check box.**

   If you choose this option, you will need to type a password to turn off the screen saver and access your computer. If you don't want to password-protect your screen saver, skip to Step 11.

   Password-protecting your screen saver can prevent people from using your computer when your screen saver is running, but don't count on a password-protected screen saver to protect your computer, because an intruder can just turn your computer off and on again to avoid any password-protected screen saver.

8. **Click the Change button.**

   A Change Password dialog box appears.

9. **Type the identical password in the New Password and Confirm New Password text boxes and then click OK.**

   A dialog box appears to inform you that you have successfully changed your screen saver's password.

10. **Click OK.**

    The Display Properties dialog box appears again.

11. **Click the Preview button.**

    Your monitor shows how the screen saver looks when it fills the entire screen.

12. **Press Enter.**

    The Display Properties dialog box appears again.

13. **Click OK.**

    Your chosen screen saver will now run whenever your computer is idle for the amount of time you specified in Step 6.

Installing a screen saver for the Macintosh

Unlike Windows, the Macintosh operating system does not include a built-in screen-saver program. As a result, installing a Macintosh screen saver requires installing the actual program that controls the screen saver plus any images and sounds that you want your screen saver to play.

Most Macintosh screen-saver-creation programs provide their own specific instructions for installing the program, but in general, you need to follow these steps:

1. **Copy the screen-saver program into the Control Panels or Startup Items folder located inside your System Folder.**

   This ensures that the next time you start your Macintosh, the screen saver program will load and be able to detect when your computer has been idle for a specific period of time.

2. **Copy any additional files (such as graphic or sound files) inside the System Folder.**

   This ensures that the screen-saver program can find the graphic and sound files it needs to play when your computer goes idle.

3. **Open the screen-saver program to specify settings such as the amount of time to wait before running.**

   With many screen-saver programs, you need to click the Apple menu and choose Control Panels and the name of your screen-saver program to display a Settings or Preferences dialog box, as shown in Figure 14-5.

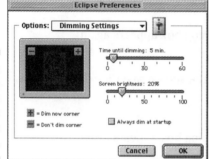

Figure 14-5:
Defining
the settings
for a
Macintosh
screen saver.

Choosing a Screen-Saver-Creation Program

Like all types of programs, screen-saver-creation programs vary widely in ease of use and number and types of features offered. Before you buy any screen-saver-creation program, download the trial version or experiment with different free versions offered by other companies. By toying around with a screen-saver-creation program, you can see which features you like and want and which ones you don't need.

To show you some of the different screen savers people have created using various screen-saver-creation programs, visit Mac Screensavers (www.macscreensavers.com) and ScreenSaver Gallery (www.screensavergallery.com). Both Web sites provide plenty of screen savers that you can download and install on your own computer.

By studying these screen savers from others, you may get ideas for creating your own screen savers. Then you can post them on these Web sites for other people to enjoy as well.

Windows programs

If the idea of creating your own screen saver with your computer appeals to your sense of wonder and adventure, then browse through the following list of companies that sell or give away screen-saver-creation programs. By experimenting with these programs, you can create your own screen savers or use (and modify) the sample screen savers that come with each program:

TECHNICAL STUFF

Search for extraterrestrials

The University of California, Berkeley, has developed one of the more creative uses for screen savers. Because screen savers start running whenever the computer is idle, scientists involved in SETI (Search for Extraterrestrial Intelligence) research have created a free screen saver called SETI@home (http://setiathome.ssl.berkeley.edu).

The idea behind SETI is that if scientists constantly scan the skies for radio signals, they may one day pick up a signal that provides proof that intelligent life exists somewhere in outer space. Unfortunately, most of the radio signals that SETI picks up are random signals created by natural causes. The trick is to sift through the multitude of radio signals and find one that actually was generated by intelligent life.

Because analyzing this mass of data requires massive computing resources, the scientists at the University of California, Berkeley, decided to break up the analysis into small chunks of data and have each chunk of data examined by the multitude of personal computers in the world.

So the SETI@home project provides a free screen saver that anyone can load on his or her Windows or Macintosh computer. Periodically, the screen saver connects to the University of California, Berkeley, server to download data to analyze. When the computer is idle, the SETI@home screen saver runs and starts searching its current chunk of radio signal data for signs of extraterrestrial life, such as specific and regular patterns. (In the movie "Contact," that pattern consisted of signals that counted out a series of prime numbers starting with one, three, five, seven, and so on. The logic behind prime numbers is that the chance of random radio signals broadcasting prime numbers is extremely low, hence the evidence that the signals must have come from intelligent life.)

If your computer doesn't find any signs of intelligent life, the SETI@home screen saver sends the data back to the University of California, Berkeley, and grabs another packet of data to analyze. By using the combined computer resources of people scattered all over the planet, scientists hope to sort through the data faster than they could possibly do on their own.

Who knows? Your computer may one day prove that intelligent life really does exist in the universe after all. By helping find intelligent life on other planets, you could be part of a major accomplishment that could get you and your personal computer into the history books.

- ✔ 123 Slide Master & Screensaver (www.n-media.com/slide.htm)
- ✔ Active Media Eclipse (www.active-media-online.com)
- ✔ AVI/MPG Screensaver (www.softdd.com/aviscrn/index.htm)
- ✔ Axialis Professional Screensaver Producer (www.axialis.com/ssp/index.html)
- ✔ GraFX Saver (www.cdhnow.com/gs.html)

✔ JPG Screensaver and SST Screensaver Toolbox (www.midnightblue.com/jpgsaver.htm)

The JPG Screensaver program is free to use and copy without any restrictions. However the SST Screensaver Toolbox program is shareware and requires payment to use.

✔ Simple Viewer (www.blown.com/simple)

✔ Slides Shower (http://members.aol.com/doanc/slshower.html)

✔ Thumbstruktion Set (http://jgoware.com/thumbstructionkit.htm)

✔ WebCam Sam (www.vista-x.com)

WebCam Sam is an unusual screen-saver program that can connect to Web cams located around the world and display those Web cam images to create a screen saver for your computer, as shown in Figure 14-6. Best of all, WebCam Sam is free.

✔ WinCycler (http://208.141.54.156/html/download.html)

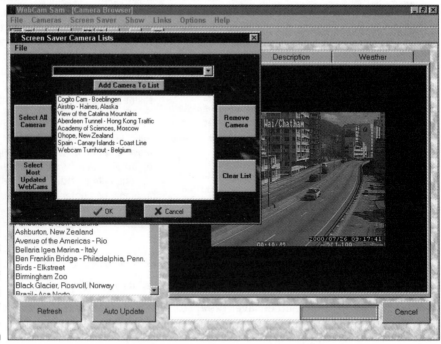

Figure 14-6: WebCam Sam can create a screen saver that shows you live views of Web cams from all over the planet.

Macintosh programs

Although the Macintosh comes with the built-in ability to blank-out its screen when the computer is idle, you may still want to create your own screen savers to give away to others or use for your own computer. Browse through the following Web sites where you can download free or trial versions of screen-saver-creation programs for your Macintosh.

- Eclipse (www.ambrosiasw.com)
- Photos4us (www.zoetek.com/entrance/Photos4us)

Advanced Computer Programming: Writing Your Own Screen-Saver-Creation Program

Computer programmers can't resist a challenge. When the first commercial screen saving programs appeared, programmers around the world immediately wanted to know how they worked, so they could write their own programs to create and display screen savers.

After the first hardy batch of programmers taught themselves the technical details of controlling the monitor and working with the operating system, they published articles and released the source code of their programs so anyone could read, study, and create their own screen-saver-creation programs absolutely free.

As with any type of program, you can write a screen-saver-creation program using any programming language such as C/C++, Pascal, BASIC, or assembly language. After you choose a programming language, the next step is to get a compiler for your programming language. Table 14-1 lists some of the more popular language compilers available.

Although the technical details involved in writing a screen-saver-creation program are far beyond the scope of this book (if you need help figuring out how to program a computer, consider buying *Beginning Programming For Dummies, C For Dummies, C++ For Dummies,* or *Visual Basic For Dummies,* all published by IDG Books Worldwide), take a look at the following Web sites that offer tips, explanations, and source code for actual working screen-saver-creation programs that you can study, copy, and modify on your own.

Table 14-1	Popular Language Compilers		
Compiler Name	**Web Site**	**Languages Used**	**Operating System**
CodeWarrior	www.metrowerks.com	C/C++ and Java	Windows and Macintosh
C++ Builder	www.borland.com	C/C++	Windows and Linux
Delphi	www.borland.com	Pascal	Windows and Linux
RealBasic	www.realbasic.com	BASIC	Macintosh
Visual Basic	www.microsoft.com	BASIC	Windows
Visual C++	www.microsoft.com	C/C++	Windows

The main difference between separate screen-saver-creation programs and the source code for the screen-saver-creation programs I discuss in the following section is that separate screen-saver-creation programs provide a fancy user interface to help you select the images and sound files you want your screen saver program to play.

The following screen-saver-creation programs simply provide the source code to create a screen saver, which means you still have to write the actual program commands to define how you want your screen saver to behave, such as which images to play, how long to wait before running, or how bright or dark to display a graphic image.

If you want to create your own screen savers quickly and easily, get a separate screen-saver-creation program with a fancy user interface. If you want to find out more about programming, then dig into the source code for a screen-saver-creation program and see how good of a programmer you really are.

A complete screen saver framework using MFC

This Web site provides the source code for a Visual C++ screen-saver-creation program that makes Windows screen savers. You can download the Visual C++ source code from

```
http://codeguru.earthweb.com/misc/scrfrmwk.shtml
```

MFC stands for Microsoft Foundation Classes, which consists of C++ code that forms the foundation of nearly all programs written in Visual C++, including Microsoft Word, Excel, and Windows.

Inprise Corporation

This Web site provides a technical paper — called *Creating a 32-Bit Screen Saver in 32-Bit Delphi,* written by Borland's technical support staff — that explains how to write a Windows screen saver program using Delphi. You can read the technical paper and copy the Delphi source code to the screen-saver-creation program from

```
http://community.borland.com/article/0,1410,19534,00.html
```

Nubz screen saver

This Web site provides the source code for a screen-saver-creation program written in the RealBasic language for the Macintosh. You can download the RealBasic source code from

```
www.nubz.org/news.html
```

Scrplus/BCB Screensaver Development Kit

This Web site provides a Borland C++ Builder add-on program source code to help you create Windows screen savers using the C++ programming language. You can download a free trial version of the add-on program, or buy the commercial version if you plan on distributing your screen savers commercially. To download the trial version of the program or to read more about this screen saver development kit, visit

```
www.wischik.com/scr/scrbcb.html
```

Visual Basic Screensaver Tutorial

This Web site provides explanations and actual source code for creating a Windows screen saver using the Visual Basic programming language. You can read the technical article and download the Visual basic source code from

```
http://members.xoom.com/micahcarrick/tutsaver.htm
```

Chapter 15

Sending Video by E-Mail

. . . .

. . . .

*A*lthough posting your Web cam images to a Web site or chatting with friends or strangers in a videoconference can be a great way of communicating, you may have noticed the limitations of these wonderful technologies. If you have a slow modem, viewing a video file from a Web page can be frustrating because you wait seemingly forever for the video file to download to your computer. Videoconferencing isn't much better because the video often appears chunky and fuzzy. The problem with slow-loading and poor-quality video boils down to bandwidth. 56K modems simply don't have the speed necessary for sending and displaying live video images very well.

Until everyone on the Internet has a fast connection (such as a cable or DSL modem), the next best solution is video e-mail, which enables you to send and receive video files by e-mail. Unlike videoconferencing, which requires all participants to attend the meeting in real time, you can send video e-mail at any time and people can view your video e-mail at their convenience.

Want to show someone a video of your dog giving birth to puppies? Don't waste time posting the video on a Web site. Instead, send the video via e-mail directly to the people who want to see it. The next time you have something important or exciting to say, send a video e-mail instead of a boring, text-only e-mail.

In this chapter, you learn how to send a video file, captured from your Web cam, to your friends and relatives using e-mail. You'll learn how to use your current e-mail program to send video files and the advantages of using a specialized video e-mail program instead.

Just remember that plain-text e-mail is always smaller than video e-mail. A typical text e-mail message may take up only 5 kilobytes of storage space while a typical video e-mail message may gobble up a minimum of 400 kilobytes (or more) of storage space. As a general rule, don't send video e-mail to people with slow Internet connections, such as an ancient 33.6 Kbps or slower modem. You don't want them to spend a lot of time downloading your video e-mail, just to see a short video of you saying hello, for example.

Sending Videos as File Attachments

The simplest way to send a video file by e-mail is to use a file attachment. The basic steps for doing this are as follows:

1. **Capture a video or still image with your Web cam.**

   Most Web cams come with software that enables you to view and capture videos or still images as shown in Figure 15-1. Chapter 4 provides more information about capturing a video with a Web cam.

2. **Start your e-mail program.**

3. **Create a new e-mail message.**

   You may want to type a short text message to explain what type of file the recipient is receiving.

Figure 15-1:
A Web cam program can save an entire video or a single image.

4. Choose the command to add a file attachment to your e-mail.

Most e-mail programs enable you to add a file attachment by clicking a paperclip icon in the toolbar or by choosing a command such as Insert⇨ File Attachment as shown in Figure 15-2. A dialog box appears.

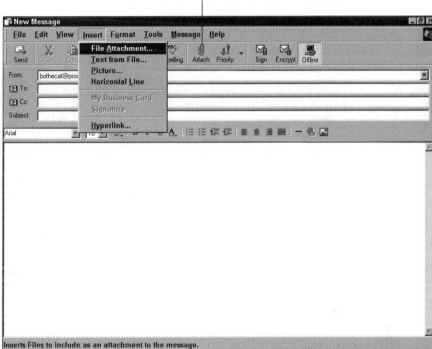

File Attachment icon

Figure 15-2: Microsoft Outlook Express gives you two ways to add a file attachment to an e-mail message.

5. Select the video or still image file that you want to attach to your e-mail message.

File attachments aren't limited to video files. You can send still images, such as those captured from your Web cam, audio files that you recorded from your computer's microphone, word processor documents, or anything else that you may have created in another program.

6. Send your e-mail message.

Most e-mail programs have a Send icon that you can click or a command such as File⇨Send Message.

When someone receives your video file, he or she may need to use a video player, such as Windows Media Player or RealPlayer (depending on the video file format you used), to play your video. To retrieve a video player, follow these steps:

1. **Visit the Web site containing the video player that you want to download.**

   To download Windows Media Player, visit `www.microsoft.com`. To download the QuickTime player, visit `www.apple.com`. To download RealPlayer, visit `real.com`.

2. **Start downloading the program.**

   You may need to browse through the Web site to find the link to the video player that you want to download.

   When the File Download dialog box appears, Windows users can download and install a program by clicking the Run This Program from Its Current Location radio button and then clicking OK to start the download process.

3. **Run the installation or setup program that comes with the video player.**

Because video files gobble up megabytes of disk space, you want to compress your video files using a special video compression program such as Media Cleaner (`www.terran.com`). See Chapter 4 for more information about compressing video files. Ordinary file compression programs, such as WinZip or StuffIt, don't compress video files very much.

Unfortunately, sending a video as an attachment may prove confusing to the novice receiving your video file. Because novices may not understand the different video file formats that exist or know how to load the video player, they may not be able to view any video files you send them.

If you're sending a video file to a Macintosh user, save your video as a QuickTime file. Every new Macintosh comes with the QuickTime player program preinstalled, so Macintosh users can always view QuickTime files. On the other hand, if you're sending video to a Windows user, save the video as an AVI or ASF file, because the latest version of Windows comes with the Windows Media Player, which is specifically designed for running AVI and ASF files.

If you need to send video files to both Macintosh and Windows users, use either the QuickTime or AVI file format. Both QuickTime and the Windows Media Player can display QuickTime and AVI files, but QuickTime can't display ASF files.

If you don't want to bother capturing and compressing your video files and don't want to burden recipients with the hassle of loading and running a video player program, you may want to use the free services of two Web sites that offer prerecorded video files that you can send to others, along with a typed message, via e-mail. These two Web sites are Feelingz (www.feelingz. com/feelingz) and VideoGreetings (www.videogreetings.com), as shown in Figure 15-3.

Both Web sites offer silly, romantic, and sentimental videos that you may want to share with others, such as a video of a dog playing the guitar, a rainbow appearing over a waterfall, or a surfer riding the waves. Prerecorded videos help spice up any message you send.

Before your recipients can view any video e-mail you send from the Feelingz Web site, they need to download a free copy of the FeelzPlayer program, available on the Feelingz Web site. If you think that the recipients of your video e-mail may not be comfortable doing this on their own, then you may want to use the VideoGreetings Web site instead.

Both video e-mail Web sites mentioned here offer a variety of prerecorded videos for different occasions, such as birthdays, weddings, graduations, or simple greetings. After you send a prerecorded video, the recipient receives an e-mail that contains a link. By clicking that link, the recipient can view the video file that you sent.

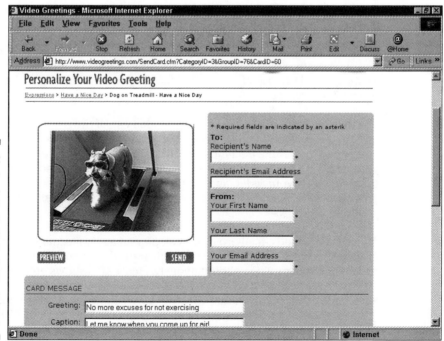

Figure 15-3: With Video-Greetings, you can send a video clip and a message to any e-mail account, absolutely free.

If you have an interesting video that you think others may enjoy watching, such as a clown falling on his face or a car smashing into a wall, submit it to the VideoGreetings site. If VideoGreetings chooses your video, you could win $1,000. VideoGreetings will then offer your video for others to use to send video e-mail to their friends.

Because both sites change their video selections regularly, you can find different videos to send to your friends every day (instead of doing work at your computer, as you're supposed to). If you want to send more offbeat video e-mail, visit the Like Television site (www.liketelevision.com/cards/card.html), which lets you send someone a clip from an old black-and-white TV show or movie, such as Jack Nicholson's cameo appearance in the movie *Little Shop of Horrors* or Marilyn Monroe singing "Happy Birthday" to President Kennedy.

Using Video E-Mail

Although sending a video file as an attachment to your normal e-mail is possible, the cumbersome steps involved in compressing and attaching your video files to an e-mail message can be annoying. Even worse is sending a video file to a friend only to find that your friend doesn't have (or isn't comfortable using) the right video file player to display your file.

As an alternative to using ordinary e-mail programs, try using a special video e-mail program. Video e-mail programs either work in conjunction with your existing e-mail program (such as Outlook Express) or as a separate e-mail program altogether.

The main advantage of using a special video e-mail program is that you don't have to worry about going through the cumbersome process of attaching your video file to an e-mail message. Instead, you just click on the video file you want, type the e-mail address you want to send it to, and the video e-mail program sends your video and message on its way. As with normal e-mail programs, video e-mail programs give you room to type a text message, as shown in Figure 15-4.

Additionally, video e-mail programs can play an audio file, display a still image, or display a video, so you can communicate with someone using text, sound, and still images or video simultaneously. Figure 15-5 shows an example.

Some of the things you should consider when choosing a video e-mail program is whether it will work with your particular computer and Web browser, the type of video file format you can send, whether the program can compress your video files, what type of video editing features it has (so you can type messages that appear on your video), and whether it has audio recording (so you can record your voice to play while the video plays at the same time).

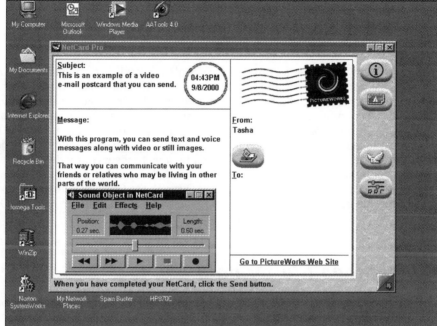

Figure 15-4:
With a video
e-mail
program,
you can
type a
message
or record
an audio
message to
go along
with your
still images
or video.

Figure 15-5:
The NetCard
Pro program
can display
an AVI
file on a
screen that
is separate
from any
text message
you may
have typed.

Working with your computer and Web browser

Many video e-mail programs can only work with specific operating systems, such as Windows and Macintosh, or with specific e-mail and browser programs, such as Netscape Navigator and Internet Explorer. For example, if you try to send video e-mail from a Macintosh to someone who uses a Web-based e-mail account such as HotMail or Yahoo!, that person may not be able to see your video file. Similarly, if you send a video e-mail from Windows to a Macintosh user, the Macintosh user may not be able to view your video e-mail, depending on the video e-mail program you used. Some video e-mail programs will only work with Internet Explorer and Outlook (or Outlook Express), therefore, if you send a video e-mail to someone who uses Eudora or America Online, he or she won't be able to see your video e-mail either.

Video file formats

When selecting a video e-mail program, you need to know what types of file formats those programs handle. If a video e-mail program can't use the same video file format that your Web cam uses, you won't be able to use that particular video e-mail program.

If you send a video file to someone, chances are good that the recipient won't know how to view that video file. For that reason, many video e-mail programs include a video player program that is sent with your video file. That way, recipients can play your videos right away without worrying about downloading and running a separate video player program first.

Some video e-mail programs give you the option of not including a built-in video player with every video e-mail that you send. That way, you can reduce the total size of your video e-mail. Just make sure that the recipients of your video e-mail already have the proper video player installed. If not, they won't be able to see your video.

Some video e-mail programs include a built-in video player, which can only use one specific video file format, such as AVI or QuickTime. If you have a video file stored in QuickTime, but your video e-mail program uses only AVI files, you have to convert that QuickTime video file to the AVI format first. Many video compression programs (see Chapter 5) not only compress your videos but also convert them between different file formats.

For even greater convenience, some video e-mail programs, such as Cresta Cards Video Greetings (www.cardsalive.com), can record a video directly from your Web cam. That way, you don't have to save your video as a separate file (or worry about video file formats) and then load that file into your video e-mail program later.

Video file compression

Video files are huge. Just a few seconds of a typical AVI video can gobble up a megabyte or more of disk space. If you e-mail such a bloated file to someone who's using a slow 56K modem, the download can take a while (ranging from several minutes for a one megabyte file to up to an hour or more for several megabytes worth of data), which may annoy the recipient of your video e-mail or just cause him or her to delete the whole thing without bothering to download it first.

To solve this problem, some video e-mail programs automatically compress video files while others require that you first run a separate program to compress the files. To learn more about compressing a video, see Chapter 5.

The smaller your file, the faster it downloads. When compressing video files, use a special video compression program such as Media Cleaner (www.terran.com).

Video editing capabilities

To spice up your video, many video e-mail programs offer limited video editing capabilities, such as allowing you to add borders or titles to individual frames that make up your video.

Titles can appear at the beginning to introduce your video, at the end to emphasize important points, or over a portion of your video to add explanations or descriptions, as shown in Figure 15-6.

Borders put color or patterns around one or more frames of your video to produce different themes, as shown in Figure 15-7.

No one will see your titles if they appear on only a single frame and the video plays too fast. To make certain that your titles are seen, either spread the titles over several frames or be sure that your video plays slowly enough for viewers to read at a normal pace.

Figure 15-6:
Titles can
add a
description
over an
individual
frame in
your video.

Figure 15-7:
Borders and
themes
customize
the appear-
ance of your
video for
special
occasions,
such as
birthdays
or holiday
announce-
ments.

Audio recording

Because watching a silent video seems as old fashioned as watching a silent
movie, video e-mail programs can also record audio messages to go along

with your text and video message. To use the audio recording feature, you need a microphone and a sound card, and your recipient just needs a sound card and speakers. Both sound cards and speakers are usually included with most computers these days although you may need to buy a microphone separately.

Sound quality can vary greatly among different computers and speakers, so be sure to speak clearly and slowly. That way, your recipients will be able to understand your message no matter how slow the receiving computer or how poor the quality of the speakers.

Finding Video E-Mail Software

Chances are your Web cam comes with a CD-ROM full of bundled software that includes a video e-mail program. If so, try that video e-mail program first — the manufacturer has already tested it to make sure it works correctly with your Web cam.

If you find that you need features other than those available in the video e-mail program that comes with your Web cam, browse through the Web sites discussed in this section and compare the different video e-mail programs.

Some of the video e-mail programs in this section offer shareware or trial versions that you can download and use for free. Others require you to buy the program, sight unseen, before you can try them on your computer.

To show you how their programs work, many companies let you send a sample video e-mail to your own e-mail address. That way, you can see how a particular video e-mail program appears in your e-mail and runs on your computer, as shown in Figure 15-8.

Because video e-mail programs often vary widely in the features they offer and how easy (or complicated) they are to use, feel free to take your time studying video e-mail programs from different companies. Some of the more popular video e-mail programs are listed here.

CoolCards

This program is one of the few *cross-platform* (compatible with Windows and Macintosh) video e-mail programs that enable you to send a still image (not a video file) as an e-mail message — along with text — to any Windows or Macintosh user. Download the program at www.coolcards.com.

Figure 15-8:
When you
double-click
a video
e-mail, the
computer
loads
Windows
Media
Player to
display your
video.

CVideo-Mail

Designed exclusively for Windows, this program does not offer a shareware
or trial version that you can test. However, you can send yourself a video
e-mail from the Web site so you can see how the video e-mail looks on your
computer. Visit the Web page and read more about the program at www.
cvideomail.com.

CrystalGrams

This program is a Windows-only video e-mail program that provides a free
demo that you can download and try on your own computer. CrystalGrams
gives you the option of sending your video e-mail by itself (to save space) or
in conjunction with a built-in video player, to ensure that your recipient can
view your video. Download the demo at www.crystalnet.com.

PhoneFree

This program offers not only video e-mail, but also videoconferencing and
free phone calls over the Internet. The main drawback is that to receive video

e-mail, both parties must have a copy of PhoneFree, and the program only works for Windows (although a Macintosh version is being developed. Download the program at `www.phonefree.com`.

SeeMail

This program is one of the few video e-mail programs available for both Windows and Macintosh. Although you can send sample video e-mail messages to yourself and friends from the SeeMail Web site, you can't try the program unless you buy it first. Read more about the program at `www.seemailinc.com`.

Super Voice

Super Voice is a Windows-only video e-mail program, and the Web site offers a free trial version that you can download to see if the program works with your computer. Visit the Web page and download the program at `www.supervoice.com`.

Video Control 98

This program is another Windows-only video e-mail program, and the Web site offers a free demo version of the program that you can download and test on your computer. Visit the Web page and download the program at `www.stefra.com`.

Video Express

Video Express is a Windows-only program, and one of the few video e-mail programs that offers streaming video. Streaming video is a nice feature because no matter how large your video file, recipients will be able to see it without waiting for the entire file to download first. Download a trial version of the program or buy the commercial version from the Web page at `www.imagemind.com`.

Videogram Creator

Although this program is designed only for Windows, Videogram Creator gives you the option to view video e-mail using a built-in player or a separate streaming video player. The built-in player ensures that anyone with a Windows-based PC can view your video, but the streaming video player can show people your video without forcing them to first download the whole file. Download the program at www.alaris.com.

VideoLink Mail

VideoLink Mail is another Windows-only video e-mail program that actually works with the ancient Windows 3.1 program, as well as with newer versions of Windows. Although no free demo or trial version is available to download, you can purchase the program online at www.smithmicro.com.

VideoMail

VideoMail is one of the few Windows-based video e-mail programs that store video files in the RealVideo format, which means that Macintosh and Linux users who have the RealPlayer program can receive your video e-mail. Best of all, you can download a free trial version of the program to see whether you like it. Go to www.chillisoft.com.au.

VideoMail Express

VideoMail Express is a Windows-only video e-mail program that offers plenty of colorful, cartoon-style themes to spice up your videos. VideoMail Express even includes its own e-mail capabilities, so you can send your video right away, without going through your normal e-mail program first. Check out www.4csoft.com.

Visualize Video and Visualize Mail

These two Windows-only video e-mail programs do not offer a trial or demo version for you to download and try, unfortunately. Visit these Web sites and read about the programs at www.visualmail.bizland.com and www.visualizevideo.com/cvmail.html.

Voice E-Mail

This Windows-only video e-mail program has two drawbacks: It requires recipients to download a free Voice E-Mail player program that can view (but not create) any video files that you send them using the Voice E-Mail program, and there isn't a free version of the Voice E-Mail program that you can test to see how it works. To purchase Voice E-Mail online, go to www.bonzi.com.

Chapter 16

Spicing Up Your Web Pages with Animated GIFs

*I*n the early days, Web pages contained nothing but text and looked about as interesting as pages ripped out of a telephone book. Then people started adding pictures to spice up the appearance of their Web pages.

However, ordinary graphic images sustain only a minimal level of interest, so Web designers went one step further and created animated *Graphics Interchange Format (GIF)* files. Unlike ordinary GIF files, which display a static image, animated GIFs display (what else?) animation.

Nearly all Web cams capture and save images as GIF files. By capturing multiple GIF images, you can use your Web cam to create your own animated GIF images that you can post on your Web site. This chapter explains how to capture GIF images from your Web cam and turn them into animated GIF files.

Creating an Animated GIF

Animated GIF images work by cramming multiple images into a single GIF file. When you view that file, the multiple images appear one after another in rapid succession, creating the illusion of animation.

Some people pronounce GIF with a soft *g* sound, as in giraffe. Others pronounce it with a hard *g* sound. Both ways are considered correct and proper etiquette among computer enthusiasts.

TECHNICAL STUFF

Flash: The alternate animation file format

Animated GIF files are great for small anima-tions, such as icons that blink, jiggle, or rock from side to side. But if you want to create more sophisticated animations, such as full-length cartoons, you're better off using another file format, such as Flash, a new Web animation standard developed by the friendly folks at Macromedia (www.macromedia.com).

Unlike animated GIF files, Flash files can include sound while providing fancier animation. The drawback is that to view Flash animation, people need to download the free Flash plug-in. If you want to create Flash animation, you also have to buy the Flash program, which costs several hundred dollars.

Unless you need the additional features of Flash, you may find that animated GIF files are suitable for a wide variety of common tasks, such as dis-playing twirling buttons or flashing icons. But if you find that animated GIF files limit your cre-ativity, you may want to invest the time and money to get Flash.

Because an animated GIF consists of a single file, adding it to a Web page is just as easy as adding any image file. All you have to do is insert the GIF file into your Web page by using the following HTML code:

```
<img src="dancingcat.gif">
```

REMEMBER

For more information about HTML tabs, pick up a copy of *HTML For Dummies* by Ed Tittel.

Although GIF animation can only display images in a fixed location (an ani-mated GIF image can't cartwheel across your Web page), the animation can still be interesting enough to catch your eye. In fact, many banner ads use animated GIF files because of their small size and their independence from any special plug-in program needed for viewing them.

Getting started

Before you create an animated GIF, you need to decide what type of anima-tion you want to make:

- **Smooth animation.** A single image appears to move on its own, such as a man walking or a ball bouncing up and down.

- **Discrete animation.** Different images appear and disappear. Discrete ani-mation is often used for banner ads that change at different intervals. For example, first an ad for a credit card appears, then an ad for an online bookseller appears, and then an ad for an online computer retailer appears.

To make an animated GIF file, you need two or more graphics files, with each file representing a single frame (much like a frame in a movie).

The more frames you use, the smoother your animation looks, but the larger your animated GIF file becomes, too.

All GIF files you use to make up your single animated GIF should be the same size, such as 160 x 120 pixels. If you use different size GIF files, your final animation image won't appear uniform, and the animated image will appears go from large to small to large again, which may disorient the viewer. Of course, if that's the type of jarring effect you want, feel free to make your GIF files different sizes and see how the final result looks.

To help you smash multiple GIF images into a single animated GIF file, you need a special GIF animation program such as GIF Builder (Macintosh), GIF Construction Set (Windows), or Ulead GIF Animator (Windows). This chapter provides a brief introduction to using GIF Builder and GIF Construction Set to help you understand some of the different features and procedures needed to create an animated GIF file.

Compressing your GIF files

Because animated GIF files are designed for Web pages, you want your animated GIF file to be as small as possible. The larger your animated GIF file, the longer it will take for the animated GIF file to appear in a Web browser.

The best way to create the smallest animated GIF file possible is to take time to optimize the size of your separate GIF files. That way when you shove a bunch of them into a single file, the single animated GIF file will be small enough to be downloaded quickly.

The simplest way to shrink a GIF file is to reduce the number of colors used. The fewer colors you use, the smaller the file. For example, a black and white picture takes up less space than a picture with lots of colors.

To reduce the number of colors used in a GIF file, use a graphics program such as Adobe Photoshop. The basic steps for reducing colors in a GIF file are as follows:

1. **Start your graphics program.**

2. **Load the image (such as a GIF file) that you want to shrink (by reducing the number of colors used).**

3. **Choose File⇨Save As.**

   A Save As dialog box appears.

4. **Click the File Type list box and choose GIF.**

   Some programs refer to GIF files as CompuServe images or as Graphics Interchange Format.

5. **Click the Options button.**

   In some programs, you have to click an Options check box and then click the OK or Save button. An Options dialog box appears, as shown in Figure 16-1.

6. **Choose to use fewer colors, such as 16 colors instead of 256 colors.**

   Some programs provide a list box to choose colors while others display radio buttons.

7. **Click OK or Save to save your GIF file.**

When you shrink a GIF file by using fewer colors, you also lower the resolution and image clarity. You may want to experiment with your GIF files to see if reducing colors makes your GIF image look really bad. Some programs, such as Adobe Photoshop, give you the option to choose the exact number of colors to use, as shown in Figure 16-2.

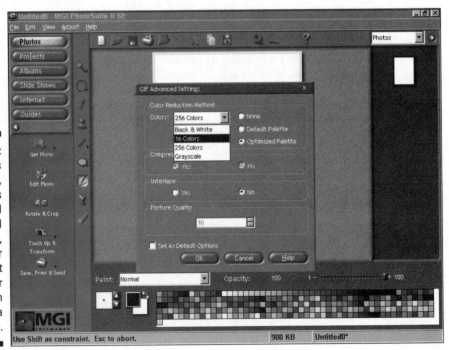

Figure 16-1: Graphics programs, such as the MGI PhotoSuite II SE program, offer different options for saving an image as a GIF file.

Figure 16-2:
Many
graphics
programs,
such as
Adobe
Photoshop,
give you
the option
of saving a
GIF file
using fewer
colors.

Another trick to reduce the file size of an animated GIF file is to use a technique known as *cutout animation*. Instead of creating multiple images in which only one portion of an image changes, you create images that focus on the changing portion, rather than the entire background.

For example, suppose you want to create an animation of a man waving his hand. The first image shows the man with his hand near his waist. The second image shows the man with his hand rising. The third image shows the man with his hand near the top of his head, as shown in Figure 16-3.

Rather than create three separate images, cutout animation uses a single background image (the man) and displays three different images of just the hand and arm in different positions. Because the image of the man's hand and arm is much smaller than an image of the entire man, the resulting GIF files is smaller, thus reducing the size of the overall animated GIF file at the same time.

To create cutout animation, you need a graphics program, such as Adobe Photoshop or Jasc Software's Paint Shop Pro, along with a GIF animation program. The general steps for creating cutout animation are as follows:

1. **Create a graphic file that contains everything you want to display.**

   For example, if you want to create cutout animation of a man waving his hand, use your graphics program to create a graphic file containing the man and his hand.

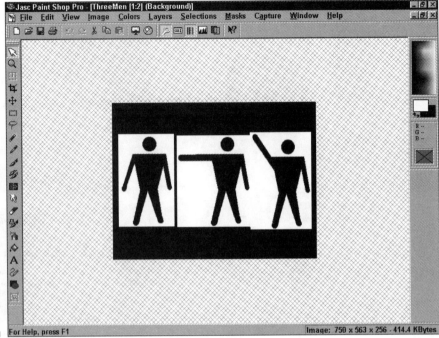

Figure 16-3:
Three GIF files give the illusion of animation when viewed in rapid succession.

2. **Copy only the portion of the image that you want to move and save this as a separate file.**

   In the previous example of the man waving his hand, you copy just the hand and save the hand as a separate file.

3. **Modify the image you saved in Step 2 by rotating or moving the image, and save it as a separate file.**

   If you want to create the animation of a waving hand, you have to create a third file that contains the hand in a slightly different position from the file you saved in Step 2.

4. **Repeat Step 3 as often as necessary to create the desired visual effect.**

   In the waving hand example, one image might show the hand pointing down, a second image might show the hand pointing to the right, and a third image might show the hand pointing straight up.

5. **Combine all your separate files into a single animated GIF file using your GIF animation program.**

In the old days, people used cutout animation to create those antiquated cartoons in which only the character's lips move or a single arm waves up and down while the rest of the image remains stationary. Such cutout animation helped keep production costs down, but it detracted from the realism.

Using a GIF animation program

After you create and optimize the size of your multiple GIF images, the next step is to load them into your GIF animation program. To create an animated GIF file, you may need to define the following information for your GIF animation program:

- ✔ **Number of frames.** This information tells how many frames are in the GIF animation program, considering that each frame consists of a single image originally stored in a separate file.

- ✔ **Interframe delay.** This information defines how much time elapses between frames.

- ✔ **Frame rate.** This information determines how fast the animation runs. A high frame rate displays more frames per second, which can make animation appear to run smoother.

- ✔ **Looping.** This information determines how many times the animated sequence runs, such as once, three times, or indefinitely.

If you don't loop your animation (which means it will only play once and then stop), just remember that the last frame is the final image people will see, so either make it memorable (displaying a corporate logo, for example) or have it disappear into the background, so it doesn't distract the viewer from the rest of your Web page. If you have an animated GIF file display the words "Welcome" in different languages, you may want the last image to match the background, so the word "Welcome" doesn't remain on your Web page.

- ✔ **Special effects.** This information determines any special transition effects between one frame and the next, such as Hollywood movie-style dissolves, wipes, peels, or pushes.

Testing your animated GIF

Despite so-called standards, nothing is really predictable in the computer world except that nothing ever works exactly as you hope it will. So before you start happily posting your animated GIF on your Web pages, take a moment to test it on as many different browsers and computers as possible.

Depending on the browser (Netscape Navigator versus Internet Explorer, for example) and the computer (Windows versus Macintosh), the playing speed can vary widely. Make sure your animations look good no matter which browser someone may be using.

Also, make sure that the colors in your animated GIF appear as they should. If one or more colors look bad, you may have to edit your original images and pick a color that most browsers can display properly. (Basic colors such as red, blue, and green are usually okay. But when you choose really bizarre colors, you may run into problems.)

If you use a color that another computer monitor can't display, that color may appear speckled or otherwise distorted because the computer is trying to use the best approximate color instead. This process is called *dithering*.

If you're really worried about colors that may not appear correctly on other people's computers, make sure you only use one of the 216 colors considered to be browser safe. For more information, visit the Browser Safe Palette (BSP) Web site at `http://the-light.com/netcol.html`.

Creating an Animated GIF with GIF Construction Set for Windows

A popular shareware GIF animation program for Windows is GIF Construction Set, which is available from `www.mindworkshop.com/alchemy/alchemy.html`.

Although GIF Construction Set may offer slightly different commands and features, browse through the upcoming steps just to get an idea of how GIF animation programs work. After you know how one GIF animation program works, you'll be able to evaluate other GIF animation programs as well.

By studying some of the features used in GIF Construction Set, along with GIF Builder for the Macintosh (described later in this chapter), you can see some of the ways different programs let you create and edit any images that you want to save in an animated GIF file.

GIF Construction Set is shareware, so if you plan to use the program regularly, support the programmers and send in your registration fee.

Creating an animated GIF file

GIF Construction Set provides an Animation Wizard that guides you step-by-step through importing graphic images stored in various file formats and turning them into a single animated GIF file. To create an animated GIF file, follow these steps:

1. **Choose File⇨Animation Wizard.**

   An Animation Wizard dialog box appears.

2. **Click Next.**

   The dialog box asks if you want to create your animated GIF file for a Web page or for other uses. If you create an animated GIF file for a Web page, the file is smaller but may lose some clarity and resolution.

3. **Click a radio button to choose an option (either to save your file for a Web page or for other uses) and then click Next.**

   The dialog box appears and asks how many times you want your animated GIF file to run. The choices are: Loop Indefinitely or Animate Once and Stop.

4. **Click the radio button to choose an option (either Loop Indefinitely or Animate Once and Stop) and then click Next.**

   The dialog box asks you to choose the color palette you want to use. If you choose an option like Photorealistic, your animated GIF file is larger (and has a higher resolution) than if you choose a different option such as Drawn in Sixteen Colors.

5. **Click the radio button to choose an option and then click Next.**

   The dialog box asks how long of a delay you want before showing the next image of your animated GIF file.

6. **Click on a time delay, such as 50 hundredths-of-a-second and click Next.**

   The dialog box asks you to select the graphic files you want to store in your animated GIF file.

7. **Click Select.**

   An Open dialog box appears.

8. **Select the graphic files you want to include in your animated GIF file.**

   You can choose graphic images stored in different file formats if you click in the Files of Type list box and choose a file format to use such as GIF, PCX, or BMP. Repeat Step 8 as often as necessary to include all the graphic files you want to include in the animated GIF file.

   If you hold down the Ctrl key while clicking a file, you can select more than one file at a time.

9. **Click Open when you're done choosing all the graphic images you want to store in your animated GIF file.**

   The Open dialog box appears again.

10. **Click Cancel.**

    The Open dialog box disappears, and the Animation Wizard dialog box appears again.

11. **Click Next.**

    The Animation Wizard dialog box tells you that it's done and ready to create your animated GIF file.

12. **Click Done.**

    GIF Construction Set displays the images of your animated GIF file in a separate window within the GIF Construction Set program.

13. **Chooose File⇨Save.**

    The Save As dialog box appears.

14. **Type a name for your animated GIF file in the File Name box.**

    You may want to change folders or drives to store your animated GIF file in a specific location.

15. **Click Save.**

    GIF Construction Set saves your animated GIF file in your chosen location.

Rotating an image in an animated GIF file

After you create an animated GIF file with your chosen images, you may want to rotate, resize, or change the colors of the individual images in your animated GIF file. To rotate an image, follow these steps:

1. **Choose File⇨Open.**

   The Open dialog box appears.

2. **Click the animated GIF file you want to edit and click Open.**

   Your chosen animated GIF file appears in a window, showing all the separate images that make up the entire animated GIF file, as shown in Figure 16-4.

3. **Click the image that you want to rotate.**

   GIF Construction Set highlights your chosen image.

4. **Choose Block⇨Flip and Rotate.**

   A Flip and Rotate dialog box appears, as shown in Figure 16-5.

5. **Click a radio button to choose an option (such as Flip Horizontal) and click OK.**

   Your chosen image flips around.

If you don't like the way your image looks, choose Edit⇨Undo to reverse any changes you made to your image.

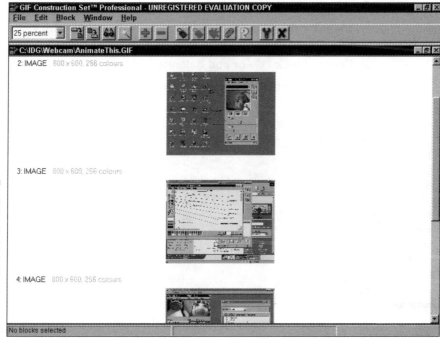

Figure 16-4:
GIF
Construction
Set displays
the
individual
images of an
animated
GIF file.

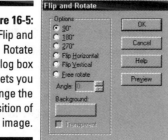

Figure 16-5:
The Flip and
Rotate
dialog box
lets you
change the
position of
an image.

Adjusting the color of an image

If you're not quite happy with the way your image looks, try adjusting the colors by making it look darker or lighter, adding a soft red hue, or sharpening the contrast. To modify the image, follow these steps:

1. Choose File⇨Open.

The Open dialog box appears.

2. **Select the animated GIF file you want to edit and click Open.**

   Your chosen animated GIF file appears in a window, showing all the separate images that make up the entire animated GIF file.

3. **Choose Block⇨Color and Balance.**

   The Colour and Balance dialog box appears, as shown in Figure 16-6.

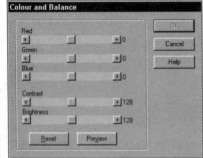

4. **Drag the scroll bar in the options you want to modify (such as the Red content or Contrast value).**

5. **Click Preview.**

   GIF Construction Set displays all the images in your animated GIF file using the color changes you chose in Step 4.

6. **Press Esc to stop the preview.**

   The Colour and Balance dialog box appears again.

7. **Click Reset if you don't like the changes you made, or click OK to save the changes you made.**

Previewing your animation

Before posting your animated GIF for everyone to see, take a few seconds to preview it, just to make sure your animation looks the way you intended. To preview your animation, follow these steps:

1. **Choose Block⇨View.**

   Your animated GIF plays on the screen.

2. **Press Esc to stop the animation.**

Creating an Animated GIF with GIF Builder for the Macintosh

One of the most popular animated GIF programs for the Macintosh is GIF Builder, which is a freeware program that you can download from many Web sites, such as Tucows (`www.tucows.com`) or Download.com (`www.download.com`).

Even if you don't have a Macintosh or don't plan to use GIF Builder, take a few moments anyway to browse through the steps required to create an animated GIF with GIF Builder. That way, you can better understand how an actual program works in creating an animated GIF file.

You can also use GIF Builder to convert a QuickTime movie into an animated GIF file. Because you want your animated GIF file to be as small as possible (so it loads quickly), make sure your QuickTime movie is short and simple, so it creates a small, animated GIF file.

Loading images

GIF Builder can load graphic images stored in PICT, TIFF, GIF, or Photoshop file formats. Because GIF Builder displays your images in the order that you load them, you may want to number your graphic files, such as Image1, Image2, Image3, and so on.

To load an image, follow these steps:

1. **Choose File⇨Add Frame.**

   A dialog box appears.

2. **Click the graphic file you want to add and click Open.**

3. **Repeat Step 2 for each graphic image you want to include in your animated GIF file.**

   GIF Builder displays your graphic images in the Frames window, as shown in Figure 16-7.

To rearrange your frames, delete one or more frames by clicking the frames and pressing Delete. Then choose the Add Frame command again. Remember, the Delete command doesn't physically delete the file, but just removes it from the Frames window.

Figure 16-7:
The Frames
window
shows you
the order,
size, and
time delay
of each
frame.

	Frames				
18 frames	Length: 1.80 s	Size: 80x80		Loop: forever	
Name	Size	Position	Disp.	Delay	Transp.
Frame 3	75x75	(3; 3)	N	10	1
Frame 4	69x68	(5; 6)	N	10	1
Frame 5	78x78	(1; 1)	N	10	1
Frame 6	80x80	(0; 0)	N	10	1
Frame 7	78x78	(1; 1)	N	10	1
Frame 8	68x69	(6; 6)	N	10	1
Frame 9	75x75	(2; 2)	N	10	1
Frame 10	80x80	(0; 0)	N	10	1
Frame 11	80x80	(0; 0)	N	10	1
Frame 12	75x75	(3; 3)	N	10	1
Frame 13	69x68	(5; 6)	N	10	1
Frame 14	78x78	(1; 1)	N	10	1
Frame 15	80x80	(0; 0)	N	10	1
Frame 16	78x78	(1; 1)	N	10	1
Frame 17	68x69	(6; 6)	N	10	1
Frame 18	75x75	(2; 2)	N	10	1

Modifying individual frames

After you load the graphic images you want in the correct order, you may want to modify the way individual frames appear. To change the length of time the frame appears on the screen, follow these steps:

1. **In the Frames window, click the frame that you want to modify.**

2. **Choose Options⇨Interframe Delay.**

   An Interframe Delay dialog box appears, as shown in Figure 16-8.

3. **Type a value in the text box and click OK.**

   The time delay is measured in hundredths-of-a-second intervals. So if you type in 50, the time delay is 0.5 seconds.

The exact length of time a frame appears on the screen depends partly on the speed of the computer, so consider the interframe delay a general guideline rather than a definite time period.

Figure 16-8:
The
Interframe
Delay dialog
box enables
you to
define
exactly how
long you
want a
particular
frame to
remain on
the screen.

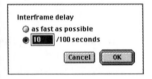

Interframe delay
○ as fast as possible
● [10] /100 seconds
[Cancel] [OK]

You can also modify the appearance of a frame by using a filter. GIF Builder provides two types of filters:

✔ **Static filter.** This filter changes the way a frame looks, such as by flipping it upside-down or rotating it 90 degrees.

✔ **Dynamic filter.** This filter changes the way a frame appears when the animated GIF runs, such as appearing blurry at first and gradually appearing more sharply focused.

To choose a filter, follow these steps:

1. **In the Frames window, click the frame that you want to modify.**

2. **Choose Effects⇨Static Filters (or Dynamic Filters) and then choose the type of filter you want, such as Blur, Flip, or Tiles, as shown in Figure 16-9.**

   As its name implies, a static filter changes the appearance of the frame you choose. A dynamic filter inserts additional frames into your animated GIF file to create the illusion of motion or change. Depending on the type of filter you choose, a dialog box appears.

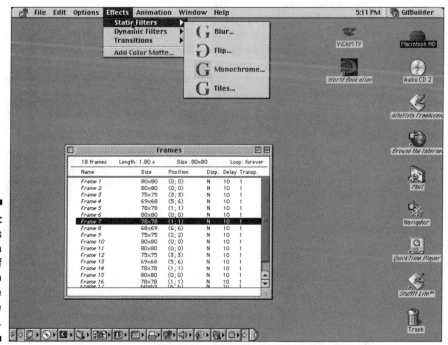

Figure 16-9:
Static filters give you a variety of ways to change the appearance of a frame.

3. **Select the options you want (such as those displayed in Figure 16-10) and then click OK.**

   You may want to take some time to experiment with the different options available for each filter, to see how they affect the appearance of your animated GIF file.

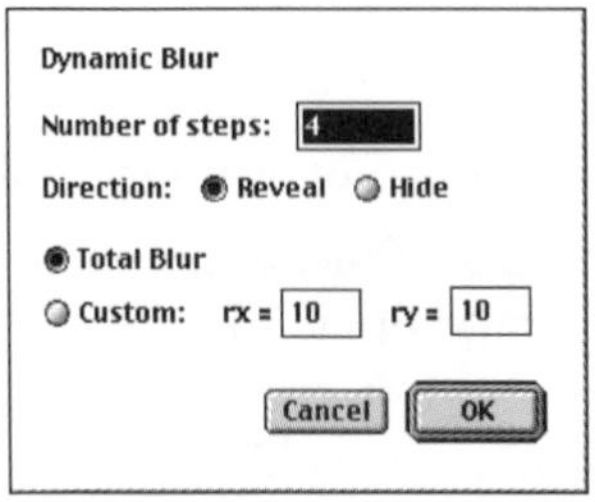

Figure 16-10:
The
Dynamic
Blur dialog
box gives
you a variety
of options to
modify the
blur effect
on a frame.

Dynamic Blur

Number of steps: [4]

Direction: ● Reveal ○ Hide

● Total Blur
○ Custom: rx = [10] ry = [10]

[Cancel] [OK]

Adding transitions

Transitions define the way your animated GIF file switches from one frame to another. To choose a transition, follow these steps:

1. **In the Frames window, click the frame that you want to apply a transition to.**

2. **Choose Effects⇨Transitions and choose the option you want, such as Peel, Wipe, or Dissolve.**

   Depending on the option you choose, a dialog box appears, as shown in Figure 16-11. See the "Transitions" section later in this chapter for more information about different transition effects and how they appear on the screen.

3. **Select the options you want and then click OK.**

Previewing your animation

Before you save your animation in a single animated GIF file, take some time to preview the way it looks by following these steps:

1. **Choose Window⇨Preview Window.**

   The Preview window appears.

2. **Choose Animation⇨Start to see how your animated GIF file looks**

Figure 16-11:
The Peel
dialog box
gives you a
variety of
options to
modify the
direction of
the peel on
a frame.

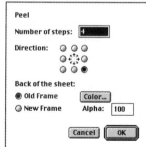

You can press   +T to step through your animation frame by frame.

After you're satisfied with the way your animation looks, you may want to use looping to make the animation repeat several times. To loop animation, follow these steps:

1. Choose Options⇨Loop.

A Looping dialog box appears, as shown in Figure 16-12.

Figure 16-12:
The Looping
dialog box
lets you set
an animated
GIF file to
play multiple
times.

2. Click a radio button, such as Forever or No (which plays your animated GIF file only once).

If you click the bottom radio button, you can type a number in the text box, such as 5, to set the exact number of times you want the animated GIF to loop.

3. Click OK.

You may want to preview your animation (see the earlier "Previewing your animation" section) to see how your animated GIF looks.

Saving your file

After you're convinced that your animation is exactly as you want it, save the entire animation as a single GIF file. To save your animation, follow these steps:

1. **Choose File⇨Save.**

   If this is the first time you're saving a file, the Save dialog box appears. Otherwise, the program just saves your file, and you can skip Step 2.

2. **Type a name for your file and click Save.**

Evaluating GIF Animation Programs

You can find a wide variety of GIF animation programs for both Windows and Macintosh. Fortunately, most of these programs come in shareware versions that you can try out, to evaluate the programs, and see what features you like best. By comparing several different GIF animation programs, you can look for the following:

✔ How easy a program is to use. (Load graphic images into the program and see how much you can get done without reading any of the program's online help. Then browse through the program's Help file to see if it's really as helpful, clear, and comprehensive as you might like.)

✔ Whether a GIF animation program offers basic or more sophisticated graphics editing capabilities, or perhaps none at all (in which case you need a separate graphics editing program).

✔ The types of animation features a program may offer. (One program may let you have graphic images appear to slide into view from left to right, or vice versa, while another program may not offer this option.)

✔ The final size of an animated GIF file that a program creates. Even if different GIF animation programs use the same images, the size of the final animated GIF file can vary widely. So if small file sizes are crucial to you, test to see which programs create the smallest animated GIF files.

File import and conversion

Some GIF animation programs can combine only multiple GIF files into a single animated GIF file. This situation means you have to waste time converting each graphic image into a GIF file before you can save each one as part of an animated GIF file.

Other GIF animation programs can import graphic images stored in a variety of different formats, including BMP, GIF, JPEG, PICT, or Adobe Photoshop file format. That way, you don't have to waste time converting the graphic images to GIF files.

Some GIF animation programs can even take an existing AVI (Audio Video Interleave) or QuickTime movie file, which you can capture straight from your Web cam, and convert it into an animated GIF file. As an alternative, you can selectively strip out individual frames from an AVI or QuickTime movie and store those frames as part of your animated GIF file. By selectively using individual frames from a video captured by your Web cam, you can keep your animated GIF file small (because you aren't using an entire video).

Frame preview

Each time you add a graphic file, your GIF animation program stores the graphic as a single frame. Unfortunately, some GIF animation programs, such as GIF Builder, only list the order of your frames, without showing you what each frame looks like (refer to Figure 16-7).

Other programs, such as GIF Movie Gear, show you the contents of each frame as well as its relative position to the rest of the frames in your animated GIF file, as shown in Figure 16-13. Because you can see the contents of each frame, you are better able to move, delete, and rearrange the individual frames of your animated GIF file.

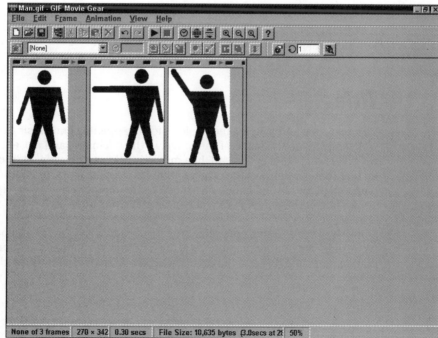

Figure 16-13:
GIF Movie Gear shows the order and contents of the frames in your animation.

Frame manipulation

To give you as many choices as possible for the way your frames look, most GIF animation programs provide a variety of commands for manipulating the appearance of your frames. For example, some common ways to manipulate a frame include flipping, rotating, blurring, reversing colors (dark areas become lighter and light areas become darker), resizing, or cropping. Figure 16-14 shows the available frame manipulation commands found in the GIF Construction Set program.

Transitions

To make your GIF animations look more like Hollywood-style productions, many GIF animation programs provide transitions between individual frames. That way, rather than one frame popping into view and then another frame abruptly replacing it, you can create a smoother transition between two frames. Some examples of transitions include the following:

- **Blur.** The first frame blurs and disappears, gradually revealing the next frame underneath.

- **Peel.** The first frame peels away, like a page being ripped from a calendar, revealing the next frame underneath.

- **Slide.** The first frame slides away to one side (right, left, top, bottom, and so on), revealing the next frame underneath.

- **Break.** The first frame breaks in two, revealing the next frame underneath.

Titles

The next time you watch a movie, look for the opening and closing titles, which introduce the name of the movie at the beginning and close the movie with a list of credits at the end. In a movie, a title can provide additional information that isn't part of the original film, such as the name of your topic, the date and place of the filming, or who filmed or directed the video. Figure 16-15 shows one of the many ways you can display your titles.

Similarly, titles can give your animated GIF an extra level of professional quality by introducing your animation, inserting additional comments within your animation, or displaying additional text when your animation is finished playing.

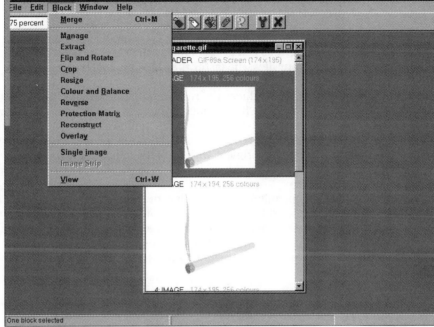

Figure 16-14:
Common frame manipulation commands found in most GIF animation programs, in this case GIF Construction Set Professional.

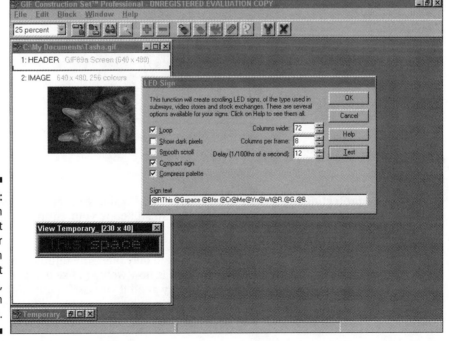

Figure 16-15:
Titles can display text in your animation in different formats, such as an LED sign.

File compression and protection

Besides cramming all your graphic images into a single GIF file, some GIF animation programs can also compress the file to make it even smaller. The smaller your files, the faster they load on a Web page.

Compressing a file reduces the resolution of the images in your animated GIF file. If you compress a file too much, the image quality may suffer as a result. A simple black-and-white picture of the moon can be compressed much more than a colorful picture of a bouquet of flowers, because colors take up space. You may have to experiment with each file individually to see how much you can compress it before the image starts to degrade and look really bad.

Compressing an animated GIF file has the added benefit of making it (slightly) more difficult for other people to strip out the individual files that make up your animated GIF file. For greater protection, some GIF animation programs offer special protection, which scrambles your GIF images without affecting their quality, as shown in Figure 16-16.

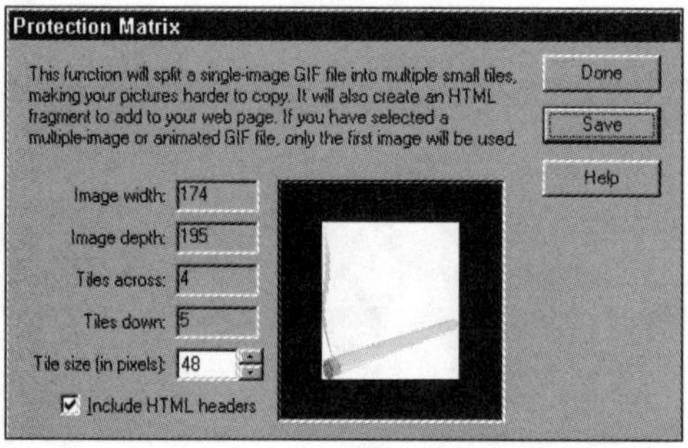

Figure 16-16:
Some animated GIF programs can protect the individual frames of your animated GIF file, so others can't copy them.

By protecting the images in your animated GIF file, you can stop people from copying your work (although others can still copy your entire animated GIF file).

No matter how many features a program may offer, the ultimate measure of which program is better than another is how well you like using it. The best program in the world won't do you any good if you can't understand how to find even the simplest commands, so don't be afraid to try different programs and use whatever program you like best.

Chapter 17

A Simple Introduction to Image Editing

Most people know how to edit text. Just add, delete, copy, insert, and maybe change fonts, colors, or type styles (such as *italics,* <u>underline</u>, or **bold**) and you're done. Believe it or not, editing graphic images isn't that much more difficult. The toughest part (just as in editing text) is deciding what to cut out, what to modify, and what to keep to improve the overall quality.

Because many people don't consider themselves artistically inclined, they may be afraid to edit any images that they capture from their Web cam. But even if you're a complete novice when it comes to editing graphic images (or using a computer for that matter), relax. This chapter gently guides you toward a basic familiarity with the different image-editing functions that you can perform on Web cam images.

Nearly all image-editing programs have a special Undo command (often Ctrl+Z or Edit⇨Undo) that can reverse your last command. The Undo command can liberate you by enabling you to experiment without worrying that you'll ruin your images. If something goes drastically wrong, just choose Undo to eliminate the last change you made to your image.

For high-powered image editing, the standard is an expensive program called Photoshop (www.adobe.com). However, if you're on a budget, some inexpensive image-editing programs include Paint Shop Pro (www.jasc.com), PhotoDraw (www.microsoft.com), and Digital Darkroom (www.microfrontier.com) for Windows. For the Macintosh, take a look at Color It! or Digital Darkroom (www.microfrontier.com). The best image editor for Linux is The GIMP (www.gimp.org).

Selecting Parts of Your Image

Before you edit a graphic image, such as a still image captured from your Web cam, select the part of the image that you want to modify (or you can select the entire image). The most common selection tools available in image-editing programs include the following:

- ✔ Rectangle
- ✔ Ellipse
- ✔ Freehand
- ✔ Magic Wand

Two basic selection tools found in every image-editing program are the rectangle and the ellipse, which let you select a rectangular or elliptical part of an image, respectively, as shown in Figure 17-1.

To select a perfect square or circle, choose your image-editing program's rectangular or elliptical selection tool and hold down the Ctrl or Shift key as you drag the mouse over the part of the image that you want to alter.

Not every image you want to alter can fit within the confines of a rectangular or elliptical shape, so image-editing programs also provide a freehand selection tool. This tool lets you use the mouse to draw the outline of the portion of the image you want to select, a process as tedious and clumsy as trying to draw a picture using an Etch-A-Sketch.

The freehand selection tool isn't always exact or precise enough to trace around irregularly shaped objects. However, some of the more advanced image-editing programs, such as Adobe Photoshop, offer a Magic Wand feature. The Magic Wand works by clicking one part of an image and having your image-editing program automatically select any adjoining portions of that image that contain approximately the same colors. Using the Magic Wand selection tool, you can quickly select irregularly shaped parts of an image, as shown in Figure 17-2. For example, you can use the Magic Wand selection tool to do things such as pick out a person's face from a crowd, highlight a black spot on a Dalmatian, or select a single cloud in the sky.

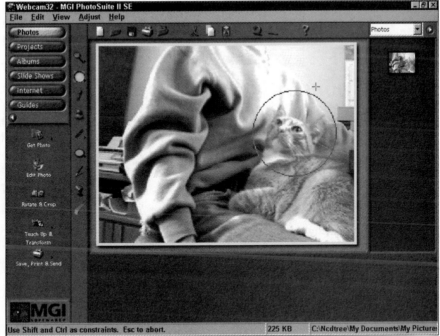

Figure 17-1:
A basic
selection
tool
available in
image
editing
programs
lets you
select an
elliptical
portion of
your image.

Figure 17-2:
The Magic
Wand
selection tool
automatically
selects a
portion of an
image based
on similar
adjacent
colors.

One common use for any selection tool (especially the Magic Wand) is to strip away nonessential parts of an image. If you captured a picture of your dog, you can remove the background completely, leaving only your dog in the image.

Manipulating an image

After you select all or part of an image, you can physically manipulate the selected portion of the image by using any of the following methods:

- Moving the image to another part of the screen.
- Rotating the image or flipping it around, as shown in Figure 17-3.
- Resizing the image to make it larger or smaller.
- Cutting the image to remove it altogether.
- Copying and moving the image for further manipulation.

Changing colors

One of the simplest — yet most drastic — ways to alter an image is to change one or more colors. You can change colors dramatically, for example, by making the black and white stripes on a zebra appear as purple and yellow, or you can change colors more conservatively, for example, by touching up a woman's face so her lips appear glossy red while the rest of her face appears in black and white.

Because Web cams don't always capture the highest quality images, you can use an image-editing program to alter the colors in your image, such as brightening up an otherwise dark picture or touching up a person's face so he or she doesn't look pale.

To change the color of your selected image, you have two choices: Either choose from a palette of existing colors (red, blue, green, yellow, and so on) or create your own colors by using a more sophisticated image-editing program, as shown in Figure 17-4.

A more tedious but exact method of coloring an image is to color an image pixel-by-pixel, as shown in Figure 17-5. This method gives you absolute control over the coloring of an image but can be extremely time consuming.

Rather than switch to different colors, you may want to keep your existing colors but alter their hue, tint, brightness, or saturation, as shown in Figure 17-6. Altering these characteristics can make your image look darker and more sinister, for example, or lighter and more cheerful, depending on the changes you make.

Figure 17-3:
Rotating a selected portion of an image can drastically alter the appearance of your image.

Figure 17-4:
You can create your own mixture of colors to color part of your image.

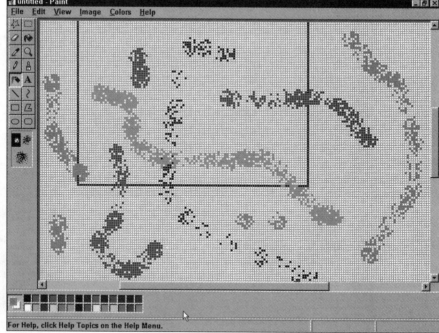

Figure 17-5:
Coloring individual pixels gives you complete control over the appearance of an image.

Figure 17-6:
The hue, saturation, brightness, and tint of an image can be adjusted to change its appearance.

Using Filters

Sometimes physically moving, enlarging, rotating, or coloring an image doesn't do enough to achieve the effect you want. If you need to alter the appearance of an entire image, you may want to use a filter instead.

Filters distort your image's appearance, enabling you to change your image in unique and sometimes bizarre ways. The purpose of applying a filter is to uniformly modify the way the image looks.

For example, you can add cracking and yellowing to the image so that it looks like an ancient black-and-white photograph, or make the image look as if it were stained glass, as shown in Figure 17-7. By using filters, you can turn any image you capture from your Web cam into a work of art, or at least something more interesting than a snapshot.

Some common ways that filters alter the appearance of an image include the following:

- ✔ **Changing the texture.** You can make an image appear to have been painted or drawn on tiles, stained glass, or a grainy piece of paper.

- ✔ **Changing the type of tool that appears to have drawn the image.** You can make an image appear to have been drawn using a piece of charcoal, a paintbrush, or watercolors.

- ✔ **Blurring or sharpening the image.** You can soften or sharpen the edges of an image to give it a gentler or harsher appearance.

- ✔ **Altering the viewpoint.** You can make an image look as if you're seeing it underwater, through a layer of fog, or through the eyes of a drunken sailor.

Figure 17-8 shows one image filtered to look as if it were made of stained glass and a second, identical image filtered to look as if it were drawn using charcoal.

Many image-editing programs offer special features to remove red eye (caused by flash reflecting off a person's eyes), dust spots, other imperfections that may have been saved as part of a scanned image, or scratches commonly found in old black-and-white photographs. Check to see if your image-editing program offers these features, because they can enable you to touch up an image quickly, without doing a lot of work.

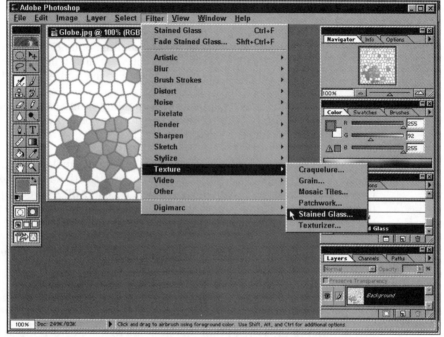

Figure 17-7: Filters distort the overall appearance of an image, giving it an interesting look.

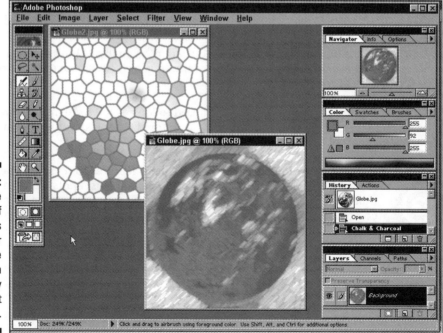

Figure 17-8: Creative uses of filters can alter the same image in drastically different ways.

Adding Text, Lines, and Other Objects

Perhaps the simplest way to alter an image is to add your own text, lines, shapes, or other objects and colors to an existing image. Most image-editing programs offer the following features:

- **Adding text.** This feature enables you to type text directly on an image to make a caption or title. Text can appear as plain characters or as wildly creative designs, such as rainbow-colored letters that appear chiseled in stone.

- **Adding pictures.** You can add another picture (such as a cloud, corporate logo, or burning building) to an existing picture, or you can superimpose interesting images, such as a man who appears to be riding an airplane like a horse.

- **Drawing lines.** Lines can point out or label interesting items, such as separate parts of a computer or a human body, so readers can quickly find those parts. You can also use lines to emphasize parts of your picture, for example, by drawing a circle around a face or highlighting text inside a box.

Some image-editing programs, such as Photoshop, give you the option of using *layers,* which are like transparent sheets of plastic that artists use to draw different items on. For example, one sheet may have a drawing of a park bench, another of a person sitting down, and a third of a city skyline in the background. By dividing a picture into layers, you focus on drawing and editing one item at a time, without the risk of accidentally messing up any other items in your picture.

Whether you plan to use the simple image-editing program that comes with your computer, such as Microsoft Paint, or spend several hundred dollars to get a professional-quality tool such as Adobe Photoshop, feel free to experiment. Make two copies of your files and then edit only one copy. That way, if you really mess up the image, you can always go back and start over with a fresh copy of the original.

The best way to understand your image-editing program is to practice by editing as many pictures as you can. As with anything else, you get better at image editing the more often you practice your skill. So don't wait. Grab your Web cam, take some pictures, and exercise your creativity with your favorite image-editing program.

Part V
The Part of Tens

The 5th Wave   By Rich Tennant

"Well that's typical. Ever since I started teleconferencing with my parents, my mother keeps looking for a toolbar function that brushes the hair off my forehead."

In this part . . .

To spark your imagination further, this part of the book provides links to some unique Web cam sites that you may want to visit so you can find even more ideas for using your Web cam. If all of this sounds good, but you still can't get your Web cam to work properly, this part of the book also provides a few handy tips for troubleshooting your Web cam. That way, you won't be left out of the fun of using a Web cam with your personal computer.

Chapter 18

Ten (Or So) Cool Web Cam Resources

● ●

In This Chapter

▶ Taking a Web cam outdoors

▶ Showcasing Web cam movies

▶ Understanding streaming video

▶ Sharing ideas in newsgroups

▶ Shopping from video specialty stores

▶ Researching more about video equipment

● ●

*P*eople find many unusual and diverse uses for their Web cams and often feature their findings on Web sites. At these Web sites you can discover more about filmmaking techniques, video editing, and Web cam tips. After studying some of the information provided at these Web sites, you may find yourself using your Web cam in ways that you never dreamed possible.

Taking a Web Cam with You

The WebCam Cookbook (www.teleport.com/~samc/bike) site keeps track of some of the more unusual uses people have found for Web cams, such as mounting a Web cam on a bike and bicycling across Cuba or installing a Web cam inside a New York City taxicab.

Besides offering links to hundreds of interesting (instead of useless and boring) Web cams around the world, the WebCam Cookbook also provides links to manufacturers of various equipment that may be useful for setting up a wireless or outdoor Web cam. Visit this Web site as soon as you can and find out more about all the unusual uses and equipment for Web cams that keep popping up around the world.

If the idea of wearing a Web cam interests you, visit the International Wearable Computing WWW Site (www.wearcam.org) and discover how to turn your Web cam into a roving eye that you can take with you wherever you go.

For example, 38-year-old Davo Karnicar became the first man in history to ski down Mount Everest, and he documented his feat on his Web site, Ski Everest 2000 (www.everest.simobil.si). Not only did Karnicar capture the feat by placing cameras along the mountain, but he also strapped a wireless Web cam to his helmet, broadcasting his descent over the Internet.

Although you may not want to ski down Mount Everest with a Web cam attached to your head, think of all the interesting and curious uses you may find for a wireless Web cam, and maybe you'll find yourself recording a bit of your own history, with you in the starring role.

Showcasing Your Own Movies

Digital photography has given people the freedom to create complete films and experiment with different techniques, without the expense or trouble of editing or creating special effects manually.

To find out about filmmaking techniques without moving to Hollywood, visit the Cyber Film School site (www.cyberfilmschool.com). This site provides the latest Hollywood headlines; software templates for budgeting and creating films; interviews with famous directors; and tips for raising funds, creating fake blood, or creating a musical score for your movie.

For a Yahoo!-like directory catering specifically to films and movie making, visit the iFilm site (http://iFilm.com). Here you can find information about film festivals, Hollywood gossip, and more importantly, how to post your own movie on the Internet for everyone to view and judge.

Another Web site dedicated to showcasing the works of independent filmmakers is the Internet Film Community (www.inetfilm.com). If you've made a particularly interesting video, feel free to post it on this Web site so others can view your video as well.

Finding Out More About Streaming Video

If you want to find out more about streaming video, visit the iCanStream site (www.icanstream.com), where both beginners and professionals can acquire the skills and tools they need to make and post video for the Internet.

Read interviews with professionals and discover how they create their videos, films, streaming Web sites, and multimedia presentations. Or browse through the collection of streaming video files to see what other people have done right (and what they may have done wrong).

Streaming Video World (`www.streamingmediaworld.com`) also offers plenty of news, product reviews, and technical articles to help you better understand the different ways you can use streaming video to spice up your Web site.

Sharing Ideas in a Newsgroup

Usenet newsgroups are places where people can share their ideas and tips with other Web cam and video enthusiasts. If there's nobody around you who can help you with your Web cam questions or problems, go online and maybe someone from another part of the world can answer your questions and provide you with the advice you need. Some popular Web cam-related topics discussed in these various Usenet newsgroups include desktop cameras, sound cards, and videoconferencing.

Desktop cameras

Newsgroups provide plenty of tips, advice, and stories from people all over the world who have used all sorts of video equipment from a variety of different manufacturers. Although only the `alt.comp.periphs.webcam` newsgroup specifically focuses on Web cams, visit the following newsgroups to find plenty of people willing to share their experiences with using any type of video recording device.

 `alt.comp.periphs.webcam` — offers information specific to using Web cams.

 `rec.video` — offers discussions of different video components.

 `rec.video.desktop` — provides tips and information about video editing and production using desktop cameras and equipment.

 `rec.video.marketplace` — helps you buy, sell, or trade used video equipment.

 `rec.video.production` — provides information about producing professional quality videos.

 `rec.video.professional` — offers a forum for video professionals to share tips and tricks with each other.

Soundcards

Along with printers, soundcards tend to be one of the more troublesome accessories for your computer. Sometimes the sound doesn't come out right and sometimes there isn't any sound at all. Rather than get mad or frustrated, visit one of the following newsgroups dedicated to soundcards. Hopefully you'll find the information you need to get your soundcard working properly without going crazy in the process.

`comp.sys.ibm.pc.soundcard.misc` — offers general information about buying and using a sound card for MS-DOS and Windows.

`comp.sys.ibm.pc.soundcard.tech` — is devoted to answering technical questions and solving problems involving various soundcards.

Videoconferencing

Videoconferencing is one of the latest uses for Web cams. The following newsgroups offer a common forum for videoconferencing enthusiasts to share ideas, advice, and suggestions:

`alt.multimedia.cu-seeme` — lets you exchange messages in a newsgroup dedicated just to CU-SeeMe software users.

`comp.dcom.videoconf` — is a general-purpose newsgroup covering all aspects of videoconferencing, from software and hardware to techniques for making your videoconference special.

`microsoft.public.internet.netmeeting` — is a special newsgroup providing support and discussion forums for Microsoft NetMeeting users.

Videoconferencing in Education and Business

Although many people use videoconferencing just to chat with others, you can also use your Web cam and videoconferencing program to educate yourself. Pacific Bell offers its Videoconferencing for Learning site (`www.kn.pacbell.com/wired/vidconf`), which provides ideas for learning, examples of people and schools using videoconferencing, and links that explain how schools and universities all over the world have used videoconferencing. Learn a foreign language, watch a play, listen to a lecture, or just see how videoconferencing can supplement or possibly replace traditional classroom instruction.

For a practical example of how videoconferencing can save time, visit the Web Traffic School site (`http://Webtrafficschool.com`). Unlike other traffic schools on the Internet, Web Traffic School uses streaming video so you can learn traffic safety laws without having to read pages of text or listen to a boring instructor. Sit back, relax, and watch a driving safety video in the comfort of your own home.

For a more business-oriented look at videoconferencing, visit the Videoconference.com site (`www.videoconference.com`), which lists video-conferencing conferences and the names of various videoconferencing products.

Whether you want to find out more about videoconferencing for education or business, one of these Web sites can give you all the information you need to justify sitting in front of your computer a little bit longer each day.

Shopping from a Video Specialist

Although you can buy video equipment and software directly from the manufacturer or through a mail order house, you're better off using a mail order or e-commerce retailer that specializes in video, such as VideoGuys (`www.videoguys.com`).

Not only does the VideoGuys Web site sell video equipment and software at slightly lower prices than retail, but it also provides a huge selection of products so you can compare features and prices to get the right item for your needs.

Elite Video (`www.elitevideo.com`) offers another source for buying hard-to-find video products and programs at reasonable prices. This Web site also provides a forum where anyone can ask questions or share video-making tips with others, so everyone can learn and increase his or her skills.

Finding Out More about Video Equipment

The Australian magazine *VideoCamera* (`www.videocamera.com.au`) provides plenty of tips for buying and evaluating video-making equipment, and for shooting your own video. Although the magazine focuses mostly on hand-held video camcorders, the magazine does provide tutorials that show you how to edit a video and how to mix in sound.

The online magazine *Hyperzine* (www.hyperzine.com) provides similar comparisons and technical specifications of the latest video equipment. In addition, you can write and leave messages for other video enthusiasts and even post classified ads to help you look for a video-related job or buy and sell equipment.

For another magazine that provides articles and reviews of different video equipment, visit *VideoMaker* (www.videomaker.com). Shop for instruction books or videos, buy video accessories, and find out where to attend the nearest videoconference.

If you want to go from the simple visual quality of Web cams to the higher end of video production, take a peek at *VideoCamera* or *Hyperzine* for additional guidance and information.

Chapter 19

Ten Cool Ideas for Using Your Web Cam

*J*ust pointing a Web cam at your face, your pet, or out a window may seem interesting at first, but eventually you may want to explore other ways to use your Web cam. That's what this chapter is about — giving you unique ideas for putting your Web cam to work in creative and interesting ways. Remember, no matter what you decide to do with your Web cam, have fun!

Setting Up a Baby Cam

For some odd reason, a newborn baby can cause friends, relatives, neighbors, and total strangers to appear suddenly, just to catch a glimpse of the newly arrived child. Unfortunately (or fortunately, depending on your point of view), not all of these well-wishers live nearby, so people in other cities can only view the baby through snapshots sent to them through the mail and hear of the child's latest activities through telephone conversations.

Instead of relying on these archaic methods of communication, you can point your Web cam at your baby and post live videos of your child to a Web site for everyone to see and admire, as shown in Figure 19-1.

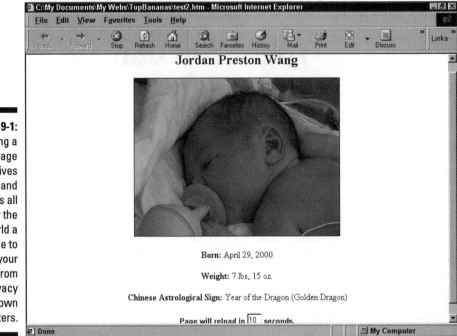

Not only can this Web site show live video of the baby, but you can also provide still images and list facts about the child. That way people can read this information on your Web page instead of calling you for the same information over the phone. Such a baby cam can provide everyone with instant access to your baby, without having to physically show up at your house. (Now if you could just hold family reunions this way. . . .)

Protecting Your Child

When people drop their child off at a daycare center, they often wonder what their child does during the day. Because parents can't always see how their child is treated, they may wish that their daycare center would install Web cams so they could see exactly what their child is doing at any moment in time.

That's the idea behind KinderCam (`www.kindercam.com`), a new business that has installed Web cams in daycare centers in several states, including North Carolina, Kansas, Texas, Nevada, Ohio, Missouri, Tennessee, Florida, Kentucky, Georgia, Massachusetts, Washington, Virginia, and Louisiana.

If you drop off your child at a daycare center that uses KinderCam's Web cams, you can peek in on the child's activities using your Web browser and a secret password. That way, you can see your child playing with others, learning new lessons, and growing up while you're at work.

You can also use this same idea to set up a Web cam in your own house to watch what your nanny or baby-sitter does with your child in your absence. Set up a hidden Web cam, post the images to a Web site, and you, your spouse, and any relatives or friends can sneak a quick peek at your house to make sure your child is safe in the hands of the nanny or baby-sitter.

Protecting Your Home or Business

Banks, convenience stores, and gas stations use video cameras to protect their premises, so why shouldn't you? Just aim your Web cam at a prominent place in your home or business (such as your bedroom or cash register) and have your Web cam record all activities.

For example, at the 1997 COMDEX convention in Las Vegas, Prescient Systems set up video surveillance software called GOTCHA! (`www.gotchanow.com`) in the Silicon Vision booth to demonstrate this use with Silicon Vision's high-quality iCam digital video cameras.

The booth staff members set up GOTCHA! on Sunday night to watch over the valuable equipment within the booth area. Sometime early the following Monday morning, thieves entered the area and escaped with several PCs.

Fortunately, the cameras and GOTCHA! recorded the entire theft. Prescient Systems and Silicon Vision simply handed over the video file to the police, which provided the actual images of the suspects.

Besides catching burglars, Web cams can also secretly record other household members engaging in forbidden activities, nosy landlords prowling around your apartment, or mischievous pets destroying your belongings.

If you get really lucky, not only will you know the identity of a criminal breaking into your home, but if the person winds up doing something really stupid, you could win $10,000 if you enter the recorded activities on a television show such as *America's Funniest Home Videos*.

Protecting the Environment

The environmental organization Greenpeace accused both the French and British governments of dumping hundreds of millions of liters of radioactive waste into the English Channel each year from the French nuclear reprocessing facility (owned by the French government company Cogema) at La Hague, off the Normandy coast, and into the Irish Sea from the Sellafield reprocessing plant (owned by the British government company British Nuclear Fuels Ltd.) in northern England.

To help publicize such activities, Greenpeace installed a Web cam to capture the alleged radioactive waste discharges from the French nuclear reprocessing facility run by Cogema. These images were then sent to an environmental meeting in Copenhagen where ministers from 15 European countries were meeting to discuss a proposal by Denmark to ban sea dumping of radioactive waste from land pipes. In addition, these live Web cam images were also posted on the Greenpeace Web site (www.greenpeace.org) for the whole world to see.

Two days after Greenpeace installed the Web cam and began transmitting the pictures, divers from Cogema allegedly cut the Web cam cable, halting the transmission of the images shown in Figure 19-2, claiming that the Web cam affected plant safety and could disturb the environmental balance.

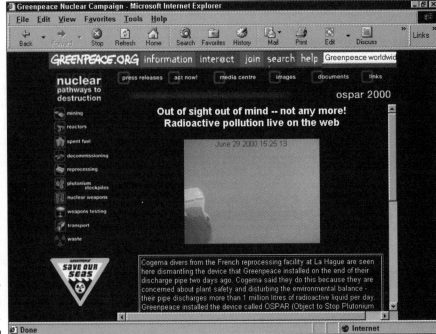

Figure 19-2:
The last images from the Greenpeace Web cam before French divers allegedly cut the cable.

To dispel its secretive image, Cogema (`www.cogemalahague.fr`) installed ten permanent Web cams at the reprocessing site, but they neglected to install one near the discharge pipe, where Greenpeace believes 500 million liters of radioactive waste pours into the sea every year.

By aiming a Web cam at law-breaking corporations, government agencies, or individuals, some people have helped expose the culprits and embarrass them into taking action.

Offering Virtual Technical Support

Although "virtual technical support" may suggest calling a computer manufacturer for help and never getting your questions answered or calls returned, the phrase actually means repairing a device from a distance.

Unlike providing technical support over the telephone, virtual technical support enables people to see, hear, and read information simultaneously, in the hopes that this bombardment of information through multiple senses may help uncover a solution to the current problem.

For example, the U.S. Navy uses virtual technical support to maximize its existing technical personnel. Previously, whenever a vital piece of equipment broke down on a ship at sea, the Navy had to fly a technician to the scene. Not only did this take time and money, but doing so also effectively removed the technician from solving any other problems in the meantime.

That's when the Navy developed its TeleMaintenance service, which uses videoconferencing software to connect repair technicians at the scene of the problem with specialists on shore. Technicians can share digital images and diagrams of the problem and use video to display a real-time view of the damaged equipment.

Anytime you need to share information, knowledge, or expertise from a distance, consider hooking up your Web cam and using videoconferencing to solve the problem. Whether you're a computer repairperson, a tax accountant, or a plumber, you can use videoconferencing to help more people in a shorter amount of time, without having to leave your computer.

Broadcasting Your Own News

Interesting news occurs every day around the world. If you capture a particularly interesting video, such as a tornado ripping through a trailer park or shopping mall, your local news station will likely want a copy to broadcast. However, your local news stations may not be interested in broadcasting all types of videos that you may capture, so you can skip the middleman and broadcast those yourself over the Internet, as shown in Figure 19-3.

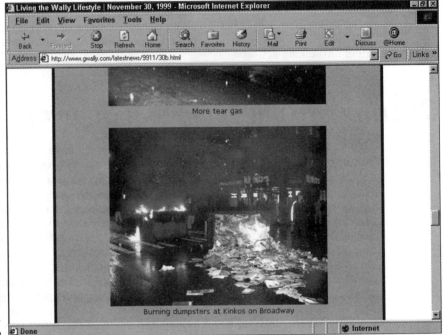

Figure 19-3: Still images from the riots that occurred during the World Trade Organization summit in Seattle.

You can broadcast video, still images, and news about events that your local news station doesn't cover.

Visit the Free Speech Internet Television organization (www.freespeech.org), which set up its own Web site claiming to counter the views of ordinary audio and visual media, which it argues are more interested in keeping stockholders and advertisers happy than reporting actual facts.

Free Speech Internet Television provides alternative media organizations a way to air their views. At the Web site, you can read articles and view video files of mini-documentaries that argue against commercial logging on Federal lands, expose the existence of sweat shops in New York City, or detail the rebellion of the Zapatista National Liberation Army against the Mexican government.

If you want to make a political statement, think of all the creative ways you can capture video through your Web cam and provide information to people all over the world. As the video footage of Rodney King and Los Angeles police officers proved, even a short video can have a lasting impact on the rest of the world.

Putting on Your Own Show

If you ever dreamed of hosting your own show, like Oprah Winfrey or Jay Leno, don't wait for a television network to discover you. Get started right away by broadcasting your show on a Web site using a Web cam.

Jennifer Ringley, the woman who helped make Web cams popular when she used her Web cam to broadcast her life through the Internet, runs a bi-weekly show called *JenniShow.*

On *JenniShow,* viewers see Jennifer visit the house used to film the final scene from the movie, *The Blair Witch Project,* fly an airplane, or listen to her chat with friends. Like the original JenniCam, *JenniShow* provides a peek into the life of Jennifer when she's not in front of her normal Web cam.

While *JenniShow* is popular enough to broadcast through its own Web site, many show and event promoters go through a special Web site dubbed Live on the Net (`http://liveonthenet.com`), which provides a one-stop Web site listing everyone's shows for viewers to watch.

Through Live on the Net, you can watch aspiring musicians perform their songs in a coffeehouse, watch minor league baseball games, or see award presentations for the best in country music.

Armed with a Web cam and a little imagination, you can make your name and face a household word through the Internet.

Making a Sales Presentation

Traveling sales representatives often carry samples of their products, brochures, and videotapes showing how their products work. The amount of information a sales representative can carry is often limited to his or her physical endurance and carrying limitations.

Rather than burden sales people with numerous videotapes to show potential clients, businesses can store all sales presentations on a company Web site, so customers can view video demonstrations over and over again from the convenience of their personal computer.

Video sales presentations can also show clients places located in other parts of the city, state, country, or world. Many real estate sales agents use video presentations to show clients homes and other properties, so they don't have to take the time to visit these locations in person.

In case you sell a factory machine (such as an automatic chicken plucker), don't just tell your clients the benefits of your machine. Let them see it live in action at a real factory through a Web cam.

The next time you need to show a demonstration or show someone an image that the person might not normally get to see, you can use your Web cam to convince others and close that all-important sale.

Conducting a Science Experiment

The next time you need to conduct a science experiment for a school project or science fair, capture it with your Web cam so people can see how you conducted your experiment and arrived at your conclusions.

For example, if your experiment involves testing the effects of different types of music on the growth of plants, use your Web cam and time-lapse photography to show plants thriving under the influence of classical music or withering up and dying under the bombardment of heavy metal or rap music. (Or use your Web cam to show your parents withering up and cringing under the bombardment of heavy metal or rap music.)

By viewing the video of the actual results of your experiment, rather than still images or boring written reports, people can better understand what your experiment proves.

Some satirical variations on the science experiment use for a Web cam include the Amazing Wall Cam (www.compassnet.com/~rdeneefe/wallcam.htm), which lets you watch a wall in someone's house, or the WebCam Cinemaplex (www.mich.com/~rrreibel/sudcinma.htm), which provides three Web cams — so you can watch paint peel off a wall, grass grow outside, or continental drift occur before your eyes from a satellite view of the Earth, as shown in Figure 19-4.

Figure 19-4:
Watch the
plates in the
Earth's crust
shift and
move
through the
wonders of
a Web cam!

Smile! You're on Camera!

One of the most innovative and frequently copied ideas was the groundbreaking humor of *Candid Camera* (www.candidcamera.com), which first began as a radio program in 1947 and then became a weekly television show that recently has been revived.

The premise behind *Candid Camera* was to catch people in unusual situations, just to record their often confused, puzzled, or hilarious reactions.

If you want to have a little fun along the lines of *Candid Camera,* plan your trick, set up your victim, and wait for your Web cam to record the action.

One popular trick is to hide a Web cam somewhere in your house to catch family members doing something they're not supposed to do. As Figure 19-5 shows, you can hide your Web cam in your kitchen and record someone sneaking in for a fattening snack that they swore off for their diet.

Figure 19-5:
By secretly installing a Web cam in your house, you can record what people do when you're not around.

If the idea of catching people doing something they shouldn't be doing amuses you, install a Web cam in a unique spot today! (Just make sure you don't break any laws in the process. Remember, secretly capturing someone with your Web cam may be amusing to you, but could cause you legal headaches in the future. Then again, keep in mind that any embarrassing moment that you can record about others, others can record about you, too. If you're ever in doubt about the legalities of using your Web cam, take some time to consult with legal experts. You may be glad you did.)

Chapter 20

Ten Troubleshooting Tips for Your Web Cam

*A*lthough Web cams are fairly reliable and easy to set up, don't be surprised if your Web cam doesn't work, you can't see pictures clearly, or the whole process of videoconferencing seems to be more trouble than it's worth.

Before you toss your Web cam out the window or into the garbage can, browse through this chapter to see if you can salvage your Web cam and get it working correctly.

Web cams, like any computer accessory, may be faulty — don't be afraid to return a defective Web cam and try a new one.

No Video Images Appear

One of the most common problems with Web cams is hooking them up and finding that nothing appears on your computer screen. Assuming you don't have a completely defective Web cam in the first place, Web cams may refuse to display any images for a number of different reasons, including an improperly installed device driver, loose or improperly connected cable, defective ports, or a firewall blocking the transmission.

Web cam device driver improperly installed

Your computer may not know how to use your Web cam until you install a special device driver program for your particular Web cam. Your Web cam should come with the device driver stored on a CD-ROM or floppy disk.

Before you connect your Web cam to your computer, install the device driver. You may have to restart your computer after installing the device driver. Sometimes reinstalling the same device driver can fix problems as well.

Because device drivers are nothing more than programs, don't be surprised to find that the device driver doesn't work on your particular computer (for some bizarre technical reason). Sometimes device drivers don't like a particular chip installed on a computer; sometimes device drivers only work with certain versions of an operating system (such as Windows 98 but not Windows NT); and sometimes device drivers conflict with previously installed device drivers for other accessories such as printers, scanners, or external storage devices such as Zip drives.

If you installed the device driver for your Web cam, and you still can't see any video images through it, visit the Web site of your Web cam's manufacturer. You may need to download and install a newer version of the device driver. If that doesn't work, the Web cam manufacturer's Web site may have posted various solutions that have worked for other people; and if you follow these instructions, they may work for you as well.

Device drivers are often designed for a particular Web cam brand and model. So even if you get a device driver from the company that made your Web cam, make sure you get the right device driver for your particular Web cam model.

For some Web cam programs, you may need to manually select the Web cam driver before the program can receive images from your Web cam, as shown in Figure 20-1.

Loose or improperly connected cable

Make sure the Web cam is securely connected to the USB, parallel, or serial port of your computer. Because computers are unpredictably temperamental beasts, try plugging the Web cam into a different but identical port. For example, most computers have two USB ports, so if your Web cam doesn't work with the first USB port, try the other USB port.

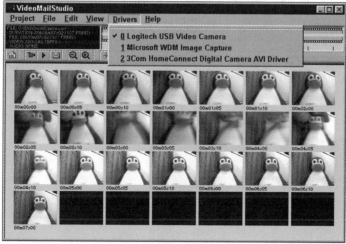

Figure 20-1:
Some
Web cam
programs
require you
to manually
choose your
Web cam
driver
through a
pull-down
menu.

iMac computers have two groups of built-in USB ports: one on its side and another used to connect the keyboard and mouse to the computer. Always plug your Web cam into the built-in USB ports on the side rather than into the keyboard port because the keyboard USB port may not have enough power to run a Web cam.

Defective ports

Sometimes the problem isn't with your Web cam but with your computer's ports. In particular, USB ports on Windows-based computers need a device driver installed to make them work.

Windows 98 includes a device driver for using USB ports. However, Windows 95 needs a USB Supplement file included with the Windows 95 OEM Service Release (OSR) updates. If you don't have this USB Supplement file installed, Windows 95 won't recognize any USB ports on your computer.

To see if your Windows-based computer recognizes that your USB ports even exist, follow these steps:

1. **Right-click the My Computer icon on the Windows desktop and choose Properties.**

   The System Properties dialog box appears.

2. **Click the Device Manager tab.**

3. **Click the View Devices by Type radio button.**

4. **Scroll down the list until you see an icon and label for Universal Serial Bus controllers, as shown in Figure 20-2.**

   If you don't see this icon or label, your computer either doesn't have any USB ports or the proper USB device drivers haven't been installed.

5. **Click OK.**

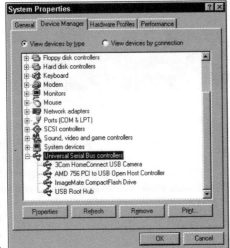

Figure 20-2:
Checking
for the
existence of
USB ports
on a
Windows
computer.

Firewall blocking your transmissions

If you have a firewall protecting your computer, the firewall may think your video transmissions belong to a hacker who's secretly transmitting information out of your computer. As a result, the firewall may block your video transmissions.

This problem is most likely to occur when you're running a videoconferencing program, because most firewalls are preconfigured to allow normal Web browsing activity to occur but aren't configured to handle transmissions from videoconferencing programs. Thus when a firewall detects videoconferencing data, it may inadvertently assume the data is unauthorized or coming from a hacker, and simply block that data. To solve this problem, you may need to turn off or modify your firewall to allow the video transmissions to go through.

Turning off or weakening the security of your firewall is usually a very bad idea because it can leave your computer wide open to an attack from an outside intruder. Unless you're absolutely sure that your computer won't become a target of an outside intruder, keep your firewall as secure as possible. If possible, try to configure your firewall to allow data from your videoconferencing program to go through. That way, you can keep the protection of your firewall while also being able to enjoy the benefits of videoconferencing.

Video Appears Jerky

Web cam advertising may give you the illusion that Web cam images look as crisp, clear, and sharp as images that appear on your television. The reality is that Web cams are still an evolving technology, which means they give you images of much lower quality than those you get from ordinary video cameras.

So if the images from your Web cam appear chunky, jerky, or just plain horrible, don't despair. To improve your Web cam images, look into such culprits as a slow processor, a slow modem, or a slow parallel port. You can also improve jerky images by keeping your movements to a minimum.

Slow processor

The faster and more advanced your processor, the faster everything on your computer runs. So if you're still limping along with an ancient Pentium processor running at 133 MHz, don't be surprised that your Web cam images don't seem as responsive as the exact same Web cam running on your friend's Athlon computer running at 950 MHz.

Short of buying a brand new computer or upgrading to a faster processor, some ways to speed up a slow processor include adding more memory (RAM) or shutting down as many programs as possible to free up more memory and processing power for your Web cam.

Slow modem

Videoconferencing is one technology that depends heavily on a variety of factors (most of which are out of your control) to display images from your Web cam. Although you can't do anything about inherent bottlenecks or problems with the Internet, you can speed up your own connection to the Internet.

The slower your Internet connection, the slower your Web cam transmits images over the Internet through a videoconference or Web site. If you want to improve the quality of your Web cam images, get a faster modem, such as a 56K modem. Or better yet, get a high-speed Internet connection such as a DSL or cable modem.

If you can't afford a faster modem or Internet connection, try to avoid peak periods of Internet usage, such as during the evening, on holidays, or on weekends. Fewer people crowding the Internet at any given time means that your Web cam can transmit images faster. Also if you shut down as many programs as possible that you don't need at the moment, you can free up memory for your Web cam and offset (to a certain extent) the slowness of your Internet connection.

Sometimes if you disconnect and then reconnect to the Internet, you can magically get a faster connection (or at least a faster connection than your previous connection). Occasionally when you dial the phone, you may hear static on the line or you may hear voices from an entirely different conversation. Because these problems can disrupt voice conversations, they can disrupt computer connections too, so by hanging up and dialing again, you may get lucky and get a much better phone connection for your computer.

Slow parallel port

If possible, get a Web cam that connects to a USB port, because USB ports transfer data faster than parallel or serial ports. If you're stuck with a Web cam that connects to a parallel port, expect images to appear jerky, because parallel ports aren't always fast enough to transfer video images in real time.

Just to make matters more confusing, you may have one of three different kinds of parallel ports: SPP (Standard Parallel Port), EPP (Extended Parallel Port), or ECP (Extended Capability Port).

SPP ports are the most primitive parallel ports and were only designed for connecting to a printer. The EPP and ECP ports are extensions to the SPP standard and transmit information faster. To determine what type of parallel port you have on a Windows-based computer, follow these steps:

1. **Click the Start button on the Windows taskbar and choose Programs⇨ Accessories⇨System Tools⇨System Information.**

   A Microsoft System Information window appears.

2. **Click the plus sign to the left of the Components heading that appears on the left side of the window.**

   A list of subheadings appears.

3. **Click Ports.**

The Microsoft System Information window may pause temporarily as it gathers information about your port types.

You may want to click the Basic Information radio button to avoid looking at more technical details than you may care to know about your computer ports.

4. **Scroll down until you see the listing for your printer (parallel) ports.**

If your parallel port is an SPP, the listing just says Printer Port (LPT1) or something similar. If your parallel port is an EPP or ECP printer port, the listing says EPP Printer Port (LPT1) or ECP Printer Port (LPT1).

Keep your movements to a minimum

If you move too quickly, your Web cam images may appear slightly delayed, blurry, or jerky. As a general rule, limit your movements, so your images aren't too disconcerting to watch. If you wave your hands around and constantly change positions in your chair, anyone watching your Web cam images may see nothing but blurry images.

Videoconferencing Problems

In its current state, videoconferencing taxes the resources of most computers, so if you try videoconferencing and find that the images are fuzzy and the audio is muffled, congratulate yourself for being a videoconferencing pioneer. Videoconferencing works best when all users are connected through a local area network. If you use an Internet connection such as a cable modem or an ordinary 56K modem, the transfer speed of both video and audio will always be slower than through a dedicated network.

Still, if you want to use videoconferencing for fun or business, consider switching from full-duplex to half-duplex or avoiding long-distance calling to make your videoconferencing experience more enjoyable and less excruciating.

Switch from full-duplex to half-duplex

Ideally, you want to use full-duplex mode when videoconferencing because this feature allows you to speak and receive audio simultaneously. However, because this can slow down your computer, you can try speeding up your computer (and the transmission of your video images) by switching to half-duplex mode, as shown in Figure 20-3.

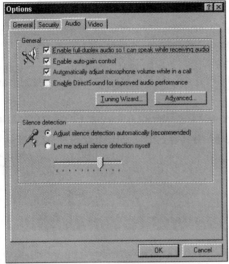

With half-duplex mode, you must stop talking before the other person can start talking. Half-duplex mode is like using a "walkie-talkie," so only one person can speak at a time. Although inconvenient, half-duplex mode can speed up your video images slightly.

Avoid calling long distance if possible

Although videoconferencing may seem like an ideal way to make long-distance phone calls for free (and with video added as well), the reality is that the greater the distance between the two parties, the lower the quality of your video images.

This problem occurs because of the way the Internet works. Instead of connecting you directly with another computer, the Internet uses several intermediary computers that transfer data between you and the other person. The more computers between you and someone else, the slower your transmission speed is. For short distances, only one or two computers may be between you and another person, but for long distances (such as connecting to a computer on another continent), half a dozen or more computers may exist between you and the other person.

To see how many different computers may exist between you and someone else, you can run a special program called Trace Route, which not only shows you the number of computers in between you and someone else, but also how much time it takes to transfer data from one computer to another.

To run the Trace Route program from within Windows, follow these steps:

1. **Connect to the Internet.**

2. **Click the Start button on the Windows taskbar and choose Programs⇨ MS-DOS Prompt.**

   An MS-DOS Prompt window appears.

3. **Type** tracert **followed by the IP address of the computer you want to contact, and press Enter.**

   For example, if the IP address of the other computer is 192.108.254.1, you type **tracert 192.108.254.1** and press Enter. The trace route program shows the number of intermediary computers between you and the computer you want to contact, along with the transmission rates of each computer, measured in milliseconds (ms), as shown below.

```
C:\WINDOWS>tracert 192.108.254.1
Tracing route to cisco.teleport.com [192.108.254.1]
over a maximum of 30 hops:
  1     17 ms      42 ms      13 ms   cr3-
        hfc3.fed1.sdca.home.net [24.0.39.1]
  2     22 ms      16 ms      27 ms   bb1-
        ge3-0.rdc1.sdca.home.net [24.5.247.33]
  3     43 ms      17 ms      54 ms   c1-
        pos4-0.sndgca1.home.net [24.7.74.101]
  4     22 ms      15 ms      11 ms   c1-
        pos1-0.anhmca1.home.net [24.7.64.69]
  5     27 ms      25 ms      25 ms   24.7.65.165
  6     37 ms      30 ms      17 ms
        200.ATM1-0.BR2.SJC1.ALTER.NET [137.39.91.61]
  7     28 ms      25 ms      21 ms
        154.ATM2-0.XR2.SJC1.ALTER.NET [152.63.51.186]
  8     34 ms      21 ms      33 ms   193.at-2-0-
        0.TR4.SCL1.ALTER.NET [152.63.48.254]
  9     92 ms      53 ms      62 ms
        207.ATM6-0.TR2.SEA1.ALTER.NET [152.63.3.225]
 10     76 ms      55 ms      67 ms
        198.ATM7-0.XR2.SEA4.ALTER.NET [146.188.200.213]
 11     69 ms      66 ms      64 ms   192.ATM8-0-
        0.GW1.POR2.ALTER.NET [146.188.200.189]
 12     84 ms      52 ms      57 ms   cisco.teleport.com
        [192.108.254.1]
```

The more computers between you and your final destination, the more likely your video images will slow down (or be lost altogether) during transmission. Any computer with a slow transmission rate (anything more than 250 ms) will likely cause delays with your video transmissions as well.

Each time you run the Trace Route program, you get different results because traffic on the Internet constantly changes. If you find that your Internet connection is running particularly slow, the Trace Route program can show you how many other computers your data is passing through and how much time it takes for each computer to transfer data.

If you want to run the Trace Route program on a Macintosh, you need to download an Internet utility such as iNetTools from WildPackets (`www.wildpackets.com/products/iNetTools.html`).

Your Internet service provider may actually be located in another part of the world than you are, even if you connect by dialing a local access number. For example, information sent through an America Online account always passes through AOL's main computers in Virginia. So if you're in Los Angeles and try to connect to someone in San Diego, your data has to pass through AOL's computers in Virginia first.

Part VI
Appendixes

The 5th Wave   By Rich Tennant

"Remember— if you're updating the family Web site, no more animated GIFs of your sister swinging from a tree and scratching her armpits!"

In this part . . .

This last part of the book provides information about different Web cam manufacturers so that you can visit their Web sites and see what these companies have to say about their own Web cams. By browsing through different Web cam Web sites, you can see which companies offer the best deals and the most feature-packed Web cam.

In case you don't understand some of the terms that Web cam manufacturers use, flip through the glossary in this part of the book. Computer companies love using multi-syllable words in place of a simple word, so the glossary can help you decipher the technical details and understand what the heck some of these companies are trying to tell you.

Finally, to help you get the most out of your Web cam, a CD-ROM in a plastic sleeve is included in the back of this book. As long as you don't break the CD-ROM while trying to peel it out of its plastic cocoon, you will have several megabytes of different freeware and shareware programs that you can use with your Web cam.

Appendix A

Web Cam Manufacturers

● ●

*W*eb cams are quickly becoming a popular commodity. But as with all computer accessories, not all Web cams are alike. Before buying a Web cam, browse through this appendix, visit different Web sites, and consider which Web cams offer you the most for your money.

Rather than buying directly from the manufacturer, consider buying a Web cam through a mail-order company, which may offer you a discount off the retail price and also help you avoid paying sales tax.

Web cam companies always post the latest device drivers for their Web cams on their Web sites. You may want to download the latest version of the device driver for your Web cam before connecting the Web cam to your computer. If your camera starts acting flaky, you lose the CD-ROM that came with your Web cam, your entire hard drive gets wiped out, or your computer totally crashes, you will have to visit the Web site of your Web cam manufacturer to download the device driver you need.

3Com

Although 3Com's HomeConnect PC Digital Web is designed for Windows users, the 3Com Web site offers software drivers that you can download to run this Web cam from a Macintosh.

3Com originally marketed the popular Palm hand-held computers, until they spun-off the division into a separate company. 3Com runs its own live radio broadcast show that focuses on networking and other exciting computer products that 3Com sells. If you catch the right broadcast, maybe you can even hear the 3Com DJs talking about the wonderful Web cams made by the friendly folks at 3Com. The contact information is

> 3Com
> 5400 Bayfront Plaza
> P.O. Box 58145
> Santa Clara, CA 95052-8145
> Phone: (408) 326-5000
> Fax: (408) 326-5001
> Web site: www.3com.com

Creative Technologies

Creative Technologies sells two varieties of Web cams: a stationary model and a portable model that runs off batteries and doubles as a digital camera for capturing still images. Another nice feature of the portable model is that it includes a built-in voice recorder, so you can take it along with you and add voice notes to go along with any still images you capture.

For example, a real estate agent may take pictures of different properties and record a short note about each one, saving him or her the time and trouble of writing down notes (and the risk of losing them).

If you visit the Creative Technologies Web site, you can even take a virtual tour of the corporate headquarters (presumably captured with the company's own Web cams). The contact information is

> Creative Technologies
> 31 International Business Park
> Creative Resource
> Singapore 609921
> Phone: (65) 8954000
> Fax: (65) 8954000
> Web site: www.creative.com

D-Link Systems

D-Link Systems sells a wide variety of networking equipment such as routers, hubs, and print servers, in addition to Web cam/digital camera combinations. By using this Web cam, you can capture images directly to your computer or take your Web cam with you and use it as a digital camera to capture still and video images. The company's contact information is

> D-Link Systems
> 53 Discovery Drive
> Irvine, CA 92618
> Phone: (949) 788-0805
> Fax: (949) 753-7033
> Web site: www.dlink.com

Eastman Kodak Company

As part of its move toward the world of digital photography, Kodak offers its own digital camera for those who like the security and comfort of buying a brand name long associated with photography. If you visit the company's Web site, you can also find out the interesting history behind Eastman Kodak. Perhaps, over time, you'll even get to see whether this company makes a successful transition away from film to pure digital photography. The contact information is

Eastman Kodak Company
343 State St.
Rochester, NY 14650
Phone: (716) 724-4000
Web site: www.kodak.com

Hawking Technology

Hawking Technology sells a wide range of Web cams, in addition to networking equipment. One of the latest Hawking models is a combination Web cam and digital camera, which you can detach from your computer to take pictures wherever you go. The contact information is

Hawking Technology
6A Faraday
Irvine, CA 92618
Phone: (949) 580-0888
Fax: (949) 580-0880
Web site: www.hawkingtech.com
E-mail: info@hawkingtech.com

Intel Corporation

Flush with cash from its microprocessor business, Intel has branched out into selling a variety of other products — including Web cams, networking equipment, and language compilers.

By visiting Intel's Web site, you can read actual success stories from happy Intel Web cam customers, including a story about a family who uses Web cams to share "virtual" Thanksgiving dinners between three separate states; a business executive who uses videoconferencing to stay in touch with his wife and twins when he's on the road; and a real estate agent who sends video e-mails of available properties to prospective clients. The company's contact information is

Intel Corporation
2200 Mission College Blvd. RN6-37
Santa Clara, CA 95052-8119
Phone: (408) 765-8080
Fax: (408) 765-1399
Web site: www.intel.com

Kensington Technology Group

Kensington Technology Group makes a variety of computer accessories for Windows and Macintosh computers and is one of the few companies that sells Web cams for both Windows and Macintosh computers. The company's contact information is

Kensington Technology Group
2855 Campus Drive
San Mateo, CA 94403
Phone: (650) 572-2700
Fax: (650) 572-9675
Web site: www.kensington.com

Logitech Inc.

Logitech has a long history of selling a variety of computer accessories — from mice and trackballs to joysticks and now Web cams. Logitech's Web cams, originally sold by Connectix, are one of the most popular Web cams in the world for both Windows and Macintosh computers. The company's contact information is

Logitech Inc.
6505 Kaiser Drive
Fremont, CA 94555
Phone: (510) 795-8500
Web site: www.logitech.com

If you're planning to hook up a Web cam to a computer running the Linux operating system, visit www.crynwr.com/qcpc, where you can find plenty of information for running Logitech Web cams with Linux.

PAR Technologies, Inc.

PAR Technologies sells a uniquely shaped, colorful Web cam that looks like a science-fiction alien spider with skinny legs and a big eye where the camera lens sticks out. These Web cams, dubbed Kritters, come in matching colors for your iMac.

Because the Macintosh is often associated with fashion and trendsetting design, PAR Technologies also provides Windows device drivers that you can download from the company's Web site. That way you can have a cool looking Kritter Web cam to go along with your beige, square box running Microsoft Windows. The company's contact information is

PAR Technologies, Inc.
15020 N. 74th St.
Scottsdale, AZ 85260
Phone: (480) 922-0044
Fax: (480) 922-1090
Web site: www.irez.com

Xirlink Corporate Headquarters

You may wonder whether you want to trust buying anything from a company with a name that sounds like a bad *Star Trek* character. But take heart. You may never have heard of Xirlink because it markets its Web cams under the IBM and Earthlink brand names.

If you visit the Xirlink Web site, you can download Macintosh device drivers for your Web cam so you can hook up a Xirlink Web cam to a Macintosh. The next time you buy a Web cam, check the package carefully. You may actually be buying a Xirlink Web cam without knowing it. The company's contact information is

Xirlink Corporate Headquarters
2210 O'Toole Avenue
San Jose, CA 95131
Web site: www.xirlink.com

Appendix B

About the CD-ROM

*H*ere's just some of the stuff available on the *Web Cams For Dummies* CD-ROM:

- ✔ StealthWatch, a freeware program for Windows that turns your Web cam into a security camera to monitor your computer, a door, or any other area that you want to monitor.
- ✔ StripCam, a great freeware program for the Macintosh to control your Web cam and post your images on the Internet.
- ✔ TrueTech WebCam, a great freeware program for Windows to control your Web cam and post your images on the Internet.
- ✔ After Effects, a demo program for Windows and the Macintosh that lets you add Hollywood-style special effects to any videos that you capture from your Web cam.
- ✔ Media Cleaner Pro, a demo for Windows and the Macintosh to show you how to compress videos, so you can post them on Web sites or send them by e-mail.
- ✔ Microsoft NetMeeting, a freeware program for Windows so you can use your Web cam to chat and see others in a videoconference.

System Requirements

Make sure that your computer meets the minimum system requirements listed below. If your computer doesn't match up to most of these requirements, you may have problems using the contents of the CD-ROM.

- ✔ A PC with a Pentium or faster processor, or a Mac OS computer with a 68040 or faster processor.
- ✔ Microsoft Windows 95 or later, or Mac OS system software 7.55 or later.
- ✔ At least 32MB of total RAM installed on your computer.

✔ At least 150MB of hard drive space available to install all the software from this CD-ROM. (You need less space if you don't install every program.)

✔ A CD-ROM drive — double-speed (2x) or faster.

✔ A sound card for PCs. (Mac OS computers have built-in sound support.)

✔ A monitor capable of displaying at least 256 colors or grayscale.

✔ A modem with a speed of at least 14,400 kbps.

If you need more information on the basics, check out *PCs For Dummies,* 7th Edition, by Dan Gookin; *Macs For Dummies,* 7th Edition, by David Pogue; *iMac For Dummies,* by David Pogue; *Windows Me Millennium Edition For Dummies, Windows 98 For Dummies,* or *Windows 95 For Dummies,* 2nd Edition, all by Andy Rathbone (all published by IDG Books Worldwide, Inc.).

Using the CD-ROM with Microsoft Windows

To install the items from the CD-ROM to your hard drive, follow these steps:

1. **Insert the CD-ROM into your computer's CD-ROM drive.**

2. **Open your browser.**

   If you do not have a browser, you can find Microsoft Internet Explorer and Netscape Communicator on the CD. They are located in the Programs folders at the root of the CD.

3. **Click Start⇨Run.**

4. **In the dialog box that appears, type *D:\START.HTM*.**

   Replace *D* with whatever drive letter your CD-ROM uses. (If you don't know the letter, find out how your CD-ROM drive is listed under My Computer.

5. **Read through the license agreement, nod your head, and then click the Accept button if you want to use the CD-ROM.**

   After you click Accept, you jump to the main menu. This action displays the file that will walk you through the contents of the CD-ROM.

6. **To navigate within the interface, simply click any topic of interest to take you to an explanation of the files on the CD and how to use or install them.**

7. **To install the software from the CD-ROM, simply click the software name.**

   You see two options — the option to run or open the file from the current location or the option to save the file to your hard drive. Choose to run or open the file from its current location and the installation will continue. After you finish with the interface, simply close your browser as usual.

   Eject the CD-ROM. Carefully place it back in the plastic jacket of the book for safekeeping.

In order to run some of the programs on the *Web Cams For Dummies* CD-ROM, you may need to keep the CD-ROM inside your CD-ROM drive. This is a good thing. Otherwise, the installed program would have required you to install a very large chunk of the program to your hard drive, which could have kept you from installing other software.

Using the CD-ROM with Mac OS

To install the items from the CD-ROM to your hard drive, follow these steps:

1. **Insert the CD-ROM into your computer's CD-ROM drive.**

   In a moment, an icon representing the CD-ROM you just inserted appears on your Mac desktop. Chances are, the icon looks like a CD-ROM.

2. **Double-click the CD-ROM icon to show the CD-ROM's contents.**

3. **Double-click the License Agreement icon.**

   This is the license that you are agreeing to by using the CD-ROM. You can close this window after you look over the agreement.

4. **Double-click the Read Me First icon.**

   The Read Me First text file contains information about the CD-ROM's programs and any last-minute instructions you may need in order to correctly install them.

5. **To install most programs, open the program folder and double-click the icon called "Install" or "Installer."**

   Sometimes the installers are actually self-extracting archives, which just means that the program files have been bundled up into an archive, and this self-extractor unbundles the files and places them on your hard drive. This kind of program is often called a .sea. Double-click anything with .sea in the title, and it will run just like an installer.

6. **Some programs don't come with installers. For those, just drag the program's folder from the CD-ROM window and drop it on your hard drive icon.**

After you install the programs you want, you can eject the CD-ROM. Carefully place it back in the plastic jacket of the book for safekeeping.

What You'll Find

Shareware programs are fully functional, free trial versions of copyrighted programs. If you like particular programs, register with their authors for a nominal fee and receive licenses, enhanced versions, and technical support. *Freeware programs* are free, copyrighted games, applications, and utilities. You can copy them to as many PCs as you like — free — but they have no technical support. GNU software is governed by its own license, which is included inside the folder of the GNU software. There are no restrictions on distribution of this software. See the GNU license for more details. Trial, demo, or evaluation versions are usually limited either by time or functionality (such as being unable to save projects).

Here's a summary of the software on this CD-ROM arranged by category. If you use Windows, the CD-ROM interface helps you install software easily. (If you have no idea what I'm talking about when I say "CD-ROM interface," flip back a page or two to find the section, "Using the CD-ROM with Microsoft Windows.")

If you use a Mac OS computer, you can take advantage of the easy Mac interface to quickly install the programs.

Web cam programs

CamShot WebCam HTTP Server, from BroadGun Software (http://broadgun.com/camshot)

For Windows. Shareware. CamShot WebCam HTTP Server is a versatile Web cam program that can post your images to a Web site or turn your Web cam into a surveillance tool for protecting your computer or making sure people are behaving correctly.

CoolCam, from YUV422 Software (http://hometown.aol.com/yuv422/coolcam.html)

For Mac. Shareware. CoolCam is a Macintosh Web cam program that can post images from your Web cam to a Web site.

Eyes&Ears, from AckNak Technologies (www.intech2.com)

For Windows. Shareware. Eyes&Ears can turn your Web cam and microphone into a complete surveillance system for capturing visual images and sound to protect your personal property.

HomeWatcherLite, from HomeWatcher.com (www.homewatcher.com)

For Windows. Trial. HomeWatcherLite turns your Web cam into a surveillance tool by capturing images periodically and time-stamping them.

iVista, from InetCam (www.homewatcher.com)

For Windows. Trial. iVista is a unique program that allows live video and audio streaming from your Web cam, with the proper hardware. With iVista, you can provide live video on your Web site.

KABCam, from KAB Software (www.kabsoftware.com)

For Windows. Shareware. KABCam automates the process of posting images from your Web cam to a Web site.

NetSnap, from PeleSoft (www.netsnap.com)

For Windows. Trial. NetSnap posts images from your Web cam to a Web site or captures images periodically to monitor a scene or object.

Oculus, from Poubelle Software (www.intlweb.com/Oculus2)

For Mac. Shareware. Oculus is a full-featured Web cam program for posting images to a Web site, capturing movement detected by your Web cam, or simply controlling your Web cam from your Macintosh.

SiteCam, from NuSpectra Multimedia, Inc. (www.nuspectra.com)

For Mac. Trial. A full-featured Web cam program that offers streaming video and audio, so people can see and hear live images and sounds from your Web cam and computer microphone.

StealthWatch, from CompuTrust International, Inc. (www.stealthwatch.com)

For Windows. Freeware. StealthWatch turns your Web cam into a security device by taking pictures periodically and storing them on the Internet for future reference. As soon as StealthWatch detects a change in images from your Web cam, it starts snapping pictures, so you can catch a thief or intruder in the act.

StripCam, from David Van Brink (www.stripcam.org)

For Mac. Freeware. StripCam is a small, easy-to-use program for capturing images from your Web cam and posting them on a Web site from your Macintosh.

TrueTech WebCam, from TrueTech B.V. (www.truetech.com)

For Windows. Freeware. TrueTech WebCam allows you to control your Web cam and post images to a Web site. A professional version of the program includes streaming audio and video capabilities.

Video Capturix, from Capturix (www.capturix.com)

For Windows. Demo. Video Capturix captures video or still images from your Web cam and time-stamps them to store as .jpeg, .bmp, or .avi files.

WebCam-Control-Center, from Marc Schneider Entertainment (www.marcweb.de/)

For Windows. Trial. WebCam-Control-Center offers two features: automatic uploading of images captured from your Web cam and motion-detection surveillance to capture images when your Web cam detects a change, such as someone moving.

WebCamNow.com Video Broadcaster, from WebCamNow.com (www.webcamnow.com)

For Windows. Freeware. WebCamNow broadcasts live video from your Web cam to the WebCamNow.com Web site where everyone can view your images.

WebCamToo, from PaperJet Software (webcam.paperjet.com)

For Mac. Freeware. WebCamToo is a unique Macintosh Web cam program that includes complete source code, in case you want to modify, update, or just study how the program works.

Web cam games

GameCam SE, from RealityFusion, Inc. (www.realityfusion.com)

For Windows. Special edition. GameCam SE uses your Web cam to put your image inside a video game that you can play against the computer or against another person.

Video editors

Adobe After Effects, from Adobe Systems, Inc. (www.adobe.com)

For Mac and Windows. Trial version. After Effects creates visual effects to add to any of your existing videos captured from your Web cam.

MainVision, from Main Concept GmbH (www.adobe.com)

For Windows. Demo. MainVision provides various filters, shading, and color options for modifying pictures in a video or still image.

MovieWorks Interactive, from Interactive Solutions (www.movieworks.com)

For Mac. Trial. MovieWorks Interactive includes a video editor, paint program, sound editor, and animation program to help you create videos that can play on both Windows and Macintosh computers.

MyFlix, from Mediaware (www.mediaware.com.au)

For Windows. Trial. MyFlix is designed for editing MPEG video files.

Personal AVI Editor, from FlickerFree Multimedia Products (www.flickerfree.com)

For Windows. Shareware. Personal AVI Editor can import .avi and .bmp files and combine them in an .avi video file.

Adobe Premiere, from Adobe Systems, Inc. (www.adobe.com)

For Mac and Windows. Tryout version. Premiere is a popular tool used by professional video editors to manipulate a video, frame by frame.

QuickEditor, from Mathias Tschopp (http://wild.ch/quickeditor)

For Mac and Windows. Shareware. QuickEditor is designed for editing QuickTime video files.

VideoFramer, from FlickerFree Multimedia Products ApS (www.flickerfree.com)

For Windows. Shareware. VideoFramer imports a variety of video files, still images, and audio files, so you can combine them all to create a video with a soundtrack.

Zwei-Stein, from Thugs at Bay (www.musicref.com)

For Windows. Shareware. Zwei-Stein is a multi-track video-editing program that creates RealVideo files. A professional version of the program can save video in different video file formats such as .avi or .mpeg.

Image editors

PaintShop Pro, from Jasc Software (www.jasc.com)

For Windows. Evaluation. PaintShop Pro is an easy-to-use paint program that you can use to edit any still images captured from your Web cam.

WebPainter, from Totally Hip Software (www.totallyhip.com)

For Windows and Mac. Demo. WebPainter is designed for creating graphics for use in Web pages, such as GIF, JPEG, and QuickTime files.

GIF animators

Ulead GIF Animator, from Ulead Systems (www.ulead.com)

For Windows. Trial version. Ulead GIF Animator lets you create, modify, and optimize image files to create an animated GIF file.

GIFLine Pro, from Diprod Software (www.diprode.com)

For Windows. Shareware. GIFLine Pro lets you create animated GIF files for your Web pages.

GIF Movie Gear, from Gamani Productions (www.gamani.com)

For Windows. Shareware. GIF Movie Gear lets you import still images stored in a variety of file formats and convert them into an animated GIF file.

VSE Animation Maker, from Voget Selbach Enterprises GmbH (www.vse-online.com)

For Mac. Demo. VSE Animation Maker lets you create and modify animated GIF files with your Macintosh.

Videoconferencing

NetMeeting, from Microsoft Corp. (www.microsoft.com)

For Windows. Freeware (Part of Internet Explorer). NetMeeting uses your Web cam, speakers, and microphone so you can chat with other people, see them, and type messages to them in real time.

Video compression

DVMPEG, from Darim Vision Corp. (`www.darvision.com`)

For Windows. Demo. DVMPEG compresses and saves AVI video files into MPEG video files.

Media Cleaner Pro, from Terran Interactive (`www.terran.com`)

For Mac and Windows. Demo. Media Cleaner Pro compresses videos captured by your Web cam, often shrinking a video file down in size by several megabytes or more.

Decompression utilities

Photo Crunch, from Imron Corporation (`www.imroncorp.com`)

For Windows. Shareware. Photo Crunch can compress the size of your JPEG and BMP images so you can shrink them just a little bit more to save space.

Stuffit Lite, from Aladdin Systems (`www.aladdinsys.com`)

For Mac. Freeware. Stuffit Lite is a program that lets you open previously compressed files, such as most shareware and freeware programs available over the Internet.

WinZip, from Nico Mak Computing, Inc. (`www.winzip.com`)

For Windows. Shareware. WinZip is an easy-to-use program that can compress and decompress files.

If You've Got Problems (Of the CD-ROM Kind)

I tried my best to compile programs that work on most computers with the minimum system requirements. Alas, your computer may differ, and some programs may not work properly for some reason.

The two likeliest problems are that you don't have enough memory (RAM) for the programs you want to use, or you have other programs running that are affecting installation or running of a program. If you get error messages such as Not enough memory or Setup cannot continue, try one or more of these methods and then try using the software again:

- ✔ **Turn off any antivirus software that you have on your computer.** Installers sometimes mimic virus activity and may make your computer incorrectly believe that it is being infected by a virus.

- ✔ **Close all running programs.** The more programs you're running, the less memory is available to other programs. Installers also typically update files and programs; if you keep other programs running, installation may not work properly.

- ✔ **In Windows, close the CD-ROM interface and run demos or installations directly from Windows Explorer.** The interface itself can tie up system memory, or even conflict with certain kinds of interactive demos. Use Windows Explorer to browse the files on the CD-ROM and launch installers or demos.

- ✔ **Have your local computer store add more RAM to your computer.** This is, admittedly, a drastic and somewhat expensive step. However, if you have a Windows 95 PC or a Mac OS computer with a PowerPC chip, adding more memory can really help the speed of your computer and enable more programs to run at the same time.

If you still have trouble installing the items from the CD-ROM, please call the IDG Books Worldwide Customer Care phone number: 800-762-2974 (outside the U.S.: 317-572-3993).

Glossary

● ●

AIFF: Acronym that stands for Audio Interchange File Format, which is a special digital audio file format.

animated GIF: A special GIF file that can display simple animation, such as banner ads or short cartoons. See GIF.

ASF: Acronym that stands for Advanced Streaming Format, a new Microsoft file format standard for displaying video. *See* AVI.

AVI: Acronym that stands for Audio Video Interleaved, which is a video file format developed for Microsoft. Sometimes called Video for Windows format and abbreviated as VFW. *See* ASF.

bitmap: A graphic image stored as a series of pixels. Paint-type programs create bitmap files.

BMP: Acronym that stands for BitMaP, which is a common graphics file format for storing still images.

CCD sensor: Acronym that stands for Charge-Coupled Devices sensor, which is used by Web cams to capture higher-resolution images. *See* CMOS sensor.

chat room: Area that multiple people can join so they can chat with one another.

CMOS sensor: Acronym that stands for Complimentary Metal Oxide-Silicon sensor, which is less expensive to make but captures lower-quality video images. *See* CCD sensor.

codec: Acronym that stands for compressor/decompressor, which is an algorithm for compressing video and audio data.

color support: The ability to capture or display a wide variety of different colors. The more colors a Web cam supports, the sharper the image it can capture. Color support is often cryptically described as 16-bit (which means the Web cam can display a maximum of 64,000 colors) or 24-bit (which means the Web cam can display a maximum of 16.8 million colors).

CompuServe: Online service that originally created the GIF file format. *See* GIF.

CU-SeeMe: The first program to make videoconferencing popular.

cutout animation: An animation technique in which one portion of the image changes or moves at a time.

desktop: The background image that appears whenever your computer isn't running any programs.

device driver: Special program designed to connect a peripheral, such as a Web cam, to your computer.

digital video capture speed: Defines how many frames per second (fps) a Web cam captures when recording a video. Most Web cams can capture video at 30 frames per second. The higher the fps rate, the smoother the video image will appear.

distance learning: Using a Web cam or live video image to attend class or learn from the convenience of another location.

DSL: Acronym that stands for Digital Subscriber Line, which is a fast Internet connection provided through a special telephone line.

filters: A graphics manipulation feature that can modify the way an image appears, such as making an image look as if it was painted on a stained glass surface or a tough textured surface.

FireWire port: Special port used for transferring video captured by digital video camcorders to a computer. Also called an IEEE 1394 port or an i.LINK port.

focus range: Defines how far away and how close up a Web cam can capture an image.

frame rate: Defines how many frames per second are used to capture an image. Also defines how many frames appear per second to display a video image.

FTP: Acronym that stands for File Transfer Protocol, which is the method used to transfer images from your Web cam to a Web site.

GIF: Acronym that stands for Graphics Interchange Format, a cross-platform graphics file format standard. GIF files often end with the file extension gif and are suited for displaying objects with 256 colors or fewer, such as line drawings or logos. *See* animated GIF.

Graphics file format: Special way of storing graphical images on disk. Some common still image file formats include GIF, JPEG, BMP, and PCX. Some common video file formats are AVI and QuickTime.

HTML: Acronym that stands for HyperText Markup Language, which is a special code language designed to define the appearance and layout of Web pages.

HTTP: Acronym that stands for HyperText Transfer Protocol, which is the method for transferring data from Web sites to Web browsers. *See* HTTP streaming.

HTTP streaming: A method of transferring a video file to a hard drive for display by the user. *See* RTP/RTSP streaming.

ICQ: Instant messaging program that is a play on the phrase, "I seek you." Often used to help people coordinate a videoconference.

ILS: Acronym that stands for Internet Locator Service, which is designed to help people find one another so they can join a videoconference.

iMovie: Digital video editing program that comes free with certain Macintosh models. Also available for purchase from Apple Computers.

IP address: Acronym for Internet Protocol address, which is a number that uniquely identifies your computer on the Internet.

ISP: Acronym that stands for Internet service provider, which is a company that offers Internet access. Some popular ISPs include America Online, EarthLink, and Prodigy.

iVisit: Popular and free videoconferencing program created by the same person who made CU-SeeMe.

Java applet: Small program, written in the Java programming language, that can make Web pages more interactive.

JavaScript: Programming language designed to make Web pages more interactive.

JPEG: Acronym that stands for Joint Photographic Experts Group, an alternative cross-platform graphics file format. JPEG files often end with the file extension jpg and are suited for displaying images with lots of colors, such as photographic images. *See* GIF.

Linux: Popular alternative operating system, mostly designed for hard-core computer programmers. Getting a Web cam to work under Linux may involve writing your own device drivers.

NetMeeting: Popular and free videoconferencing program developed by Microsoft. Unlike other videoconferencing programs, NetMeeting only runs under Windows.

parallel port: Port commonly used to connect a printer to your computer, although some Web cam models can connect to a parallel port as well.

PCX: Three-letter file extension used to identify a graphics file format originally created by a program called PC-Paintbrush. This file format is still commonly used today.

Pentium: Type of microprocessor commonly found in computers that run Windows. Some popular alternatives to Pentium processors (made by the Intel Corporation) are made by a company called AMD, which sells processors with names like Athlon, Duron, and K6.

PICT: Short for PICTure, this is a vector graphics format developed by Apple Computers for storing graphic images created by drawing programs. *See* vector graphics.

pixel: A tiny point of light that appears on a computer monitor. Groups of lit up pixels create images that you can see on your screen, such as a letter, a picture of your dog's face, or a Web page.

pixilation: Animation technique in which objects (usually people) are captured one frame at a time, with intervals between each movement of the object or person.

PNG: Acronym that stands for Portable Network Graphics. Programmers created PNG as a cross-platform graphics file format alternative to GIF files, although they aren't as popular or universal as GIF files yet. PNG files often end with the file extension png. *See* GIF.

PowerPC: Type of microprocessor used in Macintosh computers.

QuickTime: Video file format developed by Apple Computers as the native video file format for the Macintosh, although the format is also available for Windows. QuickTime files often end with the file extension mov or qt.

RAM: Acronym that stands for Random Access Memory, which defines how much information your computer can handle at any given time.

RealPlayer: Cross-platform program designed to run video and audio files.

RealVideo: Cross-platform video file format created by the Real.com corporation.

resolution: Defines the crispness and sharpness of an image in terms of the number of pixels used vertically and horizontally. Resolutions are often given in numbers such as 640 x 480 or 352 x 288. The larger the resolution, the sharper the image. *See* pixel.

RTP/RTSP streaming: Acronym that stands for Real-Time Transport Protocol/Real-Time Streaming Protocol, which is a method of transferring and displaying a video file to another computer as the video file arrives, rather than waiting for the entire video file to arrive before displaying it. *See* HTTP streaming.

screen saver: Special program that automatically blanks out your screen or displays a moving image on your screen whenever your computer is inactive for a certain period of time. By displaying nothing at all, or a constantly moving image, screen savers prevent images from physically burning into your monitor screen.

serial port: Port commonly used to connect a modem to your computer, although some older Web cam models can connect to a serial port as well.

stop-motion animation: Technique of capturing images between intervals during which the object being photographed is moved slightly. The overall result is that the object appears to move on its own, such as a clay monster moving by itself.

streaming server: A special computer designed to send video files to large groups of people simultaneously.

streaming video: Sending video files to another computer and displaying the video without having to wait for the entire video file to download first. *See* HTTP streaming *and* RTP/RTSP streaming.

TIFF: Acronym that stands for Tagged Image File Format, which is a graphics file format for storing bitmapped images.

time-lapse photography: Special method of capturing images to speed up a normally slow process, such as capturing an image every 24 hours so you can see the progress of a flower blooming.

USB: Acronym that stands for Universal Serial Bus, a type of connection used to connect most Web cams to a computer.

vector graphics: Method of representing pictures as lines and geometric shapes designated by numeric coordinates. As a result, vector graphics images can be resized without any loss of resolution, which bitmap images cannot. *See* bitmap.

video camera adapter: Special device that enables you to connect an ordinary video camera to your computer.

video capture card: Special video card that plugs into an expansion slot and enables your computer to capture and edit video.

videoconferencing: Communicating with others through voice and video in real time.

video e-mail: E-mail that contains a video file attached or embedded in the message.

videophone: A telephone that displays video images, so the caller and receiver can see each other.

Web cam: A video camera that connects to your computer, usually through a USB, serial, or parallel port, and displays images on your computer screen.

Web page: File that displays text, graphics, and video on the World Wide Web.

whiteboard: Feature offered by videoconferencing programs to display a common screen that all participants can write or draw on.

Windows Media Player: Program designed to run video and audio files under the Windows operating system.

Windows Movie Maker: Free video editing program that comes with Windows Millennium Edition.

Index

• *H* •

• *I* •

• W •

Notes

Notes

Notes

IDG Books Worldwide, Inc., End-User License Agreement

READ THIS. You should carefully read these terms and conditions before opening the software packet(s) included with this book ("Book"). This is a license agreement ("Agreement") between you and IDG Books Worldwide, Inc. ("IDGB"). By opening the accompanying software packet(s), you acknowledge that you have read and accept the following terms and conditions. If you do not agree and do not want to be bound by such terms and conditions, promptly return the Book and the unopened software packet(s) to the place you obtained them for a full refund.

1. **License Grant.** IDGB grants to you (either an individual or entity) a nonexclusive license to use one copy of the enclosed software program(s) (collectively, the "Software") solely for your own personal or business purposes on a single computer (whether a standard computer or a workstation component of a multiuser network). The Software is in use on a computer when it is loaded into temporary memory (RAM) or installed into permanent memory (hard disk, CD-ROM, or other storage device). IDGB reserves all rights not expressly granted herein.

2. **Ownership.** IDGB is the owner of all right, title, and interest, including copyright, in and to the compilation of the Software recorded on the disk(s) or CD-ROM ("Software Media"). Copyright to the individual programs recorded on the Software Media is owned by the author or other authorized copyright owner of each program. Ownership of the Software and all proprietary rights relating thereto remain with IDGB and its licensers.

3. **Restrictions on Use and Transfer.**

   (a) You may only (i) make one copy of the Software for backup or archival purposes, or (ii) transfer the Software to a single hard disk, provided that you keep the original for backup or archival purposes. You may not (i) rent or lease the Software, (ii) copy or reproduce the Software through a LAN or other network system or through any computer subscriber system or bulletin-board system, or (iii) modify, adapt, or create derivative works based on the Software.

   (b) You may not reverse engineer, decompile, or disassemble the Software. You may transfer the Software and user documentation on a permanent basis, provided that the transferee agrees to accept the terms and conditions of this Agreement and you retain no copies. If the Software is an update or has been updated, any transfer must include the most recent update and all prior versions.

4. **Restrictions on Use of Individual Programs.** You must follow the individual requirements and restrictions detailed for each individual program in Appendix B of this Book. These limitations are also contained in the individual license agreements recorded on the Software Media. These limitations may include a requirement that after using the program for a specified period of time, the user must pay a registration fee or discontinue use. By opening the Software packet(s), you will be agreeing to abide by the licenses and restrictions for these individual programs that are detailed in Appendix B and on the Software Media. None of the material on this Software Media or listed in this Book may ever be redistributed, in original or modified form, for commercial purposes.

Installation Instructions

The *Web Cams For Dummies* CD offers valuable information that you won't want to miss. To install the items from the CD to your hard drive, follow these steps.

For Microsoft Windows Users

1. Insert the CD into your computer's CD-ROM drive.
2. Open your browser.
3. Click Start⇨Run.
4. In the dialog box that appears, type D:\START.HTM
5. Read through the license agreement, nod your head, and then click the Accept button if you want to use the CD. After you click Accept, you'll jump to the Main Menu.
6. To navigate within the interface, simply click any topic of interest and an explanation of how to use or install the files on the CD will appear.
7. To install the software from the CD, simply click the software name.

For Mac OS Users

1. Insert the CD into your computer's CD-ROM drive.
2. Double-click the CD icon to show the CD's contents.
3. Double-click the Read Me First icon.
4. Open your browser.
5. Choose File⇨Open and select the CD entitled *Web Cams For Dummies*. Click the Links.htm file to see an explanation of all files and folders included on the CD.
6. Some programs come with installer programs. For those, simply open the program's folder on the CD and double-click the icon with the words "Install" or "Installer."

For more complete information, please see the "About the CD" appendix.

IDG BOOKS WORLDWIDE
BOOK REGISTRATION

Register
This Book
and Win!

We want to hear from you!

Visit **http://my2cents.dummies.com** to register this book and tell us how you liked it!

- Get entered in our monthly prize giveaway.

- Give us feedback about this book — tell us what you like best, what you like least, or maybe what you'd like to ask the author and us to change!

- Let us know any other *For Dummies*® topics that interest you.

Your feedback helps us determine what books to publish, tells us what coverage to add as we revise our books, and lets us know whether we're meeting your needs as a *For Dummies* reader. You're our most valuable resource, and what you have to say is important to us!

Not on the Web yet? It's easy to get started with *Dummies 101*®: *The Internet For Windows*® *98* or *The Internet For Dummies*® at local retailers everywhere.

Or let us know what you think by sending us a letter at the following address:

For Dummies Book Registration
Dummies Press
10475 Crosspoint Blvd.
Indianapolis, IN 46256

™
...FOR
DUMMIES

BESTSELLING
BOOK SERIES